"Heller plunges us lovingly and convincingly into that lost world, conjuring the youthful longings of her mother and her father, as well as her uncle's magnetism."
Julia M. Klein, *The Boston Globe*

"In *Reading Claudius*, Caroline Heller does what Rilke called the "heart-work," exploring moral accountability and the toll exacted by the fact of survival. Her family story begins in pre-war Czechoslovakia, passes through the Nazi holocaust, and continues on in postwar America, affirming that events may end but repercussions never do. A searching and humane memoir."
Sven Birkerts, author of *The Art of Time in Memoir: Then, Again*

"[...] this fine book contains moments of emotion so pure that in the end, we too fall in love with the writer's past."
Sarah Wildman, *New York Times*

"One of the time-honoured ways for the Holocaust's heirs to come to grips with its legacy is to write about it — to shine light on what's been hidden, to reconstruct the vanished world [...] This is what Caroline Heller has done."
Adam Kirsch, *Tablet Magazine*

"Caroline Heller writes with both honesty and delicacy. I was particularly enthralled by her finely drawn portrait of prewar Central Europe: a lost world whose memories are inestimably valuable and fiercely beautiful but which, without accounts like this, would fade forever."
Anne Fadiman, author of *The Spirit Catches You and You Fall Down*

"*Reading Claudius* is much more than a work of riveting personal history. It is a feat of passionate, radical integrity. Caroline Heller has wedded the greatest level of care in her scholarship to an even deeper form of search: that in which imagination becomes not only an ac′
Leah Hager Cohen, author of *No   of Others*

"A deeply felt and deeply thought m   st world with aching tenderness and re
Phillip Lopate, author of *Portrait Inside My Head*

READING CLAUDIUS

A Dual Memoir

Caroline Heller

Leapfrog Press and TSB
New York and London

Reading Claudius: A Dual Memoir
© 2021 Caroline Heller

First published in the United States by The Dial Press 2015,
an imprint of Random House,
a division of Penguin Random House LLC, New York

First published in paperback in the United States by Leapfrog Press, 2021
Leapfrog Press Inc.
P.O. Box 1293, Dunkirk, NY 14048

www.leapfrogpress.com

First published in the United Kingdom by TSB, 2021
TSB is an imprint of:
Can of Worms Enterprises Ltd
7 Peacock Yard, London SE17 3LH

www.canofworms.net

Cover design: James Shannon.
Typesetting: Prepress Plus.

ISBN: 978-1-9485852-1-7 (US paperback)
ISBN: 978-1-9116731-3-2 (UK paperback)

9 8 7 6 5 4 3 2 1

Printed and bound in the United Kingdom

For Thomas Heller

CONTENTS

PART I

The Subjective In-Between

PART II

The Unthought Known

FOREWORD

Shortly after the death of my father in 2001, I felt compelled to craft my family's story into words on the page. Initially, I tried writing the chapters out of chronological sequence. These would be the "easier" chapters, I thought. As fallible as memory is, at least I was *there*, a witnessing narrator, already part of the story. From the very beginning of embarking on the research that led to *Reading Claudius*, I agonized over how I would write about events that took place before I was born. Despite immersing myself in archives, interviews, letters, and books, when I turned to writing the chapters that focus on my parents' and uncle's early lives, I became paralyzed. Rich with information from research, I still had no way of knowing how the light looked through a window, what someone wore, the inflection of someone's voice—what the philosopher Michel de Certeau refers to as the "immense remainder" that makes lives real and a story about those lives larger than a compilation of "facts."

I experimented with different possibilities. I tried to enter the narrative at certain junctures, dispersing phrases like: "I think they told me . . . ," "I don't know with certainty, but . . . ," "There is a good chance that . . ." But the insertions created a nervous glancing-over-the-shoulder feeling in the text, an awkwardness that seemed to diminish the possibility of immersion in my parents' and uncle's early world—both for me and, I thought, for my audience.

That strategy failing, I turned to other writers. "There isn't a self-evident way of going about it," says W. G. Sebald in an interview about his efforts to narrate history. "You gather things up like a person who leaves a burning house . . . You adulterate the truth as you try to write it." Alice Munro seemed to agree, describing the process of writing her own family's story, *The View from Castle Rock,* as one of "sifting the untrustworthy evidence, linking stray names and questionable dates and anecdotes together, hanging on to threads, insisting on being joined to dead people and therefore to life." And because he brought such sly sad humor to the question of narrating a family's past, I felt particularly close to Delmore Schwartz. In my favorite of his stories, "In Dreams Begin Responsibilities," the protagonist goes to a movie theater and inexplicably finds himself watching a film about his parents' lives before he was born, rather than the movie he came to see. He starts to talk back to the screen, trying to insert himself into the narrative so that he can fashion the story into the one he wants it to be. "What are *you* doing?!" a theater usher shouts, running down the aisle toward where the man sits. "Don't you know you can't do whatever you want to do?" he scolds as he grabs the man's arm and ejects him from the theater. "You can't carry on like this!"

But how does any writer avoid "carrying on like this" as she summons the presumption and temerity to cross the border between present and past, living and dead? If she inserts herself into the story, as I tried to do, the reader will rightly ask, "What are *you* doing here?" But if she aims to be an omniscient narrator, her reader will just as rightly ask, "Where are *you*?"

I eventually made the decision to allow myself to imagine some of the historical details—the expressions and clothing, the dialogue and gestures, thoughts, and emotions, as they may have occurred in the holes left empty by those letters, interviews, and archives, and to provide detailed source notes that describe the research that contributed to the rendering of each chapter.

In *The Human Condition,* the philosopher Hannah Arendt, a dear friend of my uncle Erich who frequently visited my parents' home when I was a child, wrote that "compared with the reality which comes from being seen and heard, even the greatest forces of intimate life . . . lead an uncertain, shadowy kind of existence unless and until they are transformed, deprivatized . . . into a shape to fit them for public appearance." She calls such stories "the subjective in-between."

Though the contours of each historical chapter comprising Part I are fundamentally factual, in the everyday details I evoke, I called on my parents and uncle to subtly deputize me to be their chronicler, allowing myself to enter the subjective in-between. I did so not because I believe a writer accomplishes higher artistry or truth when she lets her imagination enter in, but because doing so seemed necessary to capture as closely as possible the spirit of what Claire Messud calls "life being lived." "At the heart of things," Messud writes, "whatever the ideas and ideologies, the violations and violence, the peculiarities of culture—always at the heart are ordinary people, and there is just life being lived: tables and bread and toilets and scissors and cigarettes and kisses." Unable to know my parents' and uncle's early world in its fullness, I tried in this way to approximate a representation of its wholeness. Doing so was my way of fulfilling a lifelong yearning to literally make my parents' world whole again, to bring back that dense mingling of the intellectual, the artistic, the social, and the political that defined their early lives—their lost Atlantis of prewar Central Europe.

I had no need to wrestle with a narrative style for the Prologue or for Part II of *Reading Claudius*. My challenge here was of a different nature: overcoming my resistance to adding my own story to that of my parents and uncle. Like many heirs of the Holocaust, I carry a sense that the drama and losses of the past eclipse what seem like (and often are) the more prosaic dramas of our more immediate present. Thus, I originally intended *Reading Claudius* to be solely about my parents' and uncle's lives, not about my own. But a price is paid for survival, and indeed keeps getting paid generationally, though not in the exact same coin. Writing the Prologue and Part II necessitated varieties of self-scrutiny that I hadn't anticipated having to undertake, transforming *Reading Claudius* into a more urgently personal undertaking, closer to my own bone. My parents' history has multiple implications for how I've been formed. But while I was shaped by my parents' darkness and carry its meanings, the darkness itself is only a part of me. It isn't synonymous with my fuller essence, which belongs to me as a creature of my own place and time. In gaining access to the past's secrets, I gained access to my own. It is from this full, complicated panorama that I wrote *Reading Claudius*.

READING CLAUDIUS

How can it be that all that is in us dies with us? How can it be that those memories . . . simply ceased to be? . . . This seems to me the greatest weakness of any supposed divine plan, the primary reason to doubt.

Claire Messud, "The Road to Damascus,"
Granta, Winter 2012

And That New Thing Is Life

In the summer of 1954, when I was four years old, my family moved from Omaha, Nebraska, where my father had completed his medical residency, to the west side of Chicago, near his new job as staff hematologist at the VA hospital. The Third Unitarian Church was a block from our apartment, and my parents joined it. On Sunday mornings, I'd sit enfolded in my mother's lap for the adult service, led by the gentle, grandfatherly minister, E. T. Buehrer, while my brother, Tom, who was six, attended Sunday school. On our way home, Tom performed new songs he'd learned—*this little liberal light of mine, I'm gonna let it shine.*

Occasionally, after services, my father declared a holiday from his medical research, which he rarely abandoned, even on weekends. We'd pick up rolls and cold cuts from Steve's Grocery, near our apartment, and drive to a nature preserve on the outskirts of Chicago. It had meandering trails bordered by wetlands and prairie grasses and, in spring and summer, bursts of wildflowers of every imaginable color. The long paths, visited by chipmunks and rabbits, which we fed with the fluffy insides of our sandwich rolls, were connected by arched wooden footbridges over small streams. Each bridge had a glass-enclosed display case fastened to its railing that contained drawings and photographs of the native wildlife and plants as well as short descriptions and, at the bottom, a line or two from a nature poem by Robert Frost, Henry Wadsworth Longfellow, Emily Dickinson.

Carrying our picnic, we'd set out along the trails, where my father, an assortment of Zim's Golden Nature Guides in his back pockets, had the habit of stopping at each display case and, in his serious, schoolmasterly way, reading every bit of information out loud, then looking down at Tom and me with an expression that implied a quiz might follow.

But by the time we got to the third or fourth wooden bridge, the muscles of my father's mouth and cheeks would relax. The dark mood that pressed heavily on our family life fell away like a mask, and a softness came over my father as his voice transitioned from the lines of the American nature poems to recitations of German poems he'd memorized long ago.

My parents had always peppered their English with fragments of German. In later years, when my uncle Erich, my father's older brother, moved to the United States and came to visit us on weekends, they often spoke German together. But here, on the nature trails, the German words flowed out in streams of joy. Our sad, stern father, our "Bau" (when my brother was a toddler, his efforts to say "Paul" produced only "Bau," and we referred to him as that all our lives), transformed into someone impish and lighthearted. He even did a little dance. I didn't want this Bau ever to leave.

The finale to the afternoon was poems by Goethe, which

Bau sang—*Is not the world still left? . . . Doth not the wondrous
arch of heaven still rise, / Now rich in shape, now shapeless to the
eyes?* Hearing my father speak Goethe's name with such
warmth and happiness, I imagined someone who smelled like
a grandfather might smell, a combination of Reverend Buehrer and Jingles from the Saturday-morning television show
Wild Bill Hickok. Bau swept the air with his make-believe conductor's baton and stretched his arms out toward my mother,
who stood on the sidelines of the stream of his activity. Though
he'd tease himself—"Only people who have a talent for singing ought to sing"—Bau's voice sounded as if it were meant
for just these words, as though in them he'd finally found a
ration of the world's store of happiness, which on other days
eluded him.

While my father sang Goethe, my mother pulled my
brother and me close in front of her and wrapped her arms
around us, facing Bau. It was hard to stay still for as long as
she held us, but I felt that she needed us to. It was as though
she were displaying us to the world, a little sanctuary of us.

In 1958, a few weeks before Christmas vacation—by then
we'd moved to a suburb called Riverside, and I was in third
grade—ninety-two children and three teachers died in a fire at
Our Lady of Angels, a Catholic elementary school on Chicago's northwest side. In the days that followed, the victims'
photographs filled the front pages of the *Chicago Sun-Times*,
which arrived at my parents' doorstep every morning. Each
evening I cut out the photos, laid them on my bedspread, and
stared at the children's faces, scrutinizing their expressions for

signs of their impending doom like a lookout sentry alert for shadows or noises in the night. I recall the photograph of one little girl in particular. She looked about my age, eight years old, had dark hair, a slightly protruding upper lip that gave her a mischievous look, deep-set, watchful eyes, and a knowing, eager expression, as if she wanted to talk to me.

I made myself look at the photos of the children each night before I went to bed, especially the face of this little girl, whose features, I realized much later, reminded me of a photograph of my mother as a child, one of the few she'd managed to take out of Germany. I was convinced that another terrible tragedy would ensue if I didn't hold the image of the girl with me as I drifted off to sleep, so I thought of her with such concentration that sometimes in dreams I watched her fall from the sky in a light brown dress, somersaulting as she fell, all the while looking at me, talking to me, trying to tell me something.

After the fire, every evening before my mother came into my room to say good night, I lined up my stuffed animals two by two, arms around each other, paws touching. Each was with a best friend in case something terrifying happened while I slept. "I won't die during the night. Tommy won't die during the night. You won't die during the night. Bau won't die during the night." Night after night, I needed my mother to sit with me at bedtime and repeat these words as if they could cancel the imagined ones the little girl might be trying to tell me. The ritual begun after the fire went on for several years, interrupted only when Uncle Erich, who didn't approve of babying children, visited. Still I dreamed of the little girl, who sometimes transformed into the image of my mother in the photo of her as a child. Then she'd be the little girl again, coming so close to my face I could feel her breath.

That Christmas season, while the lights of Riverside glowed outside, Bau read aloud to Tom and me from the English translation of *Doctor Zhivago*, which had just come out in the United States. After dinner, Bau, his head thrust a little forward from his body, as was his habit, hurried to the shelf to retrieve the book, which he kept next to his weathered copy of *War and Peace*. As I listened to the sounds of my mother cleaning up in the kitchen and through the windows watched the snow diffuse the beams of the cars and the lights of the houses on Herrick Road, my father turned the pages with a moistened index finger, looking for the exact passage where the previous reading had left off. He pulled out the silver mechanical pencil always clipped to the pocket of his jacket or shirt and carefully bracketed a section or drew a double line in the margin of the book. "Zis is something to remember," he murmured, as Tom and I ate the Scottie dog- and star-shaped Christmas cookies we'd helped my mother bake. Riverside had its Christmas pageants, and we had *Doctor Zhivago*.

The book, with its pencil marks, is in front of me now. I've opened to an early scene in which Yurii Zhivago explains his beliefs about consciousness, religion, and the meaning of memory and eternity to a dying and frightened Anna Ivanovna Gromeko, the woman who raised him. Bracketed in faded pencil is this passage: *And now listen carefully. You in others—this is your soul. This is what you are, what your con-*

sciousness has breathed and lived on and enjoyed throughout your life, your soul, your immortality in others.

Bau's purpose in reading to us from *Doctor Zhivago* may have had nothing to do with trying to relieve my agony over the deaths of the children, but sitting next to him, I felt as though, in a feat of uncommon empathy, he was addressing the words directly to me. I identified the children's faces, their eyes, mouths, noses, hair, with these words from the book and with my father's voice, which, though more serious, expressed something similar to what it conveyed when he stood on the footbridges of the nature preserve singing Goethe—that these words and what could be found in them, certainly what *he* found in them, might connect me to something even more real than the world that surrounded me.

So, what will happen to your consciousness? Your consciousness, yours, not anyone else's? Yurii Zhivago asks Anna Ivanovna in another passage bracketed by Bau's pencil strokes. *What are you conscious of in yourself? Your kidneys? Your liver? Your blood vessels? No. However far back you go in your memory, it is always in some external, active manifestations of yourself that you come across your identity—in the work of your hands, in your family, in other people . . . There will be no death because the past is over. It is already done with. What we need is something new, and that new thing is life,* Bau read in his deep, heavily accented voice, the book cradled in his lap, Tom and I seated on either side of him, our hands clasped around our knees.

And that new thing is life, my father repeated, tapping his knee, then each of ours, with his soft fist, and nodding as if renewing a bargain he'd made with himself long ago.

On a brilliant, sunny afternoon, fall 1966, I sat at my desk in my American history class, staring longingly out the tall windows, opened just a crack, that overlooked the athletic field. In the heat of early afternoon, the room smelled of formaldehyde from the biology class down the hall and grease from the cafeteria below. Grunts from boys in gym class outside pushed through the windows. I was sixteen years old, a junior at Riverside Brookfield High School. My teacher, Mr. Dombrowski, a slender, sweaty man with regal posture, pursed lips, and perfectly parted brown hair tamed with scented pomade, had a high-pitched voice that became nasal and tinny when he lectured. Even on warm days he wore a dark suit, dress shirt, and bow tie, and when he moved around our classroom, he smelled of menthol and body odor.

"Ladies and gentlemen, we've established that the colonists wanted their freedom from King George. What else? What else brought the colonies to war?" Mr. Dombrowski hoisted himself out of the chair behind his desk and grabbed a piece of chalk to begin one of his famous lists. *NUMBER 1*, he wrote, as always, in big well-formed letters and numerals, as if the very fact of the list were more important than its content. "In-dee-pen-dence!" he said as he wrote it out, adding in a vertical column underneath *#2, #3, #4, #5*. In Mr. Dombrowski's view, all historical events should have at least five clear causes. "Number two? Anyone?"

"To keep another country from taking your land away," said David Doemland, sitting to my left. Different from the robust, crew-cut boys who presided over the halls of RB, David was slight, with wispy blond curls, serious pale blue eyes, and a kind of melancholy and intelligence that inspired my fondness and loyalty. We were in several classes together.

"Ah, Mr. Doemland, you take the viewpoint of England!" Mr. Dombrowski said. "How diplomatic of you. Yes, England didn't want to lose its fine piece of property across the Atlantic. Correct, Mr. Doemland. Good!" He added David's contribution to the list. *#2: LAND OWNERSHIP.*

"Like Syria blowing up the Jews," David went on. I remember him leaning back in his seat and stretching his slender legs in the aisle. "The Jews took Syria's land. War is justified to get it back, to hold the Jews back." He crossed his arms with self-satisfaction.

"Okay, Mr. Doemland. You offer an example from current events to make a point," Mr. Dombrowski said, alluding to Syria's recent attacks on Israeli border towns that had filled the news that fall. "But since you're making a comparison," he went on, "let's define what we're talking about. For one thing, who *are* 'the Jews'?"

In little trumpet blasts of contempt, yet in the matter-of-fact tone of someone who saw himself as a spokesperson for accepted truths, David answered: "You know, kinky black hair. Hooked noses." His chest puffed with vanity. He glanced around the room as though we were all in on this, as though he hadn't a doubt that we all agreed.

Heat spread down my legs and arms and suffused my face. In high school, I was known for being shy, soft-spoken, and smart. My comments in class were careful, measured. I raised my hand to speak. At first nothing came out. Then I began to speak loudly, emphatically, as if a calling to meet this moment had lived inside me forever. "Israel is a tiny country." I might have shouted it. "Jews couldn't go anywhere else. Jews were being murdered . . ." I lost my way as my voice stuck in my throat.

"Before we proceed with our discussion," Mr. Dombrowski said in a cool and dispassionate voice, "I should ask if anyone in the class is Jewish."

His question felt intimate and perilous. David fiddled with his pencil. I didn't want anyone to look at me. In the room, which suddenly felt motionless and silent, Mr. Dombrowski's near-suffocating fragrance settled around me. I had the sensation of floating above myself, my body hidden in a shapeless brown dress. I felt my arm go up, propelled by a will of its own, then stop halfway, extended out to my right like that of a crossing guard stopping traffic. I couldn't raise it farther. I couldn't put it down.

Into the blank space of my mind—for seconds, minutes, years—nothing entered and yet, as if for the very first time, everything did. What was once confused, formless, and partial now cohered, like a primordial threat. Haughtily blond David Doemland had declared his hatred for Jews, and I knew: He was talking about me.

I don't believe my parents made a conscious decision to hide our Jewishness from my brother and me as we were growing up. Nor do I believe they made a deliberate decision not to tell us about the losses that formed their lives before we were born. Maybe it was a second's hesitancy that kept them from telling us. Perhaps more seconds accumulated until the silence became more a surrender to habit than a thought or plan.

They'd filled our house with symbols of intellectual curiosity and openness—shelves crammed with books, including the old tattered ones they'd managed to take out of Europe, heady progressive journals and program notes from concerts, lectures, and plays. But that openness and curiosity had limits. However it had been forged, there was a tacit family agreement not to ask certain questions. Tom and I fell into step with the prohibition, tiptoeing around those questions as if avoiding broken glass. Little by little, without our noticing, tiptoeing became our natural gait.

A truth that had little to do with our daily lives in Riverside, Illinois, hovered over everything but never landed quite long enough for us to touch it. I felt confounded by feelings of incompleteness. We were strangers to our parents' darkness, yet wholly formed from it. Though the losses our parents knew before we were born lay behind them, I sensed that everything else that held meaning and importance was behind them, too—behind all of us. The real narrative had already been lived, and we were its tiny afterlife.

After the war, my parents, like many Holocaust survivors, believed their engagement in the present and their hopes for the future depended in large measure on trying to forget the past. My brother and I were born only a few years after Hitler and those complicit with his goals destroyed the world that would have been our inheritance.

By the late 1970s, when Holocaust testimonies were more welcomed into public discourse in the United States, and even more so, later in our parents' lives, when they became increasingly overwhelmed by memories, they opened up more. Those outpourings, often filled with vivid detail, gave me a great deal of the material I've used to write this book. Until then the truth of the past announced itself indirectly and incompletely. Mostly it whispered in our ears: Don't ask. Just be good. Be so good that through you, their world will be made whole again.

It has taken me years to trust my understanding of all that I absorbed from my parents, and years more to engage in the research that helped me to write about their lives—travels to Czechoslovakia, Germany, and England to follow in their (and my uncle's) footsteps; interviews with people who knew them before, during, and after the war; immersion in the letters, photographs, books, and other documents that survived.

In what follows, I try to give that past coherence as a story.

They were young people finding their way in life, but when I try to imagine them then, they feel as old as Europe itself.

PART I

The Subjective In-Between

CHAPTER ONE

Arrival in Prague

Summer 1933

Liese Florsheim was nineteen years old when she first met the Heller brothers on the shores of the Alaunsee, a lake nestled among the wooded hills of the Czechoslovakian countryside. It was late June 1933, just weeks after Liese had arrived in Prague alone. She spoke not a single word of Czech and knew no one in the country, yet her parents believed that Czechoslovakia, known throughout Europe for its benevolence toward refugees, was the best place for her until life in Germany returned to normal.

She entered the city alongside thousands of Jews fleeing Hitler in Germany and moved into the Msec Castle, a fortresslike building being used as temporary housing for refugees. Soon she found a student room in an old stone building in Prague's Staré Mesto (the Old City). Across the hall lived a second-year medical student, Franta Kraus, whose fluent German made him a perfect guide to the city and to nearby Charles University, where she planned to enroll as a medical student that fall. A friend of the Hellers' since childhood, Franta invited Liese to join him and his girlfriend, Eva

Hirsch, for a swimming outing with the Heller boys and other friends.

Liese had changed into her skirted swimming suit and was lying on a towel in the warm sand, immersed in a book, by the time the others arrived at the lake—Franz Gollan and his girl-friend, Edith Abeles, Hans Posner, Paul Schülle, and Tomas Berman. She felt very much the outsider among this close-knit group of Czech students, whose families lived in the sleepy towns surrounding Prague and were part of the young na-tion's flourishing Jewish community. Most of them were bilin-gual; some, because of the lingering influence of the Hapsburg monarchy, had grown up more fluent in German than in Czech. Liese was relieved that they didn't ask many questions about the situation in Germany, instead showing their concern with their eyes and warm handshakes.

Soon Paul Heller arrived at the lake, winding his way toward them through the dense beach grass at the edge of the sand, wet reeds clinging to his legs and the straps of his sandals. He was a sturdy, gentle-faced boy with gray-green eyes and black hair combed straight back, in the style of the times, revealing shiny peaks and valleys of comb marks. He had a scattering of pim-ples and summer freckles on his sunburned nose, making him look younger than his eighteen years. Liese noticed his hesita-tion when he shook her hand, the shy tilt of his head as he took off his glasses. Erich would be late, Paul told the group apolo-getically, as if he assumed it was his brother's arrival that they more eagerly awaited. As usual, Erich had stayed up late the night before, writing, and was still asleep, he said.

"The task of morning sleep requires all Erich Heller's best energies, Liese," Franta explained as he, Eva, and Hans climbed into one of the shiny green rowboats tied to the nearby dock. "The man goes to bed with the dawn chorus, but it never seems to do him the least bit of harm."

Liese wondered about this absent fellow who, even before his arrival, seemed to command so much attention.

Paul headed for the water by himself, swimming across the lake and back before placing himself on his towel on the sand near Liese. Out of his rucksack he pulled a tin of bilberries, a thermos, and a volume of Thomas Mann stories, its pages pulling loose from the cardboard binding. Mann was all the rage among young people.

"I have the same edition," Liese told him, glancing up. "The pages are falling out of mine, too. Such a thin cover. But it's light and good for travel."

"*Tonio Kröger* just came out in leather," Paul said, an excited grin filling his face as he dried off his glasses and replaced them on his nose. "You can buy it with its own oak slipcase. Too beautiful to bring to a picnic, though!"

"Do you have a favorite?" Liese asked, sitting up and wrapping her arms around her knees. She was full-breasted and slim, with dark, wildly curly hair and intent brown eyes that shimmered when something interested her, a quality that gave a sense of something tender in her personality, something inviting.

"Depends on my mood," Paul said. "But really, I suppose, it's always been *Tonio Kröger*. Maybe because I read it first. I remember thinking then . . . Well, you come away thinking that you haven't really *lived* yet. There is all this life to live!" Paul's neck and face reddened.

"It's impossible to read *Tonio Kröger* without thinking

Mann wrote it just for you. I mean, *me,*" Liese said, and they
both laughed.

When the rowers returned, they spread out an immense
picnic—salami, rolls, bottles of wine, chestnuts, strawberries,
Paul's bilberries, chocolate (Liese's contribution), even ba-
nanas, a rarity. Franz Gollan began to whistle a tune from a
Hofmannsthal operetta while balancing a chestnut on his nose.

Paul wanted to ask Liese more questions, to talk about
other Mann stories, about the Tolstoy she was reading. He
wanted to tell her she'd just missed Prague's spring lilacs,
which blossomed into more colors than anywhere else in the
world. He wanted to recite to her the poem that had been in
his head as he swam. This happened to him often—a nonsense poem would enter his head, a Christian Morgenstern
or a Joachim Ringelnatz—and wouldn't leave until he re-
cited it out loud. This time it was Morgenstern's "The Picket
Fence."

One time there was a picket fence
With space to gaze from hence to thence.
An architect who saw this sight
Approached it suddenly one night,
Removed the spaces from the fence,
And built of them a residence.
The picket fence stood there dumbfounded
With pickets wholly unsurrounded,
A view so loathsome and obscene,
The Senate had to intervene.
The architect, however, flew
To Afri- or Americoo.

"Hence to thence" was Paul's newest favorite line with which to tease himself about his incessant need to carefully plan his future. "Hence to thence, Paul! But focus more on hence than thence!"

Erich Heller arrived soon, a tall, slender, startlingly handsome figure in a rumpled shirt and long striped swimming shorts under his open robe. His light brown hair was tousled from sleep. He couldn't stay long, he announced immediately, glancing at his wristwatch, for he was expected at a party in Prague and had to catch the six o'clock train. He took off his robe and shirt and bounded into the water before joining their feast.

"Unbedante Weise," he said to Liese, shaking her hand. All my very best to you, though I do not yet know you. Liese watched him as he shook the water from his hair and laid his towel in the warm sand beside her and Paul. She listened to his rapid-fire stories and his opinions about literature and history, which she thought showed a remarkable command of whatever subject he touched upon. He had spent much of the night before, he announced, working on an essay about Goethe, the poet he loved above all others. He felt that suddenly, that very night, he'd recognized in Goethe's work what no one else ever had.

"Oh, Erich Heller, don't show off! There's nobody here who will take notice!" said Edith.

"No, I'm entirely serious. Goethe did not comprehend his own history!" Erich said, jumping to his feet, sandwich in one hand and paper cup of wine in the other. "He would not admit to his own despair at the tragedy of Germany. Do you not see? While he foresaw the fragmentation . . ." No, this was not the word he meant. He paused, staring at the sand. "Breakdown!" He seemed to revel in this retrieval. "Breakdown! The breakdown of German culture. Do you see? Do you not see that Goethe refused to recognize this tragedy? His optimistic heart simply could not accept it. He was accused of aloofness from politics, but his only choice, if he wanted to be a poet, was to identify completely with his own inner order. Does this not sound like a lesson for us?" Erich asked, his gaze fixed dreamily on the steep wooded hills across the lake.

Turning back to his friends, he offered a toast to the lake, then another to Liese. "To our new acquaintance from Frankfurt! To optimism amid tragedy!" After polishing off his wine, he collapsed on his back, stretching his arms out in the sand.

"To the lake and to Liese!" the others added, raising their cups toward her, coaxing a smile to her face as she sat, transfixed by their sense of celebration.

"What should the lesson from Goethe be?" Edith asked Erich as she replenished everyone's paper cup, then pulled him up to a sitting position, falling back into the sand herself. "You left that part out. That we should all aspire to his inner order?"

"No one should aspire to anyone else's inner order!" He tossed a bilberry at his friend and lit a cigarette. "For *him* to create, he couldn't accept the idea of evil. He could write his poetry, his plays, only because on some level he refused to let himself comprehend real evil. I mean, look at his Mephistopheles in *Faust*. In Goethe's hands, even the devil himself was nothing but a fool."

"No one in his right mind comprehends evil," Hans said. "Goethe's not alone in that."

"To the incomprehensibility of evil and to Goethe's inner order!" Franz said, and they raised their cups again.

"But I only mean we should keep reading him," Erich said. "Even as Hitler now claims him as *his*. We can't let Hitler have him! But this is self-evident! What would Tante Ida say, Pauli?" Erich asked, turning to his brother, who'd taken off his shirt and glasses and was heading off for another swim.

" 'Life is a mess!' " Paul called back in a perfect imitation of their late father's oldest sister, the Heller family matriarch.

"And then she would scold me for wearing *fürs schlechtere* [messy clothing] to the beach when I meet such an elegant stranger," Erich said, turning to Liese.

"To Tante Ida!" said Franta. "And to finishing off the wine right here and now."

As they sat on the beach through the afternoon, debating politics, books, the best way to peel a chestnut, Liese felt the first shiver of joy she'd known in months. It surprised her. So this was what it was like to be in Czechoslovakia. A line from a Matthias Claudius poem her mother used to recite to her at bedtime came into her head: *Where the sorrow of the day you shall forget and sleep away.* Here was everything that was still normal, that belonged to everyday life—choosing what book to read, what poet to take hope from, making fun of Hitler without having to be afraid. This feeling began to thaw the frozen places in her mind, as if she were being dug up from the ice.

Lying in the sand next to Erich, Liese felt quiet and beautiful. When her eyes met his, she looked away, at the ashes falling from the end of his cigarette, or at the sand wedged between his toes, or at the soft cotton sash that tied his robe.

The sun set behind the hills, the beach lanterns were lit, a fire was built. Erich decided to skip his party in Prague that night. And so it was that Liese began to build herself a world as an émigré.

She heard from Erich a week later by way of a note Franta Kraus delivered to her room. He would be meeting friends that evening at the Café Continental. Later there would be a get-together at the apartment of his friends the Mayers. Joszi Mayer's father ran one of Prague's major newspapers, *Prager Tagblatt*, and Joszi's husband, Fredy, was the managing editor. Their apartment was the center of life for writers and social democrats. Would she accompany him?

Tall black statues stood along either side of Charles Bridge, which linked the somber Staré Mesto to the lively cafés across the river. At twilight, when the mist formed above the Vltava, the shadowy statues took on a life hidden from daylight, ominous and ghostly in appearance. But that evening, walking on the path along the river to meet Erich, Liese saw them as loving, benevolent gods.

When she got to the entrance of the café, she saw Erich sitting at a corner table, his eyes turned away from the doorway. Very good, she thought. She could find a washroom, tidy up, get her bearings, and look around before he knew she was there. Every table and almost all the seats at the bar in the center of the room were full. The Continental felt to her like a wonderfully festive university library. Most of its inhabitants were young. On the tables, amid fat beer glasses, half-full wine bottles, and wooden bowls filled with salted nuts, were stacks of newspapers, open books piled on top of each other, and handwritten sheets of paper scattered about. Other newspapers, more than she'd ever seen in one place, hung over rods attached to varnished oak pillars against the wall. On the walls themselves were dark pictures of serious faces, some of whom Liese recognized—the untamed hair and sumptuous mouth of Rainer Maria Rilke, the piercing eyes of a young Kafka.

"Liese, Liese, dear Liese," Erich called over to her before she could find the washroom. "Congratulations! We must celebrate your first visit to our spiritual sessions at seventeen Na Prikope, where we all practically live!" He pulled out a chair and motioned to her to sit, pouring a beer from the pitcher on the table into a cup and handing it to her. Still standing, she quickly licked the foam running down the outside of her cup, then felt mortified by her unguarded moment.

Seated beside Erich at the table was Hans Posner, whom she'd already met at the Alaunsee. Hans had sandy-colored curls and wore rimless glasses; he was growing a not terribly successful beard. He introduced her to his older brother, a medical student a year ahead of her. Also named Erich but nicknamed EP, he had kind eyes and a fine mustache and was smoking a short English pipe, his hands stretched over a good-sized belly.

"Liese and I are already great friends," Erich Heller told the group. He lit a cigarette and ground the lighted match into the floor with the sole of his shoe. "By chance, Liese, did you read my piece in the *Prager Tagblatt* on Tuesday? I must give you a copy if you haven't. An essay about Karl Kraus. Have you read Karl Kraus? Have you not? Have you not read Karl Kraus?" All this before Liese sat, before she spoke.

"I haven't. But of course I will. Tonight, possibly," Liese said. She was distressed by the sound of her own voice, words coming of their own accord, and they weren't even the truth. She'd read a good deal of Karl Kraus. She corrected herself. "I actually read parts of *The Last Days of Mankind* last year in school, and I enjoyed it immensely."

"Immensely?" Erich said, smiling. "You enjoyed it immensely? Tell me more, Liese. Might you choose a word, as Kafka would say, where you wouldn't be misunderstood? What does 'immensely' mean to you?"

Liese brushed her hair back with her hand and let herself down into the chair. "I enjoyed him. I liked him immensely." She was dazed for a moment, surprised that she'd repeated herself. "I don't know him well, really," she added, when in fact she'd read his play several times and discussed it at length with her best girlfriends, Lilo and Ille, in Frankfurt.

"Yes, well," continued Erich, as if speaking for her—and she found herself strangely grateful for this—"if Kafka will one day be known as the greatest writer of Prague, Kraus will be claimed as the greatest of Vienna. His satire is so very Austrian, if there can really be such a thing as '*so very Austrian*.' This is my claim!" He leaned toward Liese. "If I only had the courage, I would travel to Vienna tomorrow to insist that I become his literary biographer. Do you think he'd permit someone twenty-two to write his life story? Shall we travel there together, Liese?" He smiled at her, tilting his chair back and balancing it on two legs.

EP turned to her. "Tell us, would you, Liese, about how it is in Frankfurt. We don't know how to take some of the news. What's your impression?" he asked, never removing his pipe from the corner of his mouth.

The word "impression" took her by surprise. What was happening at home couldn't be explained as an impression. She got angry for a moment, then was overcome with the sense of isolation that had become so familiar to her since she'd come to Prague, where so few seemed to comprehend the seriousness of what was happening in Germany.

"It's terrible," she said, looking at Erich Heller, expecting to say more. "It's perfectly terrible." Again she was stunned that she'd repeated herself. She was used to being so much more articulate. She spoke directly to Erich Posner now, explaining that Hitler was able to fool so many in Germany, that he was not going away any time soon, that she and all of her friends at home believed things would get worse. She knew this conversation inside out. It was all anyone had talked about in the months before she left.

"Please," she said haltingly. It seemed to her that she might cry. She glanced behind her, aware of her shadow on the wall across from their table as the lights in the Continental were lowered. How small she looked next to the shadows of the men. How wild her hair looked. She got up to find the washroom, surprising them with her hasty exit.

Through the filmy window set deep into the wall of the tiny washroom, she could see the shape of the gargoyles looking down at her from the roof across the alley. Humiliated by her flustered state, she thought of leaving the café, crossing the main square of the Staré Mesto, and returning to her room. She even thought of boarding the train back to Frankfurt that night. She could be in her own bed, in her own home on Scheffelstrasse, before her parents and older brother awoke the next morning. It was a bad idea, she knew. The thought of the black-coated SS guards swarming the railroad station made her sick, and to draw any attention would put her family at more risk. But since coming to Prague, she had always carried the railroad timetable with her, and she opened her handbag now to touch it.

She inspected herself in the mirror, her lips so close to the glass that she fogged her own reflection. She ran icy water over her wrists and splashed it on her face. When she returned to the table, she'd tell Erich Heller some of the points she'd made in a paper about Karl Kraus that she'd written for her German class just that past spring. In it she'd imagined Kraus as the editor in chief of all the major newspapers of Europe. Had this been the case, Liese had asserted in her paper, the Nazis would not have gained power. Their propaganda would have failed. Kraus, his judgment governed by his love of clear language, would have seen right through it and convinced the German population that it was empty and false. Her teacher, Frau Eppels, had admired her passion. Yes, she knew the words she'd say when she got back to the table.

But when she returned, Erich was already waiting by the exit, eager to be off to the Mayers' apartment. "Hans, can you imagine my great good fortune! Schocken publishers in Vienna may be interested in my Kraus essay," he was saying as he bought cigarettes from the headwaiter, who counted the pencil marks he'd scratched on their table's cardboard coasters to tally up their bill. Liese was impressed that such a young man was already being considered by a major publisher.

"If only the editor weren't such a complete idiot! His interest in my essay is one of his few good ideas," Erich added, poking Hans in the upper arm and looking delighted when he noticed Liese's return. He'd taken her sweater from the back of her chair, and handed it to her now as he brushed nut crumbs from its sleeves. But it was Erich Posner who helped her into it as they walked down the winding stairs and out onto Na Prikope Street. It had started to drizzle.

Liese had always doubted her intelligence. Even as a little girl in Frankfurt, she had felt insecure about whether she would ever be smart enough to be taken seriously. Her father, so Old World that he continued to wear a standing collar long after its stylishness had faded with the defeat of Germany in World War I, was wedded to the bourgeois order in which only men were the thinkers. Proud as he was of her high marks in school, he teased her when she expressed an opinion or idea, a reaction that caused her more pain than she admitted.

Once, her father chuckled from behind his after-dinner newspaper as she tried to explain to him her intense reaction to the novel *The Forsyte Saga*—she felt that this book had taught her to understand human psychology in a new way—and she'd run to her room in tears. There, glancing at herself in the mirror, she was haunted by the feeling that she had disappeared altogether.

And she had a great many ideas. She got them from the books she read nearly every evening after school, sometimes a full novel in one sitting and several on weekend trips to her paternal grandparents' farm in Alsfeld, southwest of Frankfurt, where, under her grandmother's tutelage, she cared for their goats and chickens and the small field of cucumbers, cabbage, and potatoes. She also got ideas from Lilo and Ille, with whom she debated and discussed nearly everything. By the time they turned fourteen, they'd read all of Mann's books, then read them again, until the stories became as dear to them as any living thing. They formed a reading club which, to describe their never-ending connection, they called *Kränzchen*—their little wreath. They met after school and on weekends, dramatizing stories and plays they'd read, talking about their latest crushes and comparing them (usually unfavorably) to favorite characters from books. In these books they found their first sweethearts, sensitive, passionate young men with artistic souls—Mann's Tonio Kröger, Schiller's Prince Don Carlos, Goethe's Young Werther, Galsworthy's Jolyon Forsyte—men who they were sure would long to hear their most private thoughts.

She'd gotten still other ideas from her teachers at the Volksschule in Frankfurt, particularly from Frau Eppels and Herr Hirsch, her German teachers, whom she adored. Frau Eppels had invited Liese, Lilo, and Ille to an after-school reading group where they discussed Goethe's *Faust*. Herr Hirsch seized every opportunity to take his students out of the school building and into the city to observe as much as they could. He sometimes became so impassioned about a story or poem he was teaching them that, while they wrote at their desks, he would turn his head to the window behind his own desk and, hidden from his students—though Liese saw him—softly cry.

He had cried, too, when he came to Liese's family's apartment two months before she left for Prague. With a new mandate in place prohibiting Jews from teaching, Herr Hirsch was removed from his position before the school year ended. He had come to say good-bye before he left with his family for Paris.

Most of all, it was her mother, her "distant angel," as Liese thought of her, who gave her ideas, her mother who spurred her to think and dream. "What do you think having your eyes open means?" Irma Florsheim had often asked her daughter as Liese followed her from room to room in the apartment. Irma had asked her again as they walked in Römerberg Platz, the center of cultural life in Frankfurt, and in the city parks, as she pointed out the hummingbirds circling maple trees looking for sugar, the gray swans as tall as Liese, floating down the Main River.

"What do you think having your eyes open means, Lieschen? Does it mean just having your eyelids propped up?" she'd asked, her daughter giggling, her voice blending with her mother's as they answered together. "No, it means watching the world!"

Joszi Mayer, who greeted Liese, Erich, and the Posner brothers at the door to her apartment, was tiny, with a slight hunchback and thick black-rimmed glasses. She was considerably older than Liese, with a pale pretty face that lit up when she spoke. After seeing them in, Joszi walked them past the crowd of damp coats on the rack in the hall to show Liese around. The apartment was brightly lit and immense, occupying the entire top floor of a gabled Czech Renaissance building in the center of Wenceslaus Square. The front half was their living quarters, and tonight it was already filled with people and activity.

Joszi escorted Liese to the back of the apartment, which they'd converted into a work area. On the desks were several typewriters, bulging notebooks, and tablets of paper filled with notes. It was here, Joszi told her, that her husband, Fredy, worked; here that members of Freie Vereinigung, the Social Democratic student organization, often congregated after their coffeehouse meetings, eager for Fredy's political counsel; here, too, that Kafka's onetime love, Milena Jesenská, who was a close friend of the Mayers, had come to write; and here that Erich Heller sometimes stayed when he needed a quiet place to work during his frequent trips from Komotau to Prague over the summer.

By the time they returned to the living room, more guests had arrived, shaking rain from their hats and umbrellas. Tonight the Prague accent seemed to turn German into another language. The room was a blur of young men—there weren't many women—smelling of wet wool, musky cologne, and sweat, helping themselves to food from the buffet, which was laden with platters of beef hot from the oven, cucumbers and green peppers laid out in neat lines, bread dumplings atop braised cabbage leaves, and honey cookies filled with poppy seed jam. There were rows of beers: Plzen, Prazdroj, Bakalar, and Gambrinus.

Erich was standing across the buffet, several young men surrounding him. Liese wondered which of his features she found most appealing—his commanding voice, his forever amused expression, the pink that flushed his face when he spoke, the way he dressed: never without a tie, properly creased trousers, and well-chosen colors, like the blue-gray shirt he had on tonight. She tried to catch his eye, but he didn't see her.

"Only someone from Prague can really understand Kafka," she heard him say. "And it doesn't hurt to be an expert in alienation!"

"No one will ever accuse you of being a high-grade optimist," she heard another say.

Moving to join them, she changed course when she noticed Paul Heller standing near the door, his raincoat over his shoulder, as if either just arriving or about to depart. He was leaning over a newspaper and peeling an apple with a pocketknife. Talking with him would relax her, she thought, embolden her.

"You perform your task like a future surgeon, Paul," she said, surprising herself by kissing him on the cheek. When he looked up, he put his hands above his eyes as if the light were too bright.

"Well, I make perfect what I can make perfect," he replied. "And right now there isn't much that I can make perfect. How good to see you again, Liese." He offered her a fresh slice of the apple speared on the tip of his knife.

Erich had left his group and was walking toward them, lighting a cigarette hurriedly. "Dear, dear Liese, did you fill your plate yet? Come meet my friends Milan and Kurt; they want terribly to make your acquaintance." He stood nearly a head taller than his brother and towered over Liese. He tousled Paul's hair and straightened his brother's shirt collar. His expression communicated either tenderness or condescension, Liese couldn't tell which. As Erich steered her toward his group, she saw Paul immediately adjust the collar back to the way it had been, square his shoulders, and, offering Liese an awkward smile, walk out into the rain.

CHAPTER TWO

Twenty Železná Street

Fall 1933

Weekday mornings, when waiters were just starting to fill their café windows with trays of pastries and baskets of rolls for breakfast, it became Liese's habit to walk the ten-odd blocks between her room on Pariz Street and the Café Continental. Before her classes began, she'd go straight to the round table in the corner where Erich and her new group of friends gathered so many evenings. She sat by herself drinking thick coffee, eating hot rolls with butter, writing letters home to her parents and brother, and catching up on her studying, for she found it difficult to concentrate in the evenings when so much else, her feelings for Erich above all, competed for her attention.

Now three months into her stay in Prague, she'd been seeing him two or three times a week. He'd taken her to parties at the Mayers' apartment, to films, to concerts at the National Theater, and to the political meetings that were starting to dominate student life. They were often together at the Continental, and lately he'd invited her to his apartment to study. When they were with others, he behaved like her boyfriend, kissing her, putting his arm around her waist when they took walks. Yet for a young man so full of words, he had yet to tell her how he felt about her. He was forever hurrying off at just those moments when she felt most romantic, and afterward she would feel dejected for days.

But today she would simply assume she *was* his girlfriend. She'd decided to cook him dinner as a surprise before going to the film they planned to see—the new Charlie Chaplin, which was playing at the cinema near the toy store where her newest friend, Steffi Schlamm, worked. It was Steffi, also a recent émigré, who had encouraged her to cook a meal for Erich. Though the truth was that Liese was somewhat pampered and had rarely cooked in her life, it was so obviously the thing to do to fully win his heart that Steffi had convinced her.

Erich had suggested Liese meet him at his apartment before they headed out for a quick dinner at the Continental and then the film. Since he wouldn't be done with his dreaded taxation and municipal finance seminar until sometime after six, and her last class was over at four, he'd told her he would leave the door unlocked and she could wait for him there.

Liese planned to have dinner prepared by the time he arrived. She had bought a chicken (which she'd only have to reheat because Steffi had offered to roast it that morning), a bag of tiny new peas, crusty rye bread baked with molasses and caraway seeds, white wine, and a rum-soaked chocolate cake from Stérba, his favorite bakery. She even bought flowers and candles. She arrived at his doorway so laden with packages that her shoulders ached.

His kitchen was barely the size of a closet, with saucepans left on the stove, empty glasses and full ashtrays in the sink, a hastily pulled-off tie here, a dirty sock there. No trace of a female touch. When Erich had looked for an apartment, the only thing he'd cared about was that it have adequate wall space for bookshelves.

The living room of his apartment was nearly as small as the kitchen, with a wrought-iron table and two worn cane chairs by its single window, which looked out on the shops across Železná Street. A hardwood rocking chair and a sturdy radio-phonograph cabinet, with dozens of shellac records in thick paper sleeves leaning against it, were the only other furniture. He kept his skis in one corner, his leather suitcase in another.

On the shelves, against the spines of his books, he'd arranged picture postcards from vacation trips, photographs of sculptures, and pictures of his closest friends—including one of him and Willi Schlamm, Steffi's husband, standing with the Posner brothers in front of the vine-covered stone buildings of Charles University. Another photo showed Willi and Erich sitting at the Continental's corner table, holding up their first issue of *Die neue Weltbühne*, a left-wing anti-Nazi political journal the two had just launched in Prague. It was patterned after the Social Democratic journal, *Weltbühne*, for which Willi had written in Vienna until it was banned. The only family photo was of Paul and Erich as young boys—Paul maybe six and Erich nine or ten, sitting on either side of their father on the bench of the horse-drawn carriage Dr. Alfred Heller used for house calls.

Spotting the perfect glass for the bouquet of irises she'd brought, Liese returned to the living room to set the table. Except for heating the peas and lighting the candles, she was ready, though it was still a half hour before she could expect Erich home.

She peeked through the open door to his tiny bedroom and then, shocking herself, for she had never considered herself a bold person, entered. For such a tall man, he had a very small bed, covered by a single pumpkin-colored blanket. It didn't seem to her quite possible that he actually slept in it. His desk was up against the room's one window, which wasn't opened wide enough to dispel the smell of old cigarettes. Two mismatched wooden end tables abutted his desk, and she couldn't resist having a closer look. Spread out over them, catching the slanting light from the fading sun, were several open books, the first typed pages of the Goethe essay he seemed to be in the midst of writing, and a worn copybook filled with quotes, the most recently dated pages devoted to lines from Karl Kraus: *Language is the divining rod which discovers wells of thought . . . I and life: The case was handled chivalrously. The opponents parted without having made up.* She smiled. Erich's own way with words was a good deal like that of his literary idol, she thought.

She examined the bedroom bookshelves filled with knick-knacks and more picture postcards propped against the long rows of spines. There were few law books in evidence.

"Am I really to care about guidelines for litigation against improper farm irrigation?" he had joked with her when she asked about his classes. He never enjoyed law, he told her, studying it only because his mother felt it would be a practical profession. He happily traded in his textbooks at the end of each semester for novels and poetry.

She checked her watch. Still fifteen minutes before he might arrive home, and he was never on time. She spotted the leather edition of *Tonio Kröger* that Paul had described, weighted by an ashtray holding it open to a page where Tonio is walking home from school alone. Erich had written in the margin: *Painfully convinced of his future apart; a world without knowledge into knowledge without a world. Must it be a choice? Perhaps.* With the turn of each page, Liese imagined catching some secret whiff of Erich's soul.

When she heard his voice in the outer doorway, she was so startled that she knocked over an empty glass. She hastily put the book back under the ashtray, then bruised her shin on the corner of his bed frame, hurrying out of the room to greet him.

Erich arrived aflame with enthusiasm over a conversation he'd just had with the vendor at the newsstand. "He's a poet— the Danish boy, Kai. I never knew this. We never talked before," he announced as he kissed Liese on the forehead. "He saw ink on my fingers and asked me if I wrote. He showed me one of his poems. I had no idea he's a poet, and not a bad one!"

She took his hand to lead him from the doorway into the kitchen, then turned to him expectantly. At the sight of Liese's preparations, Erich looked dazed.

"How terribly good of you, Liese. How terribly kind," he said. "I've done nothing whatsoever to deserve this."

It became him, she thought, this look of being caught off guard. She'd never seen it before.

He crossed the room and began to fiddle with the knobs of the radio, then flipped through his record collection. "But I must tell you, the boy lives on next to nothing," he said. "A few crowns each night from the newspapers. A poet selling

newspapers. I think I've gotten him interested in Freie Vereinigung. He seems quite political."

"I'd like to meet him," she said, knowing that she'd really
like nothing less than to meet yet another of Erich's friends.
She wished she hadn't lied, at least not so automatically.

While Erich occupied himself with the phonograph, Liese
lit the candles and divided the chicken between their plates,
worrying that she should give herself a smaller portion, but
letting her appetite rule this out. "I noticed *Tonio Kröger*," she
said, deciding to confess. "I couldn't keep myself from going
into your room to see what you're working on. I hope that was
all right."

"Of course." Erich laughed as a Mozart piano concerto
filled the apartment. "And you discovered Master Kröger."

"I remember reading it for the first time when I was thirteen, memorizing lines, feeling so swelled up and poetic myself, I suppose—different, like Tonio, the outsider, looking in.
Paul and I talked about the story when we first met."

"You, Liese?" He looked at her with an amused expression.
"An outsider? But you're a well-to-do girl studying to be a
doctor. And if you don't become a doctor, you'll become
something else." He took his first sip of wine. "I didn't realize
that you felt poetic, too."

Liese flushed, feeling as dismissed as she had in the past
when talking to her father about her favorite stories. But she
went on, "I think about Tonio yearning to be like Hans Hansen, with his blond hair: *who else has blue eyes like yours, or lives
in such friendliness and harmony with the world?* This had such
meaning to me—Tonio's envy of Hans, how much he wanted
Hans to understand him, to love him just as he was." Erich got

up and returned to the phonograph, lifting the needle from the record and turning the knob of the radio across the flickering lights of several stations before settling on some American jazz. She saw he was only half listening to her, but couldn't keep herself from going on.

"Do you remember that, Erich—his wish that Hans be affected by the same things that he was affected by, the same stories, words, pictures? I'm not sure why I feel so much about all this. It's just such a beautiful story." She paused, then added: "Perhaps, too, it's that Jews always feel different somehow, always seeking the right words, our heads in books, outsiders in some way. Certainly we are now. And, of course, with this great wish to be understood."

Erich loosened his tie and undid his top button. He looked at her with an expression she'd never seen from him, eyes filled with indignation, as though what she'd said about the story were so extraordinarily wrong that she'd offended him.

"Liese, really, the story says nothing of being Jewish, but of being an artist, a writer, different in that sense." He sat back down and lit a cigarette, offering her one, though they'd hardly touched their dinner. She had no interest now in eating, and though she liked the look of holding a cigarette, she didn't enjoy smoking. "Different as in having the burden of too great a knowledge," he went on. "This burden exhausted him. It is that simple. One can't make the story what one wants it to be."

She looked straight into Erich's eyes. Holding back her anger, her tears, she expressed nothing of what she felt. He looked at her as if from some unreachable height.

"But forgive me, Liese," he said, seeming to realize he had

behaved badly. "Except for my talk with Kai and now, this dinner, it hasn't been a good day."

He put out his cigarette and returned to eating. "And really, it's just that I'm so involved in reading the story right now, perhaps for the twentieth time. Do you remember the line: *What there is left of art ought to be carefully preserved; one ought not to tempt people to read poetry who would much rather read books about the instantaneous photography of horses . . .* or whatever—the point is, about simpler matters." He paused and went on. "What was it Goethe said in *Wilhelm Meister? The human rabble ought to be afraid of stupidity if they really understood what is terrible.* Was that it?"

She stared at him, wondering if he was talking about her, hoping he couldn't read the fury that was filling her face, at the same time hoping he could.

"I don't mean you, of course," he said with a look of sudden warmth. "It's hard for me to talk about the story without feeling somehow that I possess it." Erich reached for her hand but pulled his back when she didn't offer hers in return. He fingered his empty wineglass before refilling it. "But let's change the subject. Can we agree to change the subject? The chicken is perfect. It's exactly what I needed." She turned away and looked out the open window at the foot traffic across the street. "I must say, and yes, in the service of changing the subject, that I would love to take you out for cake."

"But I've brought a cake," she said, turning back to him. Her voice came out at first as a whisper, though the thought of the beautiful rum-soaked cake she'd so carefully selected from Stérba's display case brought her back to life, reminding her that she was still hungry. It would lift her mood and maybe his.

She went into the kitchen and began to open the pink cake box tied with string, but the sound of Erich's voice stopped her.

"I've only just started to write my talk for Freie Vereinigung, and I'm anxious about time. Would you mind terribly if we saved the cake for tomorrow and you went to the film without me?" His pace quickened. "I'll walk you there, and I'll clean up as penance." He grabbed his jacket and was already heading toward the door. She replaced the cake in its box and resecured the string, feeling herself in a kind of daze as she pushed the box to the far corner of the counter, suddenly embarrassed by its festive presence.

They walked to the cinema in near silence. Passing evening strollers and workers leaving their cafés, Liese kept seeing people she thought she knew, relatives and friends from Frankfurt, and wanted to hurry toward them to look at their faces more closely, her homesickness overwhelming her anger and disappointment at how the evening was turning out. She watched a stray dog cross Vaclavske Namesti in the lights and shadows of the traffic, making it safely to the other side.

——

When she arrived home from class the next day, flowers were waiting outside the door to her room. Atop the bouquet of irises and lilies was a notecard:

Dearest Liese,
You probably understand our Tonio Kröger far better than I.
But whatever your feelings, I feel Mann's words as the idiom
of my soul. I wanted only to tell this to you, even if it ex-

pressed itself in a rather strongly scented patronizing language. Forgive me. Do you recall these lines from the second part of the story? Asked what in the world he meant to become, Tonio gave various answers, for he bore within himself the possibility of a thousand ways of life, together with the private conviction that they were all sheer impossibilities. I sometimes hold this conviction about myself, dear Liese. You console me as much as Thomas Mann does. More so. It is this time! I don't know how any of us will survive with our sanity intact. Again, forgive me.

Yours, Erich

She did forgive. If he was condescending, it was only because he had no choice but to be. *Ódu Sevéneli,* one of the first Czech phrases she'd memorized: having a soul, having a soul full of feeling and understanding. This was the most powerful thing about him; where others might see arrogance, she saw this. She would forgive him almost anything.

CHAPTER THREE

Freie Vereinigung

Late Fall 1933

The Charles University Freie Vereinigung meetings started late in the evening, after the libraries had closed for the night and the students had packed up their books. During the summer of 1933, the members started alternating their meetings among coffeehouses scattered throughout Prague. Since Hitler had come to power, the Czech and Jewish students, always at odds politically, found themselves united by a common enemy. Nothing revealed these new ties more than their willingness to merge their coffeehouse gatherings. That night the joint meeting would be held at Café Union, where Czech-speaking students had long gravitated.

Handwritten notices were fastened to the streetlight in front of the neoclassical building. As Liese approached the entrance, she inhaled gusts of tobacco, coffee, grease, and yeasty beer, all mingled with the scent of old plumbing. Bottles and glasses glistened in the café's dim lighting as she made her way across the crowded main room and through the dusty velvet curtains to a back room that had been set up for the meeting. It had a low curved ceiling, walls decorated with stippled mirrors, and heavy pine tables and chairs, nearly all occupied. Above the tables hung blazing red art nouveau lamps. The house phonograph played at full volume, but against the clamor of voices, the music was difficult to hear.

Erich stood at the center of the bar in the back of the room, embroiled in conversation with Hans and Erich Posner and several others while he searched his pockets for coins to feed, one after another, into a glass-domed nut dispenser mounted on the bar. Steffi Schlamm, waving her cigarette in the air, motioned Liese to the table near the front, where she sat with Willi and several young men Liese recognized from the Mayers' parties. Steffi pulled Liese toward her, sliding Liese's arm into the crook of her elbow as Willi, whose attention remained on his conversation with the others at the table, extended his hand absentmindedly.

Ten years older than Liese, Steffi was a gently rounded woman with a weathered, serious face and thick, high-set eyebrows that made her look eternally surprised. She'd married Willi just before both were forced to leave Vienna because of Willi's anti-Nazi writings. Some years out of school themselves, the Schlamms regularly joined the student gatherings, fulfilling the role, like Joszi and Fredy Mayer, of the seasoned older couple.

In the few months the Schlamms had lived in Prague, Erich Heller and Willi had become close, pooling their time and resources to keep *Die neue Weltbühne* afloat on a tiny budget of donations. Many a night they worked at the Schlamms' apartment in the Malá Strana, or at the Mayers', dreaming up plans to raise money to publish collections of their essays, some of which they tried out as speeches at the student meetings, before rushing them into print in the latest edition of their red-covered pocket-sized journal.

Steffi had studied child psychology and had taught in one of the most progressive children's schools in Vienna. But with the flood of immigrants seeking to escape Hitler, teaching positions were scarce in Prague, so she'd taken a job at the toy store. There, Liese often visited her after classes, pulling up a chair next to the counter as Steffi worked the cash register. Watching the mothers and children, breathing in the woody incense of the puppets on display, gazing idly at the carved horses fastened on wheels, the model train circling the room, and the dolls sitting down to tea in painted dollhouses, Liese didn't feel any pressure to keep a conversation going. Enclosed within this children's world, she could feel something rest inside of her, silencing the commotion in her head that had begun with her arrival in Prague and—with the exception of that first afternoon at the lakeside—almost never quieted.

Now, at the Union, Liese relished the sight of her spirited friend, the camphory smell of her sweater, her confident manner. Perhaps what Liese liked best of all was that Steffi seemed to embrace the role of romantic adviser.

"Erich's at the bar practicing his talk," Steffi said, her eyes serious with instruction. "Go join him!"

Liese was about to accept the challenge when Erich laid his jacket on the bar, motioned to a waiter standing nearby to lift the needle off the crackly record, and, ever-present cigarette between his lips, made his way to the front of the room. A table with a makeshift podium had been set up there, laden with literature from the Social Democratic Party, a stack of copies of the latest *Neue Weltbühne*, a bowl for contributions, and clipboards bursting with political flyers. The room was packed now: Latecomers carrying book satchels leaned against the walls, others looking up from the schoolwork they'd brought in, straining to hear what was going on. Smoke hung in the air, and cigarette ash dusted the floor and tables, making the Union's simple meals—bread dumplings swimming in gravy and sausages encased in thick rolls—look smudged and grimy. As the waiter passed, Liese whispered her order of chocolate cake and coffee. She could always bear the smell of the heavy Czech food better if she had something sweet on her own plate.

"Before tonight I thought everything important happened at the Continental," Erich said, switching to his best Czech from the German he'd spoken at the bar. "But clearly this is not in the least true. Plus, Unionka's waiters are far better-looking!"

He struck the table with a small kitchen mallet he'd taken from his mother's apartment in Komotau to call the meeting to order. "A thousand thanks, dear friends, for coming." He paused as plates were pushed away, fresh cigarettes were lit, and the room quieted.

"Anyone but dear Erich would limit himself to a hundred thanks," Steffi whispered, and Liese laughed. Erich went through the opening protocol of the meeting with polite if somewhat absent interest. Then he pulled a thin stack of typed notes, many times folded, from his shirt pocket, and motioned to those standing in back to find a place on the patch of empty floor in front of him.

Paul Heller, late for the meeting as he never was for medical classes, passed Liese's table as he headed for one of those spots, glancing at her with a lopsided smile. They seemed so little like brothers, Erich and Paul, Liese thought. Paul took life cautiously, seeming almost to dismiss himself in the shadow of Erich's larger presence. There was a melancholy in Paul's expression, a sadness that friends told her had been with him since their father's death. But he also had a buoyancy in his step and a lightness of heart that she'd seen peek out from time to time. Once, at the end of their anatomy class, after Paul got his first medical school exam back with the highest mark possible, Liese watched him break into an off-key coloratura from Dvořák's opera *Rusalka* as he left the lecture hall. "Silver moon, upon the deep, dark sky, through the vast night, you pierce your rays . . . smiling on men's homes and ways!" she heard while he nearly skipped down the hall, his head uncharacteristically high as he let his exam paper swing by his side. Now her mind wandered back to that moment, with Erich's voice filling the background. Only six months into her time in Prague, her command of Czech was far from assured. The more abstract Erich got, the less she could follow.

"Many of you will undertake serious work in the next months, campaigning for Social Democratic policies, campaigning *against* any possibility of aggression from the madman now leading Germany, helping the poor, the uneducated. But there's danger in our enthusiasm," Erich said. "So many of us *hope* without quite knowing what for. How do we ever know, I ask you, what to rightly hope for?

"We recognize some values as higher than others, of course! We recognize that fascism is evil, that Hitler is evil, and we want to find ways to push against him. But where does our sense of what is right and proper action come from?"

Erich spoke in an assured rhythm, looking up from his notes to his audience at just the right moments. Though his eyes never settled on anyone for very long, Liese hoped his glance would rest on her. Would he walk her home along the river after the meeting? Would they stop at a favorite pub for a late drink? Her face grew scarlet with pleasure when he nodded toward her, a nod that she weighed on the finest scale, replaying it for every sign of affection it carried.

"When once Confucius's disciples asked him what he would do first if he had to administer a country, he had a fascinating answer: *The first would be to correct language. If language is not correct, then what is said is not what is meant; if what is said is not what is meant then what ought to be done remains undone; if this remains undone, morals and arts decay; if morals and arts decay, justice goes astray; if justice goes astray, people stand about in helpless confusion. Hence language must not be allowed to deteriorate. This matters above everything.*"

Erich loosened his tie in his customary way and rolled up the sleeves of his light brown shirt, a perfect color match to his hair.

"A mark of earnestness, those rolled sleeves," Steffi whispered in Liese's ear as she rolled up her own with mock gravity. Willi gave her a look of slight disapproval, and with effort, she put on a more serious face. That Steffi always seemed to struggle a bit to be on her best behavior endeared her to Liese. And that she always seemed to know what she wanted to do, what she wanted to say—this was the Steffi Schlamm trait that Liese admired most.

"Tonight I want to speak to you of language and its connection to truth," Erich continued. "I ask you to think with me

about our Viennese comrade Karl Kraus, who is too often ignored today. I believe that his aphorisms, his plays, and most
of all his poems, should stand on the shelf of every one of us,
next to Goethe and Kant."

"Goethe and Kant? I think you must mean Hašek, Čapek,
and Marx!" shouted a Czech student sitting on the other side
of Liese.

"Yes, quite," said Erich. "Quite! Of course. But will you
permit me to go on? 'In case of doubt,' Kraus wrote, 'decide in
favor of what is *correct*.' What is *correct*! Is this not magnificent
instruction? That we could actually *know* what is correct?" He
stretched out the word "know," directing all his attention to
the young man who'd interrupted him. "I urge you to consider
this," Erich went on, leaning forward, "for it reveals the importance of Kraus for *us*. You see, he believes the only true
guide is language *itself*, the domain of the poet, the domain, he
argues, of the true political man as well. For Kraus, language,
passion, and thought are one and the same."

Erich looked as if he were enjoying a bracing windy day in
the mountains.

"He does not write *in* a language, but through him the
beauty and moral experience *of* language assume personal
shape. He is unwilling to bow to ideology, to fashion. He
grasps the demonic possibilities of mediocrity because it
shows itself in ideology-filled, faulty language. He grasps the
satanic depths to which inferiority may rise. He anticipated
Hitler long before anyone knew his name. How? Because of
Hitler's empty language. Human corruption, Kraus believes,
can be revealed instantly in the corruption of language, and
every correction of faulty speech induces a miniature catharsis

of the soul. We *must* emulate his faith that if we work language to its finest point of precision, it will tell us what we must know!"

The Czech student interrupted Erich again, arguing loudly that Kraus was an elitist, an apologist for the old Hapsburg regime. Marxism was the only way to counter Hitler, he claimed. Liese disagreed with him and wanted to say so, but Erich's opponent swallowed what was left of his beer and left the room, the curtains billowing behind him as he disappeared.

"For those of you still here, may I go on?" Erich asked. The stippled mirrors on the wall behind him distorted his head, with its crests of sandy hair. "I argue that seeking the purity of our language is part and parcel of seeking the truth about what is right—right thought, right action." Erich's face was filled with a furious radiance.

Coming from Erich, everything sounded so crucial, hopeful, as though the past, before Hitler, was returning, even still *becoming*. Lighting a fresh cigarette, Erich asked everyone to bear with him.

"Kraus reminds us that the world of the word teems with paradox. And yet for him, everything that truly *is*, is sayable: war, killing, but also trees, fountains, the peace of the mountaintops on a summer evening. The man who, night after night, alone at his writing desk, is besieged by the decomposition of his time, *our* time, reads Goethe, Claudius, Hölderlin, and again and again, Shakespeare's tragedies and comedies. To turn to anything less is the intellectual pretense of a spiritually impoverished age, false nourishment for the young seeking a home."

"Good God, Erich," Willi Schlamm broke in. "Trees, fountains, summer evenings!" Willi was a tightly wound man, all lean bones, nerves, and eyes, with a voice as strong as Erich's. "You speak of Kraus as if he were all the rage in political theory! Kraus's aphorisms and poetry are outdated, entirely beside the point. To believe that German literature, or heaven forbid, Shakespeare, can save us, can counter Hitler, well, we don't have that luxury anymore. Maybe someday we'll return to them, but certainly not now, Erich. We can no longer keep our own hands so clean."

"Some things *should* come to an end, Willi—naïveté, inaction! But not everything!" Erich said, looking past Willi and the roomful of people to some distant horizon. "Now, more than ever, we must claim this *luxury* as ours to keep."

His tone reminded Liese of his manner when they'd quarreled over *Tonio Kröger*—an exalted desperation. "Such idiocy," she heard Willi mumble as Steffi put her hand on his.

"I find myself in agreement with Erich," Steffi whispered to her husband, just loudly enough for Liese to hear.

Behind the bar, waiters were polishing glasses and beer mugs, and Liese saw them holding them up to the light before arranging them on the shelves. Even though this was taking place on the other side of the room, Liese worried she might break them, that although she was sitting there with Steffi eating her cake, something would overtake her and she'd fly off, overwhelming the neat rows of glassware, breaking everything in sight. It was like a dream she'd had more than once since arriving in Prague. She'd walk into a café, a classroom, a science laboratory, filled with glasses, bottles, vials, beakers, and her mere presence would cause them to break.

Once, when they were on a walk, she'd told Steffi about her dreams; Steffi had suggested it was she herself who felt breakable. "And why wouldn't you, Liese, dear child? How can any of us not?"

Erich folded his notes and asked if everyone was still awake. "I'd like to remind those of you who are that you are listening to the emotive noises of your leader who perhaps yearns too much for a world that no longer is. I have been accused of that." He raised his chin in teasing resolution. "And I'll stand accused."

The damp back of Liese's blouse clung to her skin. In the mottled mirrors that lined the walls, everyone was doubled and tripled, their faces, her own included, unrecognizable and flushed with wine and heat. The smells, the smoke, and now the words started to exhaust Liese. Her knees felt jammed under the cramped table.

"I have to stretch my legs, I'm sorry," she told Steffi. As she headed toward the bar, threading her way between legs and tables, Erich started to recite a poem by Kraus:

Where lives were subjugated by lies
I was a revolutionary—
Where norms against nature they sought to devise
I was a revolutionary;
When someone suffered I smarted within.
Where freedom became a meaningless phrase
I was a reactionary—
Where art they besmirched by their arty ways

I was a reactionary,
Backing all the way off to the origin.

———

Paul clambered to his feet from his spot on the floor of the meeting room, a stack of medical books under one arm. He'd heard much of Erich's talk before. He appreciated his brother's passion, envied his certainty, was critical of his grandiosity. One part of Erich's speech had filled him with a new sense of purpose, however: *Everything that truly is is sayable.*

Until Paul told Liese how he felt, he would be a sleepwalker. But how would he begin? His feelings for her were so disquieting that he felt pitiful and miserable. *Please excuse this force of heart. Please forgive this intruder, if he is that, and send him back to his world of imagination, but I must tell you,* he rehearsed in his mind. How flickering his confidence. He saw it, felt it. Then a moment later, his head felt like a dry dandelion, thoughts and words scattering in the air. He tried to approach her twice, only to panic and walk right past, before finally making his way back, against the current of those leaving, to where she stood at the bar. This time he stayed.

At first their talk was desultory, full of pauses and flaggings—their classes, their families—the kind of conversation Paul usually enjoyed but now only suffered.

"Erich certainly makes me think," Liese said in response to his question about her views of the meeting.

"About what?" he asked.

"Oh, God and the world," she said as she fastened her soft beret on her head at a fashionable angle, all the while eyeing

Erich. A group had gathered around him while he and Willi boxed up leftover copies of *Neue Weltbühne* and put the coins and bills from purchased copies in a leather pouch.

"*Ja*, well, that is a good combination," Paul responded. "God and the world." Catching his image in the mirror behind the bar, he thought the whole range of adolescence showed in his face. He had only contempt for himself as he realized their conversation resembled nothing he'd planned.

The music had returned, and there was a pause in activity as the bartender turned the record over. More students congregated near them, ordering fresh drinks or counting the marks on their beer mats, paying their checks and bundling up to leave. Above the bar, *putti*—plump naked babies made of granite and holding urns—looked down.

Steffi, the Posner brothers, and Franta Kraus had come over to the bar as well, kissing one another in greeting, catching up on gossip and news, for they'd been sitting far apart during the meeting. Paul glanced at his brother at the front table and saw his eyes locked with Liese's. Erich would remain there, Paul knew, debating, drinking coffee, long after most of the chairs were upside down on top of the tables and the waiters were done sweeping up the crushed cigarette ends and crumpled newspapers with their big brooms. He tried not to let his disappointment show when Willi joined them and Liese accepted the Schlamms' invitation to walk her home.

As a boy, Paul had made a bargain with "God and the world." Though it went against his nature, he vowed that he would summon the maximum optimism at his disposal. It was a technique he'd practiced since he read Hans Vaihinger in his early teens. According to Vaihinger, the only sensible approach to life was to behave "as if" it were meant to make sense, as if, all evidence to the contrary, life would treat you reasonably. Vaihinger had worked out an array of charts, graphs, and syllogisms to illuminate his "as if" principle, all of which appealed greatly to Paul.

The evening had done much to vanquish his hopes, but he was determined to act "as if" life would be tolerable even if Liese's devotion went to Erich, not to him. He took a deep breath and told himself three times not to worry as he walked over to say good night to his brother.

CHAPTER FOUR

Grab Up Life, My Child

Late Summer 1934

Our lovely child, may you be in good health. Don't worry about us, and be happy, began Albert and Irma Florsheim's birthday letter to their daughter. It arrived in her mail basket, one of many lining a wall of the front vestibule of her building, in August 1934, a few days before her twenty-first birthday. Like many of the letters from Liese's parents, it had been opened and resealed with German government-issue tape.

We know you can't write with detail, and we must be content with the hope for the future, the letter continued. *But we would be happy to hear anything about how things are going.*

Their words were always encouraging and cheerful but cryptic. *Our lives are very confined* was as far as they'd admit to any hardships. Rarely did Albert and Irma refer to Liese's letters to them, and of course they wrote nothing critical of Hitler's government. They seldom mentioned real names—*I* and *L*, Liese knew, meant Ille and Lilo. *I and L have gone abroad*, they'd written in a letter dated a few weeks before this one. *They promised they'll write to you when they're settled.*

She'd search between the lines for hidden meaning. In the

middle of the night, a seemingly insignificant detail would awaken her, her sleeping mind having endowed it with ominous meaning. She longed to call them, particularly at dusk when, as she walked home from classes in the gray twilight, the faces of the people who crossed her path were obscured just enough that she'd see her parents' features in them. But the house phone was near the entrance to the apartment of her landlady, whose son-in-law was rumored to be a Nazi. Friends offered their phones for Liese's use. Erich Posner even organized a Liese phone fund so she'd always have change in her purse to call her parents from pay phones. But as Nazi party membership grew in Prague, and as her friends' and particularly Erich Heller's anti-Nazi activities expanded, no phone felt safe. As much as she missed the sound of her parents' voices, it was almost more painful to speak to them in coded, artificial words than not to speak to them at all.

During those brief interludes when there were fewer reports of Jews and anti-Nazis being beaten or disappearing into protective custody, Albert and Irma's letters included more detail about practical matters—about daily life, their struggles to keep Albert's wine business going, their plans to send her tuition money when it was permitted again. The government was famous for granting permissions one day, only to withdraw them the next.

The birthday letter arrived as Liese was about to begin her third term of medical school. Her first year of studies had gone well, despite the many distractions. Now it was not clear whether she would be able to continue. She had enough money from her parents for one more semester, but that was it. Not that this was ever discussed in any detail in the letters they exchanged. Even their mention of sending money when it was permitted seemed risky to her. Although these less coded letters restored her parents' voices to her, she paid a price for the momentary comfort, always worrying that they'd disclosed too much for their safety.

They alluded, too, to their deliberations about leaving Frankfurt—Irma favoring it, wanting Albert to let her seek an affidavit from Hermann, her one uncle living in New York City, or to relocate to Prague until life in Germany was back to normal. "One will yet see," said Albert, as related by her mother. Liese knew that her father's faith in Germany was one on which he'd formed his life. Albert considered modern Germany—his Germany, not Hitler's—to be the most enlightened country on earth, far more emancipated than the United States, for instance. His friends who visited the U.S. were surprised how rare it was to find a Jewish professor teaching in an American university. True of England, too, he'd add. Like others in the Jewish Businessmen's Association of Frankfurt, of which he was secretary, Albert had always treated outbreaks of anti-Semitism as brief departures from Germany's post–Great War democratic principles. "The devil has appeared again," he'd say. "But it will be for only a brief visit. Unconstitutional! Certain to pass quickly!"

After all, he and thousands of other Jews had fought for Germany in the Great World War. He'd left for the front when Liese was an infant, achieving the rank of second lieutenant by the war's end. Liese vaguely remembered her father's return when she was four years old—the huge friendly stranger with the booming musical voice, the thick mustache, and the tall cap, bringing light into her mother's eyes. She remembered his handsome uniform with its high collar and the column of gold buttons running down the front, its scratchy feel when he hoisted her up on his shoulders and she wrapped her hands around his forehead, her legs sinking into the thick wool of his coat. When she rested her chin in his thinning hair, the color of ginger, she was sure it smelled like her paternal grandparents' farm in Alsfeld, where her mother had taken her often in the years he was gone. A photograph showing her father in full dress military uniform was displayed on a wall of the farm kitchen, and a similar one sat on her mother's nightstand. "Your *Vati*," her grandmother told her, and Liese diligently practiced the word. Now the uniform hung in his armoire, looking like a soldier standing at attention.

Even as Hitler consolidated his powers, even as he ordered that Nazi party officials who opposed his plans be shot, Albert still believed the dictator couldn't possibly prevail. "*Optimisten!* Trust me," he had reassured Liese on the morning, now over a year ago, when he, Irma, and Ernie had seen her off at the train station for her journey to Prague.

Liese brought the onionskin paper close to her nose, breathing in the faint smell of Albert's desk pad, leathery and old.

We have very nice acquaintances from many families, with whom we gather in different places, and in whom we can trust, and sometimes when necessary we have to cheer up one another, their birthday letter ended. *We hope to see you soon, dear child, and healthy. Grab up life, my child. Heartfelt greetings from your vater und mutter.*

She lifted it to her nose again, then added it to the letter box nestled in the folds of a nightgown at the top of her trunk.

Liese's brother, Ernie, was due to arrive on August 27, the very afternoon of her birthday. Liese was waiting for him at Masaryk Station, about a half mile beyond her apartment on Pariz Street, when his train pulled in. When the passengers disembarked, she spotted him immediately. He was carrying their father's huge brown leather suitcase in one hand and, in his other, a little bouquet of peach-colored roses, slightly wilted from the hot ride. Liese was carrying a bag of his favorite fruit dumplings, apricot, with a sprinkling of powdered sugar. She'd sampled several on her walk to the station, wiping the sugar off her lips, smoothing her skirt, and checking her appearance in the store windows.

Ernie was a big-shouldered, affable young man with soft brown eyes and an angular face, not quite handsome but pleasant and intelligent. Three years older than Liese, he was in many ways her opposite—less interested in politics and ideas, less overtly ambitious, less interested in school, though no less a lover of books and language. He seemed to his sister enviably practical and organized. For as long as she could remember, Ernie's ambition had been to join their father in the wine business. A love affair existed between her big brother and wine, and he wasn't even much of a drinker. He was enthralled by the calm, focused look in Albert's eyes while he worked, the smell of the old wood in the office cellar, the patient determination of the grapevines pushing their way through the gravelly banks of the Main River, and the hidden alchemy occurring inside the oak barrels as the grapes transformed into this most perfect of liquids.

The fascination had begun early. As a little boy, Ernie would leave the house at six each morning, while Liese was having her breakfast, to walk hand in hand with Albert to his office overlooking the river. In the hour or so before Ernie had to be in school, he perched himself on a stool across the desk from his father, while Albert, a brass spittoon by his side, tested new vintages. As he watched his father examine the contents of each tasting glass as if reassessing a piece of fine art, Ernie carefully wrote the name of each varietal in his composition book—Elbling, Silvaner, Bernkastler, Spätburgunder, Riesling—the same way other little boys might write down the names of famous soldiers or sports heroes.

When he was twelve, Ernie began to work in the warehouse after school and during summers. After affixing the labels, each depicting a shield adorned by a Star of David flanked by grapevines winding around the initials A.F. and the words *labor omnia vincit* (hard work conquers all), he'd arrange the elegant bottles in boxes soon to be sent to shops and restaurants all over Germany.

Now that Hitler had ordered a boycott of all Jewish businesses in Germany, Ernie was joining his sister in Prague, hoping to salvage the family company by finding new clients in Czechoslovakia. Seeing her brother walk toward her through the steamy exhaust of the resting trains, his shirt stained with sweat, looking so serious in his business hat and thick glasses, Liese was startled to feel, mixed with joy, a sense of shame for herself. Ernie was *doing* something for their parents, while she was only spending her father's money on school, studying, and having fun—the essence of a well-spent life, Liese's new friends had assured her, *particularly* in difficult times. Ernie had never been much of a talker with his sister. But once they'd deposited his suitcase in her room and they set out to see Prague, their year apart seemed to make Ernie capable of intimate conversation.

Like Liese, Ernie had never imagined working or studying in another country. And like Liese when she first arrived in Prague, he knew barely a word of Czech. He confessed to her the unease that gripped him whenever he allowed himself to think about how completely his father was depending on him. He also brought her up to date on all the people who'd left Frankfurt in the last months. Ille had gone to Switzerland, and Lilo had taken a cargo ship to Venezuela—they, too, leaving their parents behind. Frau Eppels was in Chile; their down-stairs neighbors, the Oppenheimers, had left without a word about where they'd gone. Ernie told her how worried he was about Albert and Irma. Albert was losing weight and aging, it seemed, by the hour. He'd shaved off his mustache and spent hours sitting upright in his favorite chair in the sitting room, a blanket wrapped around his shoulders, crying. Irma was hold-ing up better, reading a great deal, trying to stay in touch with friends, and surprising all of them with her strength. She was forever quoting lines from *War and Peace: Seize the moments of happiness; love and be loved. That is the only reality in this world. Harder and more blessed than all else is to love this life even in one's suffering.*

As Liese and Ernie sprawled out on the lawn at the edge of the Vltava, he described the new loudspeaker tower at the end of Scheffelstrasse, drawing a map on his knee with his finger to show its location, not far from their family's apartment. It was one of many the Nazis had erected, seemingly overnight, blar-ing propaganda at all hours. He recounted how he'd take side streets and alleys, sometimes adding an hour or more to his walk home from shopping or social engagements, in order to avoid saluting the SS who patrolled the main streets, or risk being beaten if he didn't. At the train station that very morning, he'd almost been arrested. "Are you Herr Fleischman?" the SS guard had asked as he inspected Ernie's passport. Ernie tried to look calm. "You are *not* Herr Fleischman?" the SS asked again as Ernie pointed to his last name on the passport and pulled out other identification papers when the guard remained unconvinced. They'd put him in a holding area until a senior officer finally decided he was indeed Herr Florsheim and allowed him to board the train just before it left the station.

"They all seem so happy and pleased with themselves, the more miserable they make us feel," he told his sister, looking to her like a young boy—an impression reinforced by the generous dustings of powder that fell from his dumpling onto his fingers, lips, and chin. Ernie tried to lighten the mood by practicing and perfecting his pronunciation of the Czech delicacy. *"Ovocne knedlicky."* The consonants, particularly the *chuh-k* sound of the "ck," produced a mist of sugar that had them both laughing with relief at the welcome turn the conversation had taken.

The afternoon was hot, but a summer storm was about to break. They eyed the clouds, but neither of them wanted to get up.

"This Erich Heller you've written us about. When will I meet him?" Ernie asked.

"In a few hours! If he doesn't pick us up by eight, the arrangement is to meet him at the regular table at the Continental. You'll love him, Ernie! You'll love my friends. They'll all be there to celebrate exams being over. But most of all to meet you," she added, seeing worry in his face.

"Are you intimate?" Ernie asked, uncharacteristically forthright. His face turned pink. "You and Erich, I mean."

Liese imagined Irma and Albert coaching their shy son. "Of course!" she said, doing her best Marlene Dietrich and turning pink herself. "Don't I have sex written all over me?"

Ernie blew his nose in response, the signal he'd employed throughout their growing-up years that his sister's teasing had stepped out of the bounds of his comfort zone. "Excuse me." He blew his nose again, returning his handkerchief to his pocket. "What I really mean is, does he love you?"

She longed to be able to say yes, he did, but in spite of Erich's regular presence in her life, in spite of his invitation to go steady, in spite of her certainty that she loved *him*, she couldn't.

"You have to pay the penalty for the first question. And you can tell Mutti no, I don't yet know what he has underneath his trousers! We haven't been that close, not even half undressed!"

The awkward truth was she and Erich were rarely alone. Erich seemed to see to that. Once he left her holding a bottle of champagne at the door of her room when he realized he was late for a political meeting. When she wanted kisses, he went on about Nietzsche's "pathos of distance"—the notion that keeping a distance could be a passionate thing. He claimed that sensations of tenderness were sometimes better felt than expressed.

In reality, she spent much more time with Erich Posner and Steffi than with Erich Heller. EP's appetite for sweets and penchant for keeping his room messy rivaled Liese's and endeared him to her. Like her, he was a lover of gardening and a lover of Tolstoy. Sometimes they'd stay up half the night at the Continental, challenging each other about Tolstoy's views. Lately the subject was *The Kreutzer Sonata*. Liese believed it to be a profound exploration of intimacy between men and women, while EP saw its meaning in far simpler terms: a proclamation against confining sexual intercourse to the institution of marriage. That argument left her more than a little worried that he was starting to feel toward her in ways she didn't feel toward him. He was such an affirming figure, relieving her self-doubt with compliments. But she wasn't attracted to him, with his sloping shoulders, prominent nose, and round belly. EP seemed blessedly unaware that these features counted against him.

But this was not the time to tell Ernie about these complications in her love life. "Oh, I do love him," she told her brother as it started to drizzle. "I just admire him so much."

They were lying under an old chestnut tree. Coaxed by the rain, several pieces of ripe fruit bounced on the ground next to them.

"But I think love is not so much a matter of admiration, you know, but—" Ernie didn't have a chance to finish before Liese took both his hands, pulled him up, and led him toward the sidewalk.

"Let's go to one of my favorite places!" she said. "Yes, I *am* changing the subject!"

They walked along Dvorakovo Nabrezi, steam rising from the storm drains at the center of the brick street, and across Charles Bridge, the black statues shiny with fresh rain. Ernie bought an umbrella from a vendor's cart, and under it they walked up the hill toward the castles and Zlatá Ulička, where a number of fortune-tellers conducted their business.

Despite not really believing in fortune-telling, Liese had visited Madame Thebes on four different occasions, especially when events in Germany seemed to be taking a turn for the worse, as they had earlier that summer, when Hitler purged the more moderate leadership of his party. Madame Thebes lived in a house no taller than a man's height, fronted by window boxes filled with poppies. Liese would sit across from her at a low table covered by silk scarves, the prettiest of which matched the one Madame Thebes wore around her head. Every so often Madame would reach into her bottomless apron pockets, pulling out crystals and amulets and vials of powdered medicines. "You have arrived under good signs," she assured Liese on her first visit soon after she'd met Erich Heller. "The heavens smile." Whatever Liese's mood when she arrived, Madame Thebes's attentive eyes, her look of confidence, her predictions of health and prosperity for Irma, Albert, and Ernie, and romance and love for Liese, always calmed her. Liese was charmed, too, she told Ernie, as she urged her reluctant brother to come with her, that Madame Thebes ended each session by sprinkling lilac-scented foot powder in her shoes. "To protect you," she'd say, kissing Liese on both cheeks and holding her hands together as if praying.

Now, as they entered her tiny house, Madame assured them both that Ernie had arrived under good signs, too. Madame closed her eyes for several minutes, holding Ernie and Liese's hands across the table; Ernie wore a skeptical look throughout. Then Madame opened her eyes with delight. She was certain they would both flourish and prosper. She encouraged them to return with the photo of their parents Liese had brought in before. She would provide Irma and Albert with new fortunes as well.

"What nonsense!" Ernie said afterward. "Though I have to admit that I feel curiously relaxed." They splurged on chocolate from the shop across the street and, in their freshly powdered shoes, headed to the university, where she showed Ernie the immense medical lecture hall of Charles University where many of her classes were held. Sitting in the back row, she pointed to where Erich Posner, Franz Gollan, Franta Kraus, and Paul Heller sat for morning lectures, closer to the front than she ever dared.

They left the university in time to watch the procession of the twelve hand-carved wooden apostles emerge from their little door under the clock tower at the center of Staré Mesto, a performance that had delighted Prague citizens one minute before every hour for over four hundred years. Except for meeting her friends, Liese could imagine no more perfect Prague event to welcome her brother.

It was dusk by the time they got back to Pariz Street. It had cooled off and stopped raining, but the afternoon heat and moisture had collected in Liese's room. The night before, she'd pushed the desk aside and made a bed of blankets and pillows on the floor for Ernie. She knew he'd refuse to put her out of her bed. She'd taken down her only wall decoration, a Van Gogh print of a chair with a rush-grass seat—*Vincent's Chair with His Pipe*—which reminded her of the chairs on the porch of her grandparents' farmhouse. She'd dusted its wood frame and leaned that and a photograph of Albert and Irma on their honeymoon against the wall next to Ernie's bed. The rest of her room was chaotic, filled with notebooks, clothes, scissors, empty inkwells, a tin of saddle soap, a single shoe on a shoe tree, hairpins, crumpled handkerchiefs, candle stubs, scraps of paper scrawled with telephone numbers. She'd kept her childhood room at home in much the same state, finding her sense of self in the clutter: This is me. I am here.

She could tell Ernie was tempted, but he refrained from teasing her about the mess, as he had always done at home. Instead he expressed admiration that she'd found a room with its own sink and with the toilet just down the hall, and he stared with wonder at the tall stack of textbooks for her fall classes—histology, physiology, embryology, neurology, topographical anatomy. Piled neatly on her desk, they, like his bed on the floor, were an oasis of order.

He made room for his suitcase and, kneeling beside it, pulled out reams of business forms, enough carefully folded clothes to last him through Prague's chilly fall, and the small Adler typewriter Albert had used in business for twenty-five years, wrapped in linens. Under them was a square package in yellow paper—a birthday gift from her parents—which Liese quickly tore open to discover a black patent leather belt; a framed photograph of Lilo, Ille, and Liese taken at the end of their first year in gymnasium; and the family book of Matthias Claudius poems. Liese plopped down on her bed and opened the weathered book to gaze at her mother's familiar underlinings in faded ink.

The moon has risen
The golden starlets sparkle

Brightly and clearly in the heavens;
The wood stands black and silent
And from the meadow rises
The white fog wondrously.

It had always been at night, when her mother read poetry to her before she fell asleep, that Liese felt the full force of Irma's tenderness toward her. Reading the Claudius poem now, she could almost feel her mother's good-night kiss on the top of her head.

"What do I wear to meet your friends?" Ernie asked. He searched through the pile of clothes on his bed, looking worried again. It was already after eight.

"How about your blue sweater?" she asked, spotting a favorite knitted by their grandmother. The familiarity, the sense of domesticity, contained in the question felt so comforting.

"And what do I talk about after I say *Guten Tag*?" His voice was muffled in wool as he pulled the sweater over his head.

"Rilke, Goethe, and Hitler are always good," Liese said, full of playfulness as she cinched her new belt around her waist.

"And after Rilke, Goethe, and Hitler?"

"With Erich Heller, that will last for hours! Then we'll plead exhaustion, come home, and go to sleep." She put her arms around him.

"I like the last part especially!" he said.

———

They were the first to arrive, her friends joining them in twos and threes. Ernie shook hands as Liese made introductions, but he entered into the conversation only when someone asked him a direct question. Even then he hesitated and repaired his sentences before finishing them. She could tell from his eyes that he wanted to take part but didn't know how.

"Ernie, I hope you realize you are about to become a member of the family, really, quite officially!" Franz said. "Our family life begins with the Continental's terrible cooking!" They admired their soggy sausages and rolls with ironic exaggeration.

Erich Heller finally arrived in time for dessert, kissing Liese as well as Steffi and the other women, putting his hand on the men's shoulders, and presenting Ernie with a bottle of wine he carried under his arm. He moved a chair between Liese and EP, spreading his arms behind them.

Steffi had ordered a plum cake for Liese's birthday, and when their favorite waiter, Georg, set it on the table, the unpeeled purple plum halves baked into the cake's surface looked to Liese like beautiful stained-glass domes. At the table, Georg decorated each slice with chocolate cream, his aim suffering and splats of cream landing on his wrist every time he got too involved in the conversation. "If you don't go like this," EP said to him, licking up imaginary chocolate from his own wrist, "I'll lose all respect for you!"

With Ernie on one side of her and Erich on the other, Liese felt a pleasure similar to what she'd felt as a child when Lilo, Ille, and she built playhouses out of sheets pinned together and draped over the Florsheims' four high-back chairs. "And if all else breaks, our little wreath stays as one." This was her *Kränzchen*'s private battle cry, the friends reciting it in unison, dissolving in giggles at the earnestness of their declarations of love and loyalty to one another. She'd felt then as if she were sitting inside a paperweight—a beautiful scene, protected and contained.

Paul Heller had taken to avoiding most occasions where he thought Erich and Liese were likely to show up together. He kept away from Liese's birthday celebration, and he kept away from the Continental, studying instead at the Manes Café overlooking the river. He stopped going to the Mayers' parties and attended Freie Vereinigung meetings less frequently, always sitting in the back. It was mostly in classes and the library that he'd see Liese.

Even in these late-summer weeks before the fall term began, Paul poured all his energy into his studies. In his first year he'd won a research assistantship usually awarded to third- or fourth-year students, and he was working late hours in Professor Heinrich Waelsch's lab, studying blood proteins under the supervision of Waelsch's research team. Never before had Paul felt so focused and able, so fully at home in a subject matter. It was exactly what he felt he needed—something on which he could bear down with all his concentration and energy so as not to think about Liese.

He'd return to his room late at night, almost light-headed. He shared the place with Richard Spitzer, another medical student, and Paul Schülle, who studied law, in a baroque-style dormitory in the medical school complex. His room was enormous compared to the bedroom he'd shared with his brother in Komotau, with vaulted ceilings and high windows. Though it was cold and needed a good scrubbing, Paul found its griminess romantic. He and Richard had intense discussions of bio-chemistry formulas, anatomy problems, and embryology findings, which were occasionally interrupted—when Paul Schülle joined in—by wistful comments about girls they'd seen at a café or concert.

With his stipend from the lab, Paul had money for theater, concerts, even opera. Until he'd come to Prague, his cultural experiences had consisted mainly of concerts given by the Komotau Orchestra, conducted by their family dentist, Dr. Fleischman, and the town's amateur theater performances, which he and Erich had attended all their lives. They seemed almost childlike in comparison to what he was accustomed to now.

He had waves of homesickness, but the aspects of Komotau life that he missed, he found a way of re-creating in Prague. He discovered a bakery that had apple strudel similar to that served at Bobby Komisch's haberdashery in Komotau, a men's clothing and hat store that also housed a café serving pastries, light lunches, and cold drinks.

Paul had created a life for himself that made him feel happy, a feeling that took some getting used to. It was hard for him even to say the word out loud. He thought of his former self and dubbed him "Tantalus," a character he'd read about in his gymnasium Greek class. Tantalus had been doomed by the gods to spend his days underneath a tree full of delicious fruit, but every time he wanted to pluck a piece to eat, the branches moved just beyond his reach. Tantalus Heller, he thought, hadn't needed wrathful gods to keep life's pleasures out of reach. He'd needed only his cautious, doubt-filled self.

Not that he wasn't still prone to worries—about politics,

about his mother's health, about whether he'd ever find a girl-friend as beautiful and easy to talk to as Liese Florsheim. His gnawed fingernails reminded him of that. And he missed his father, who had been dead for over five years, more than ever. He wished Alfred Heller could have witnessed this new phase of his life.

During his first two school terms in Prague, and now over the summer of 1934, Paul took the train home to Komotau every Friday, leaving the library or his lab bench early enough to ar-rive at the Heller family apartment before dark. His first task was to carry enough coal upstairs from his mother's cellar to heat the stove and provide hot water for the coming week. Else had been diagnosed with a mild form of leukemia shortly after Alfred's death, but her treatments had been successful, and her doctors were optimistic. He'd sit with her at his fa-ther's old medical office desk, now in the sitting room, reassur-ing her about the prognosis, which had inspired his interest in blood research, and helping her sort through the tangle of legal and financial matters Dr. Alfred Heller had left unat-tended.

Saturday mornings, he bicycled to the Alaunsee. Just as he had every summer since he was a boy, he swam the length and back before the beach grew crowded, making sure to be gone early in case Erich, Liese, and other friends showed up for an afternoon outing. Then he was off to Bobby Komisch's gen-eral store in the market square. He sat outside on the stoop and watched Bobby hold court on the sidewalk, expounding to the square's diverse cast of characters on music, books, theater, politics, and most important, the news of the town. He reported on everything Paul wanted to know—who'd gotten married, who was having a not yet public romance, who'd had a baby, who'd taken a new job, who'd left, who'd returned.

Once caught up, Paul headed to Komotau's two bookshops: Julius Mendel's, a tiny, musty shop owned by an elderly Jew; and just across the square, its rival, Deutsche Volksbuchs Handlung, specializing in German books. Even if he was now a cosmopolitan Pragueian with access to the city's biggest bookshops and libraries, he still liked to see what was new in his hometown bookstores' windows.

Saturday afternoon, when he boarded the train back to Prague, it was hard for him to say good-bye. He'd never been close to his mother, but since Alfred's death, he felt an attachment that took him by surprise.

When Paul was fourteen years old, in a section of his office partitioned off by a curtain, Alfred had shot himself in the chest. He survived but was grievously injured and died months later from the effects of the gun blast. The crowd at his funeral was so large that it seemed to Paul all of Komotau was there.

The one personal item Paul took when he left home for medical school was his father's pocket watch. He liked having it, but even more than that, he needed it to hold on to an image of Alfred that countered those he carried from the last months of his father's life. He couldn't keep the counterimage in his mind's eye longer than a few seconds at a time, but in it, Alfred was in silhouette, and Paul was next to him, their heads together, sitting on the bench of the family's horse-drawn buggy that Alfred always used for house calls, ready to begin a conversation.

CHAPTER FIVE

Everything Is Still Becoming

Spring 1936– Winter 1937

When Liese closed her eyes, the room, the sofa she lay on, and she herself seemed to be floating in a sea of black. "I need to vomit," she said.

"You go right ahead, dear girl," Steffi said in her down-to-earth voice, nodding toward Ernie with lifted eyebrows—his turn to help her get to the toilet. Steffi was reading aloud from the opening pages of a Gustav Meyrink story about a black velvet ball suspended in a glass vessel that, when in contact with certain elements, exploded into a "mathematical nothing" and sucked up all the thoughts in the room. On the way to the washroom, steadying herself on her brother's arm, Liese clung to fragments of the last sentences she had heard: *You there, interpreter, is one permitted to think of something imaginary? I wish to think of something imaginary.* When Liese returned to the sofa, pulling the wool blanket close to her chin, Steffi's silhouette transformed into that of a big pirate woman, Ernie's into their father as a young man.

Falling back to sleep, which, during the hot midsummer days of 1936, seemed to be the most basic act of her body's defense system, she dreamed she was standing in front of the Florsheim family apartment on Scheffelstrasse. It was early in the morning and the street was deserted. From the sidewalk, she could see through the windows to the sitting room, bare except for her father sitting in his chair, reading. He saw her and came to the window. "What are you doing here?" he asked.

"Resting," she said. "I've come to rest. That's all."

It was nearly three months since Liese had returned from Capri. She hadn't told her parents or even Ernie that she was spending her spring break there, alone with Erich. Franz Gollan and Edith Abeles, as well as Franta Kraus and Lisa Hirsch, had become engaged that winter. Tentative about their relationship for two and a half years, Erich had told Liese that he, too, wanted to turn the page on their romance. He wanted to consummate their love during a spring trip to the Italian island, he announced. Liese eagerly assented. She missed her last exam in chemistry, meeting Erich at Masaryk Station to catch the early train to Milan, then another to Naples, where they boarded a small tourist boat to the island.

The location was Erich's idea—his literary idols had gone to Capri for inspiration, Goethe writing poems and letters on its beaches—and it was also his idea that it be just the two of them. He was tired of politics, tired of Prague, tired of Marienbad and the Sudeten mountain settings where they always went on holidays as a group. And though his mother wanted him to spend spring break in Komotau, he told Liese that he couldn't bear the thought of it, particularly of going to the Alaunsee, where Nazi flags now lined the shore.

Still, Liese would have preferred somewhere closer. She

wanted to be able to tell Ernie how to reach her without his guessing that she and Erich were traveling alone. Not that he would have objected. Two years in Prague had transformed Liese's reserved and old-fashioned brother into a modern cosmopolitan. Ernie counted himself as a staunch advocate of premarital sex, always joking with Liese about her popularity with men and hinting that he would gladly accept her help finding a girlfriend in Prague. But she worried what he would tell their parents if Albert and Irma happened to call while she was away, and she didn't want to put him in the position of having to lie for her. So she told him she was going to the mountains with friends.

She and Erich rented a tent on a beach of tiny pebbles, overlooking huge limestone rocks jutting out of the sea. In the days before they'd left, Liese had gone to Steffi's gynecologist to be fitted with a cervical cap, which she carried in an empty cigarette case in her travel bag. She and Steffi had made quite a ceremony of wrapping the little piece of rubber, which Liese thought looked like a child's pacifier, in pastel tissue paper that Steffi brought home from the toy store.

On the train, quite out of the blue, Erich told Liese that a woman never got pregnant the first time. He hadn't brought a condom and didn't plan to buy one. It would only interfere.

Remembering that trip, Liese wondered how she could have ignored that air of condescension, even slight cruelty, and yet again let herself believe that he was right, though she knew better.

That night, outside their tent, they drank two bottles of wine, Erich quoting Nietzsche: "For any aesthetic activity to exist, a certain physiological precondition is indispensable: intoxication!" It was windy and cool for early April. Two men walking past their tent wearing paper party hats blew them kisses.

After they made love, which for Liese turned out to be anything but an "aesthetic activity"—painful, sweaty, mechanical, nothing like what she'd expected, what she'd looked forward to for so long—Erich treated her with absentminded politeness, then impenetrable silence. While she washed the blood from their towel with seawater, he announced that he needed a walk. He wanted to go alone. She walked too slowly, he said, and would prevent him from going on a walk of what he called "the right kind."

Hours passed. She searched for him on the long stretch of beach, lit only by the moon and small fires at the water's edge, but soon turned back. Every few steps, the backs of her legs tightened.

She wrapped herself in his coat outside their tent, lighting his cigarettes, taking one or two puffs before laying them in a crater she dug in the sand, long worms of ash measuring out the time.

He returned at sunrise with milk and cheese, looking exhausted and disheveled. He spoke in halting, broken sentences: "I begin to suspect that . . . I begin to suspect that I . . ."

Liese had never seen Erich at a loss for words. "I begin to suspect that I have not much grand in my composition," he blurted out finally, looking directly at her. "I can't give you what I don't have," he went on, rasping, for his voice went hoarse.

She thought at that moment that she hated him, even when her mind turned to wondering what it was that he hated in her.

While Erich remained in Capri for the week they'd planned,

she returned to Prague the next day, having decided to end the relationship; she got seasick on the tourist boat, even though the Mediterranean was as tranquil as a pond.

By June, the beginning of her ninth semester at medical school, and six weeks since that night in Capri, she was trying to ignore the meaning of the small swelling in her belly, the absence of her period the month before, the fact that since returning from Capri, she'd gone from having little appetite to wanting to wolf down thick pieces of bread and meat and to drink ice-cold Prazdroj beer, which had never tasted so good. When her period didn't return by early July, the gynecologist confirmed that she was pregnant.

She met Erich at the Palace Hotel on the corner of Jindruska and Panská on a particularly muggy afternoon. In public, neither of them had been able to bring themselves to say anything about their breakup; only Ernie and Steffi knew something of what had happened in Capri. They'd continued to see each other at the Continental and at the Mayers' parties when they were with the group, but each avoided seeing the other alone. When she'd written to Erich to request a meeting, he suggested the Palace Café, where it was less likely that they'd run into friends. It wasn't one of their regular haunts, but they'd gone there together on the nights when Karl Kraus, who'd recently traveled to Prague and become friendly with Erich, performed Offenbach operettas, transforming the staid café into a dazzling theater.

Now, arriving between lunch and dinner, they ordered rice pudding with bits of caramelized sugar floating on top. When she told him she was pregnant, his eyes rested on his pudding for several moments. Then he said, in a tone of the greatest tact and restraint, that it was for Liese to decide what she wanted to do, and that he would support her in whatever course of action she chose. "You have an abundance of good sense," he added.

Though his voice was full of sadness and tenderness, he looked neither sad nor tender but stunned, with a slightly blaming look in his eyes, Liese thought.

Moments of silence gave way to one of his famous quotes, this time from the Austrian philosopher Otto Weininger, whose books and articles he told her he'd recently discovered: "No one who is honest with himself feels bound to provide for the continuity of the human race." Then he broke down and cried. "That I should have brought any disturbance into your life, I will have always to regret," he went on.

All that held her together at that moment was the pudding, each spoonful delivering her to connectivity with herself, not the self that she'd sometimes feared might be about to vanish into thin air, but corporeal, solid, and with it the realization, always in the back of her mind since Capri, that she was not helpless without him, that she had already learned to be on her own, and would continue to learn, whether she had the baby or not.

She wanted him to see that and nothing else, least of all her longing to reach for his hand.

In the days that followed, she talked to Steffi almost every day about whether to have the baby. With Ernie, she had similar conversations, and with Madame Thebes, who offered no advice, only her certainty that the baby would be beautiful, like Liese. For the first time since coming to Prague, she tried to attend Friday-night service at the synagogue across from the small Jewish cemetery near her building, but left when she was told that women congregants could only look through the small slits behind the wall. Walking out, she broke down and cried, the praying men's harmonies drifting in the air behind her.

The doctor who performed the abortion, illegally, in a makeshift clinic down a winding alley in the Malá Strana, was a tall, middle-aged man with thinning hair and a double chin. Oddly, for all his office's shabbiness, an ornate crystal chandelier hung from the ceiling in the middle of the examination room, and she heard it tinkling as she went under the anesthesia. When she awakened, the doctor made her view the fetus, which lay, no bigger than her thumb, in an enamel bowl. His way of preventing it from happening again, he insisted, of justifying his work. He thought it was a girl, he told her. Liese fainted.

In the cab on the way home, she laid her head in her brother's lap. *"Was für ein Trottel,"* she said. What a jerk.

"Was für ein Trottel!" Ernie repeated loudly, fury ringing forth from this otherwise reserved young man.

"I meant me," Liese whispered before she fell back asleep.

———

Erich sent flowers and notes: *I have such a confusing entanglement of feelings.*

When she didn't respond, he sent more flowers, more notes. *The lack of contact between us weighs on me daily.* But what had happened in Capri, what had happened at the Palace Café, what had happened in the office down the winding alley, had released something in her. Every note, every flower, from Erich brought only anger and a sense of further distance from him.

For five days she lay on the Schlamms' sofa under a wool blanket, listening to Steffi read aloud from favorite stories, cabaret comedy on the radio, and the 78s that Willi played at night on their gramophone. Ernie appeared at the door of the Schlamms' apartment at dinnertime with bags of chocolate and sugared dumplings. He plopped himself at the foot of the sofa, occupying himself with little projects, fitting a wooden puzzle on the ring of his key chain, oiling his pocketknife. When Liese was no longer nauseated, Ernie reminded her of the paper bags that lined the Schlamms' kitchen counter. "Never let anyone tell you that you can have too many dumplings," he instructed as Steffi prepared extravagant hot meals for the four of them, decorating each with chives and nettle shoots she clipped from the herb garden on the kitchen windowsill.

In late July, Liese left the Schlamms' to return to summer classes and to her room on Pariz Street. Steffi held her tightly in her arms when she said good-bye and kissed her on both cheeks. "Head high," she said.

Dear Children,
For the past three days, blustery and rainy, then an hour or two of sun, then more storms; two sides of the weather are in

discussion with each other. Unlike promises the weather can make, we hope to answer our doubts with creativity and concentration. One will yet see. Love to Liese on your 23rd birthday. Irma and I are both well. Albert Florsheim, August 13, 1936

A few days later, another letter. Along with Albert's sister, Hedy, they had obtained stamped immigration cards to Luxembourg, Albert wrote in uncharacteristically tiny cramped handwriting, as though whispering. *Many decisions need to be made and quickly. Write, please, with your opinions on what we should pack and what better left behind. Container 28 cu. meters. Definitely we will leave behind the older table—too large and heavy, and, of course, we will leave piano behind. We want to bring the high-back chairs and Mother's blue armchair. We can break down clothing cabinet so it will take little room. We will reluctantly part with writing table—too large and heavy. Big question is green sofa. The material is no longer pretty, in need of recovering. What do you think? And the bookcase will take up little space in the container for it can be in back, behind other things, not deep, maybe 30 cm, but wide, 2 m. The kitchen utensils and candlesticks, of course, and the silver trays and tea set. Adler typewriter already with E. Wine labels, photographs, books, clothing for Mother and myself. Give your opinions. In October it should all be picked up. I think that's all there is to be decided. Heartfelt greetings, lovely children, may you remain in good health. Don't worry about us and be happy. From your father, Albert.*

At the bottom and up the sides of the thin paper, Irma had added: *Father and I greet you from full hearts. Went to a chamber music concert. It was beautiful and there is still much that is beau-*

*tiful to play. The way we look at the world remains strong. Warm-
est greetings and kisses. Mother.*

For several days in late August 1936, one letter followed
another, each addressed to them both at Pariz Street, for she
and Ernie had cautioned them that mail service to Zizkov, the
section of Prague where Ernie had taken a room, was even less
reliable than to Staré Mesto. Each letter described, in cryptic,
abbreviated form, elements of their plan.

Hedy was with them now, having given up the family farm
in Alsfeld to their closest neighbor, who would look after their
goats and chickens until Hedy could return. Albert's younger
brother, Julius, and his wife were already in Luxembourg and
had found a small apartment they could all share. At the beginning and end of the letters, the weather served as metaphor,
Liese concluded, for their inner worlds: *Today, weather terrible.
Today, weather pleasant and comfortable. Today, weather tolerable.*

Since her abortion, Liese had been avoiding her old group
of friends. But now she sought many of them out for advice
and reassurance. The Mayers and Franz Gollan thought Luxembourg an excellent "way station," as they called it, though
not a place to stay long, from what they'd heard. Duchess
Charlotte was a strong, benevolent leader, but the country
lacked good newspapers, the music, the museums, the theater
of Prague. But if they didn't apply for work permits, it would
be a straightforward matter to get from Luxembourg to
Prague. The Mayers offered their extra room, saying they
could stay indefinitely. EP, Franz, Edith, and Franta thought
the choice of time to leave was perfect, while the country was
on center stage during the Olympic Games and all accounts

indicated Hitler was on his best behavior. They would board the train accompanied by Olympic stars.

Of all the reassuring words her friends provided, it was that image that calmed her most, non-German swimmers and track stars, javelin hurlers and weight lifters befriending and protecting her parents and aunt.

She knew that whatever his diminishment in the years she'd been gone and whatever his doubts, her father's most durable strengths would be revived by the tasks involved in preparing to leave. He would surely organize their packing, dispatching Irma from room to room, his leather-covered notepad in her hand. In turn, she would update and revise lists, jotting down measurements in neat columns as they debated the merits and drawbacks of each decision down to the smallest detail. "Keeping up with Irma Florsheim is a lost cause," Albert would say at the end of each day's work, just as he had so many times when Liese was a child. "I'm in no condition to keep up with Irma Florsheim!"

She could picture her mother quietly returning the notepad to the upper-right drawer of the writing table once the day's decisions had been recorded. That was its home, after all, where the notepad could always be found and where it would be returned even if the writing table itself were left behind.

For weeks, almost as if no danger had existed before now, as if Hitler had only just arrived on the scene, Liese's fears for her parents' and aunt's safety grew exponentially, alive in everything she saw, heard, touched—in cobblestones, in music, in the already changing leaves. Though the fall classes of her fourth year had begun, medical school and the public world of Prague almost ceased to exist for her, intruded upon by her worry and anticipation of their getting out. She worried that they'd disclosed too many details in their letters, that her landlady's son-in-law had been reading them, making the necessary phone calls to Germany, that her own carelessness, whatever it may have been, would imperil them. Walking along Pariz Street, crossing Charles Bridge, descending the concrete steps to the Vltava to watch the boats, she felt as if she herself were newly at risk.

Then, as the October departure date Albert and Irma had alluded to grew closer, their letters stopped.

EP and Hans Posner offered their mother as an intermediary. Rumors swirled that Nazis had spies among all the phone operators in Prague. But the Posners reassured her that the operator who handled calls in their hometown of Karlsbad was a close family friend and could be trusted to manage communications with all possible secrecy.

It was through Annerl Posner, then, that Liese learned how the plan to leave Germany had fallen through. As the day of her family's departure approached, just before the shipment crate was to be picked up, the transport company instructed Albert and Irma to move it to a common area of the apartment building to simplify the process of collecting it. A downstairs neighbor, who had just moved into the building, complained of its presence to the police, and the crate, with all its contents, was impounded. Albert, Irma, and Hedy were ordered by the Gestapo to remain in Germany until the packing crate could be examined. In the meantime, because they were now considered enemies of the state, their savings account had also been confiscated, and they could no longer send tuition money to Prague. To challenge any of this would take months. They'd have to fill out hundreds of forms, each requiring different signatures from scores of obscure government offices. They hadn't the stomach for trying, nor, they were convinced, would it do them any good, only drawing unwanted attention to all of them that might hamper later efforts.

Though most of the news came from Irma, in the end Albert took the phone and asked Mrs. Posner to tell his children that there were many advantages to their leaving later and even to being rid of their furniture and money. They would be eating less, he joked, and therefore would take up less space when they did get out. Until such time, Mrs. Posner was to tell Liese and Ernie, they would continue to manage.

The conversation, not longer than fifteen minutes, had touched Mrs. Posner. Shortly after hanging up the phone, she said, she'd started to cry uncontrollably, as though they were the dearest of friends.

Days after Albert and Irma's failed attempt to leave Germany, Liese dropped out of medical school. With her parents no longer able to send tuition money, and she herself unable to secure one of the few work permits still available to refugees, Liese applied to the Czech government's Refugee Funds Committee to enter a new two-year social work program that was starting late that fall. Her friends—Steffi most of all—had advised that it was an eminently practical degree that could secure her work in another country should she have to emigrate. Liese packed up her room on Pariz Street and moved to a dormitory on the state school's small campus. Classes were held early in the morning, and her dormitory's curfew was so strict that only on special occasions did she see her old friends, a sacrifice almost greater than abandoning her dream of becoming a doctor.

The school had Czech- and German-language sections. Her Czech still far from perfect, Liese registered for the German section. Her two roommates were Sudeten Germans and supporters of Hitler. The majority of her classmates, she soon discovered, were Nazi sympathizers. In spite of making friends with Eve Adler, one of the few other Jewish students, who was as puckish and confident as Steffi, Liese felt a new level of loneliness. She was so uncomfortable in the presence of her roommates that she was constipated her entire first semester. The hope for the occasional sight of Eve was all that got her up in the mornings.

That winter, as snow blanketed the streets, and when the snow turned into piles of gray slush pitted with salt and sand, Mrs. Posner's occasional train trips to Prague to visit her sons were among Liese's few moments of happiness. Annerl Posner always brought a homemade pound cake iced with apricot or poppy-seed frosting, and always asked that Liese and Ernie be included in dinner plans. When they were together, Liese brought her chair as close to Mrs. Posner's as she could, and even after the last crumb of cake had been finished, she didn't want the dinner to end.

CHAPTER SIX

Where Is My Home?

Fall 1937–Fall 1938

At the beginning of Liese's second year of social work school, she, Ernie, and nearly all of their friends joined more than a million others on a windy, sunlit afternoon for the funeral procession of Tomáš Masaryk, Czechoslovakia's beloved first president. The sound of the hooves of the horses carrying his coffin and the quiet weeping of the people lining the streets on that first day of fall would stay in Liese's ears for months to come.

"His belief in democracy outstrips my own capacity to believe in anything at all!" Willi Schlamm once said at a Freie Vereinigung meeting. Liese had jotted the words down to include in one of her first letters home, hoping they would reassure her parents that in Prague, under Masaryk's watch, she was out of danger.

She had seen the president in person several times, riding his horse in the Malá Strana, strolling in the Staré Mesto with his daughters and grandchildren, or having coffee with his closest friend, the playwright Karel Čapek, at Café Louvre. Once, to her great excitement, he brushed past her as he entered the great lecture hall of Charles University and quietly took a seat not far from where she sat with Erich when Edmund Husserl and Rudolf Carnap held one of their frequent Saturday-morning philosophy debates.

She came to think of Masaryk as "paterfamilias"—bigger and more powerful than a parent but somehow so far-reaching in his sensitivities that she imagined he cared about everything that affected her life. The top of Masaryk's head sometimes replaced her father's in another of her recurring dreams, this one that she was being carried down a wide, tree-lined street in Frankfurt on a tall man's shoulders. Old and long in failing health, Masaryk had left office two years earlier, succeeded by Edvard Beneš, to whom he'd been a philosophical and political mentor. Even after stepping down, Tomáš Masaryk had retained the role of the country's spiritual leader, his humanism ringing like a bell against the nightmare unfolding across the border, his scholarly rationality making Hitler seem to many Czechs almost more absurd than threatening.

As Liese, Ernie, and the Schlamms stood shoulder to shoulder watching the funeral procession pass, Erich Heller, whom Liese had not seen in almost a year, came to stand next to her. She pulled in as close to him as she dared, and he put his arm around her shoulders. "I'm glad you arrived in Prague early enough to know it in more than one kind of light," he said, his voice solemn and warm.

That evening at the Continental, after the group of friends said their good nights, raising their beer glasses to Masaryk, licking up the foam running on the outside walls of their cups as a group salute to his love of life, Liese and Erich stayed on. They walked in Staré Mesto and sat on the bench where they'd sat many times before, watching the saints make their rounds above the clock in the tower of the old town hall. Erich encouraged her to finish her social work degree. *"Verbissen,"* he said, stick with it, bringing forth an old Komotau expression his father had said to Paul and him when they faced unpleasant tasks. He was trying hard to find *Verbissenheit* himself, he told her, having taken a mind-numbing job as a court apprentice for a Prague lawyer. "It all seems like a lot of nonsense. But I suppose for right now it's the right sort of nonsense!"

Then, as he so often had before, he added a touch of Goethe: *But naught to seek, that is my goal.* Indeed, what he wanted most of all, he told Liese, was to simply dream and let his spirit grow. And, he added, his arm stealing behind her, his spirit would grow the more abundant if she were by his side again.

Liese returned to school that night but was back the next evening for a gathering of her old friends at the Continental. She crammed all her studying into the few hours between her classes so she could take the last afternoon streetcar back to Staré Mesto, where life would begin again. She and Erich tentatively resumed their romance. She'd stay out late with Erich and her old friends, losing track of time, even putting herself at risk. She was reprimanded by the dormitory's custodian who, studying her with disapproving eyes when she got back long after the students' curfew, threatened to report her. Once the custodian refused to let her in at all, and Liese, starting to wonder whether seeing Erich again brought happiness or simply relief from pain, slept in an empty classroom, her head resting on a desk, so as not to miss a test the following morning.

With Masaryk's passing, the spirit of Prague seemed to diminish overnight. Fear grew each day that Hitler would make his move to overtake the grieving country. In a speech two months after Masaryk's death, which Liese listened to on the radio with the Schlamms and EP, Hitler openly declared his intention to do just that. The "settlement of the Austrian and Czech question," he said in the high-pitched voice they once loved to imitate, was next on his agenda.

"Prague is no place for such a clown," EP declared.

"I'm glad that argument, at least for now, is settled!" Willi replied. But none of the usual repartee followed, only silence as the four sat through the rest of the broadcast, their heads bent close together.

EP and Hans Posner, Franz Gollan, Franta Kraus, Tomas Berman, Kurt Plowitz, Paul Schülle, Paul Heller, even Fredy

Mayer, who'd lost the use of one leg to polio years before and relied on a cane, all prepared themselves to join the Czech army in the event of a German invasion. The Czech national anthem, the wistful opera aria "Where Is My Home?," could be heard through the open windows of apartments and cafés at all hours. In spite of the surging Czech patriotism, Nazi party members, particularly from the Sudetenland section of Czechoslovakia—which included not only Komotau but Karlsbad, where EP and Hans had grown up—gained a stronger foothold in Prague's political life, showing up in the Hall of the Czech Parliament in jackboots and full Reich regalia. The threat to anti-Nazis and Jews, particularly Jewish émigrés, was felt everywhere.

For the moment, Hitler made no move on Czechoslovakia. He had other plans. In March 1938, in a bloodless coup d'état led by the Austrian Nazi Party, Hitler took over Austria.

Steffi and Willi Schlamm were the first to leave, departing Prague on a night train to Brussels in July 1938. From there they hoped to find a way to get to the United States. They'd learned that Willi's name was on a list of Austrians living in Prague whom the now coordinated Austro-German government, counting on a weakened Czechoslovakian sovereignty, claimed the authority to arrest. Always decisive and rational, the Schlamms surprised their friends by turning to Madame Thebes to help them decide the most propitious hour to leave.

Liese, EP, and the Schlamms' good friend Milena Jesenská accompanied them to the Masaryk train station. The friends stayed close by the Schlamms as they stood in line to have their papers and passports processed. Steffi, who could be relied on for a merry wisecrack, was silent, her face drawn and pale. "All this stamping. So many stamps!" she finally said as the line moved at a snail's pace and the smell of ink and sweat filled the station lobby. To Liese, Willi and Steffi looked as fragile as children. She peeled oranges she'd brought, carefully separating the sections, and handed them to Steffi, Willi, Milena, and EP. She'd brought chocolate as a small gift, too, and opened the bag to share.

When their train was announced, Steffi and Willi took their friends in their arms. "We had never quite imagined it this way," Steffi said, her eyes filled with tears.

There had been no period of strain or artifice in Liese's

friendship with Steffi, no time when she had felt anything but comfort and familiarity in Steffi's presence. To lose this dear friend, who had been through so much with her and buoyed her in so many ways, felt unbearable.

After the train doors closed, Liese, Milena, and EP followed Steffi and Willi with their eyes until, searching for seats, the travelers were absorbed into the crowd.

Soon after the Schlamms' departure, Franz Gollan and Edith Abeles, with their three-month-old son, Andy, began their journey, first to England and from there to the United States, where a distant relative of Franz had offered them an affidavit of support.

Franta Kraus and Eva Hirsch left next, taking a train to France and there beginning a circuitous journey that ended in their arrival in Santiago, Chile, many weeks later.

Only days after that, in what for Liese was the hardest good-bye, Ernie, struggling to keep his father's business afloat and worried that increasingly anti-Semitic business regulations might prevent him from continuing to work at all, left Prague on the night train to Brussels, traveling through Luxembourg and France, and finally arriving at the port of Calais, where he boarded a French steamship bound for the United States. Thirteen days later, he arrived safely in Manhattan harbor, where he was met by Irma's uncle Hermann, who'd provided an affidavit and a temporary room in his family's apartment on East Eighty-third Street.

It is not an auspicious beginning, Ernie wrote to Liese his first week in the city. *I can confirm what Franz and Edith wrote us— the United States is not make-believe. I haven't yet met a gold miner or a cowboy. But I did watch the American Nazi Party march-*

ing in Central Park. "*Perhaps it is beautiful somewhere else, but I am here anyway,*" he ended his letter, quoting Wilhelm Busch's "Restless Traveler," a poem he, Liese, and other German schoolchildren used to recite as they mourned the carefree days of summer on their way to the first day of school each year.

Liese had little doubt that the day would arrive when she, too, would have to leave Prague, but for now she was staying in order to take her final social work examinations in late August.

As talk of a German invasion of Czechoslovakia escalated, Liese studied for her exams while organizing the details of her journey to America. In view of the increasing number of Nazis in Prague, communications needed to be managed with more secrecy than ever. The affidavit of support Hermann had signed for Ernie included Albert, Irma, and Liese's names in the lines provided for family members, and Ernie sent a certified copy, along with money borrowed from Uncle Hermann, to Annerl Posner's apartment for safekeeping until Liese finished school. While Albert and Irma continued their efforts to secure a visa, they insisted that Liese should leave ahead of them. She was to depart in September and follow the same route Ernie had taken, only she would travel the first leg, to Brussels, by plane, since trains traveling west from Prague were being detained in Germany.

Erich discussed going with her. If Willi's name was on a list, there was little doubt that his would soon be on one, too. But every time Hitler's activities abated and life in Prague momentarily stabilized, he changed his mind. There were good reasons for him to wait, he said. He was worried his English was so poor that he wouldn't be able to write in the United States, much less make a living there. His mother's leukemia was quiet for now but still of great concern. There was Paul to think of, too. With one more semester of medical school remaining, Paul wasn't ready to go, and Erich was reluctant to leave him behind.

When Hitler's war rhetoric escalated, he wavered again. "I don't know how to make good decisions, bad decisions, or any decisions!" Erich said. "No amount of thinking helps me to think!"

He wavered most of all when Liese told him that Hermann could include him in an amendment to the affidavit if they were married. "You deliver that news with rather too much enthusiasm," he said. It was a wearyingly hot evening in late summer. They were walking across Charles Bridge toward a café in the Malá Strana. Hearing those words, Liese felt the backs of her legs tighten, locking her knees in a way that hadn't happened since that night in Capri when she searched the beach for him. A long silence followed.

"Perhaps I didn't put that well," he added.

"Perhaps you didn't," she said, walking on without looking at him. Neither of them introduced the subject again.

As her departure date approached, her friends joined forces with Georg, the Café Continental's much loved headwaiter, to organize a surprise farewell party for Liese at the Mayers' apartment. Joszi and Fredy Mayer planned the food; Georg took charge of libations; Erich organized the gifts, which Joszi would ship to New York; and EP claimed the happy assignment of making sure Liese arrived at the Mayers' by the appointed hour.

Before they left Prague, the Schlamms, Franz, Edith, Franta and Eva, and Ernie had each insisted to their friends that elaborate good-byes would only make their leave-taking harder. "Vould you be so kindly to not make such a fuss," Ernie had told Fredy and Joszi, always the most enthusiastic party givers, in his most practiced English.

But with Liese's departure, her Prague friends were simply *going* to have a party, their only line of defense against all the farewells.

Two days before Liese's scheduled flight, EP escorted her into the Mayers' apartment, filled with the fragrance of steaming svíčková (beef in sour cream sauce) awaiting them in the center of the adjoining room. She was so overcome that she couldn't look at her friends for several minutes. Her eyes rested on the flowered wool rug where she had deposited the bulging satchel she'd brought to give to Joszi, having filled it with clothes that wouldn't fit into her trunk. When she did look up, she thought how beautiful all her friends were, how dear every detail of their appearance—the kindness in EP's eyes, the liveliness of Milena's and Eve's, Annerl's hands with their bitten fingernails, the shy gap-toothed smile of Paul Heller, whom she hadn't seen in over a year. And then there was Erich, handsome in his summer linens.

A little tower of books sat on the Mayers' coffee table. Hot and blushing, Liese accepted a glass of sherry from Fredy as he led her to the sofa and sat down beside her, nodding toward the books. Liese had been firm that no one give farewell gifts, but Fredy announced that her authority didn't stretch that far. "Let them all be charms against forgetting us," he said as he presented her with the first, an English translation of Mann's *Buddenbrooks*, gleaming shiny and perfect with uncracked spine and uncreased pages. *Read with joy. I like thinking of you where you should be. Be well. Be well,* Annerl Posner had written on the title page.

From EP came an English translation of *War and Peace. I hope all goes well for you forever,* he'd written inside. *But T. always good in impossible situations. No small thing.*

From Eve Adler came *The Education of Hyman Kaplan* by Leo Rosten. *A comic story of a new arrival to New York learning to speak English,* Eve wrote in her card. *Our social work classmates excelled at the "yes and no" questions. We must excel at the complicated ones. I shall miss you terribly.*

From Paul Heller, she received the leather-bound edition of *Tonio Kröger,* housed in its own oak slipcase, that he'd talked about when she first met him and Erich at the Alaunsee. *Postponement too often means that it does not happen at all,* he wrote on a small card inside. *I only hope life won't be withheld from us as it was from Tonio. Paul.*

Finally, from Erich and Paul Heller together came a collection of poems by John Donne bound in blue leather with embossed borders. *For Liese, most affectionately, Erich and Paul.* She fought irritation that the book wasn't from Erich alone, then fought elation when she discovered inside the book's pages several additional neatly typed-out poems on folded sheets of letter paper. *Poems that cannot but confirm the existence of a meaningful world,* Erich had written below them in his unmistakable handwriting. *So they can be with you always, and therefore, so that I can be.*

When he said good-bye to Liese at the Mayers', Paul Heller asked if he might see her alone before her flight. They squeezed their meeting, at Café Juli, into her last day in Prague. Paul arrived with wet hair and a towel tucked under his arm, fresh from his daily swim in the university pool.

After ordering coffee and pound cake soaked in chocolate sauce, he explained that he'd spent the last few days selecting medical books he thought he could do without. He wondered if he could send them to her once she was settled in New York, whether it would be a burden for her to keep them for him until things in Europe settled down. "It can't go on forever," he said, "but who knows? I may find myself in the United States one day, too." If there were any room left, he'd fill the box with a few other favorite books—his Stefan Zweig, with the little chapter on Goethe falling in love in Marienbad that Paul liked to reread every year, maybe his books of nonsense poems, and certainly, his Mann stories.

He leaned forward as if he wanted to say more, but after innumerable hesitations, he turned instead to his cake, unwrapping it carefully from its butter-soaked pastry paper. *"Fortgewürschteln!"* he said, his face and neck erupting in patches of red again. It was a "Tante Ida–ism," he explained. "We must muddle forward against the odds," he added with an antic expression, postponing his first bite of cake to describe his vibrant aunt, whom they'd toasted that day in 1933 when Liese had first met Erich and Paul at the Alaunsee.

Paul had outgrown the pimples and summer freckles that once covered his nose, Liese noted. He was growing into his own manner of handsomeness, so different from his brother's, she thought. His sweetness made her sad that she hadn't spent more time getting to know him. She was uncommonly pleased he'd asked her a favor that she could fulfill. "Of course you should send them," she assured him as she dug into her own slice of cake and they ate in silence, which she welcomed, for she suddenly felt how tired she was.

Erich accompanied her in the cab for the twenty-minute ride to Prague's small airfield on the western outskirts of the city. The kiss he gave her the moment before she was to board felt like neither a promise nor a good-bye, as if he wanted to keep his intentions hidden from her, just as he had so often before.

The late-afternoon sky above Prague was a purple blue as her plane flew into it, cloudless as far as she could see. A bridge of swallows soared below, and the river looked like a winding gray ribbon against the wooded hills.

"You are from somewhere, too?" the woman next to her asked, the question strangely resonant, but Liese couldn't respond.

Liese had never flown in a plane, had never even been to an airport. No one she knew had ever flown. Her body bounced with each patch of turbulence, and her stomach churned from the smell of the fuel.

She fingered the thin sheets of paper in her handbag and unfolded them, their corners curled from the humidity of Prague's August. Rilke's "Elegy" filled the first page of the poems Erich had typed out for her.

Ah, whom can we ever turn to
in our need? Not angels, not humans,
and already the knowing animals are aware
that we are not really at home

in our interpreted world. Perhaps there remains for us
some tree on a hillside, which every day
we can take into our vision; there remains for us
    yesterday's street
and the loyalty of a habit so much at ease
when it stayed with us that it moved in and never left.

By the time the pilot, his voice nearly drowned out by the hammering engines, announced that the flight was passing the Sudeten mountain range and would soon be crossing over Germany, the light blue paper stood between her and the world below.

CHAPTER SEVEN

The End of Czechoslovakia

September 1938–March 1939

When Liese arrived on the overnight train from Brussels to Luxembourg City to make her next rail connection to Paris, exhausted and still nauseated from her flight the previous day, she saw, to her astonishment, her mother and father standing side by side on the marble concourse of the station. They hadn't breathed a word to her of their intention to slip out of Frankfurt illegally so they could see her before she left Europe. In the seconds before Liese's mind could believe the evidence of her eyes, the concourse seemed to float away beneath her. She walked toward them, at first tentatively, as though what she was seeing could not possibly be there, then in a mad rush.

"It's as if we'd fallen out of the sky," Irma said as she took her daughter in her arms for the first time in five years and held her there for many moments.

Albert's composure disintegrated when Liese's eyes caught his. *"Ich wehr verückt!"* he said, using a lighthearted family expression that poked fun at one's flickering grasp of reality: This is so unbelievable I might be crazy! His voice wasn't light, however, but tremulous. As he held Liese's face between his hands, his body abruptly doubled over under the weight of unrestrained weeping. Taking his arm, Irma guided him to a bench on the edge of the concourse and sat down next to him, putting her hand on his knee. A baggage attendant arrived to inquire if he needed medical help. "Thank you so very much. I'm all right now," he insisted, struggling for breath, his forehead glistening with sweat. "Albert Florsheim, from Frankfurt," he said, reaching out to shake the young man's hand. "Albert Florsheim, Frankfurt. Here only for a brief visit. Thank you so very much. God bless you."

Since leaving Prague the day before, and particularly after the stopover in Brussels, where she had disembarked to the familiar faces of Steffi and Willi—who had surprised her by coming to meet her plane and escorting her to the train station for the next leg of her journey—Liese had been overtaken by a fear she could barely contain. Now, watching Albert, she felt it crushing her chest. She had never seen her father cry, never seen a look of such sorrow in his face. Though Irma's hand remained on his knee, her eyes full of care and attention, Albert looked hapless and alone. He leaned forward with his eyes closed, both hands resting on the knob of his cane. He'd always been a large man, not overweight but tall and softly bulky, with the powerful hands and shoulders of someone who'd lifted sacks of grain and potatoes in his younger years. Now, through his pressed wool trousers, his legs looked sticklike, and his jacket hung so loose that Liese could almost imagine he'd borrowed it from a much larger man. His iron-gray mustache was gone, making his face seem unprotected and unfamiliar. Liese wanted to ask her parents' forgiveness without knowing what for. She could see her father's effort, muscle by muscle, to regain his composure. He straightened his back and adjusted his jacket and tie. He'd always lived by an unyielding sense of obligation to present himself at his best. On the rare occasions when he, rather than her mother, had put Liese to bed when she was a little girl, he always chose the poem "Winter," from the book of Matthias Claudius poems Irma kept by her daughter's bedside. His eyes twinkling, he changed Old Winter's name to his own, claiming that the poet had written it about Albert, for Claudius knew that he had the strength to protect his daughter from anything that could happen in the night.

"You know the poem, too!" he'd say, coaxing Liese to recite it with him.

"No!" she'd insist. "Say it the way *you* say it!"

Old Winter [*Albert*] *is the man for me—* / *Stout-hearted, sound, and steady,* he'd say in the booming voice that added to Liese's sense of him as a man of earthshaking capabilities. *Steel nerves and bones of brass hath he:* / *Come snow, come blow, he's ready!* he'd go on, as Liese giggled with happiness. *If ever man was well, 'tis he!*

Liese eyed the bag on the floor in front of the bench where her parents sat. Several loaves of bread poked out, as well as the tips of her favorite peach-colored roses wrapped in the familiar gold paper of the Palmengarten, Frankfurt's sprawling botanical garden, where the family had often gone on weekend hikes. Irma left Albert's side for a moment to present Liese with the bouquet and take her in her arms again. She was dressed elegantly, though when she'd bent over to comfort Albert, Liese noticed the hems of three different dresses showing under her loosely fitting wool coat. Irma had lost weight, too, and around her mouth were worry lines. Her smoky silver hair, held by tortoiseshell combs, was thinning, but at fifty-five, she was far less changed than Albert. Her bearing was strong and confident, her brown eyes full of warmth.

The three made their way out of the station into a day bright with blues and greens and gently changing leaves. Liese walked between her parents, looking back and forth, not wanting to miss a word. Albert insisted on carrying Liese's suitcase, and Liese took her mother's hand.

They'd asked Annerl Posner for Liese's itinerary, Irma explained. They simply could not let their daughter cross the ocean without seeing her. It was hard enough that they hadn't said good-bye to Ernie or to Albert's brother, Julius, and his family, who had kept secret their departure from Luxembourg to Chile. During the late days of August, they explained, they'd concocted their own plan: A client of Albert's, a printer out of work because his shop had closed due to the boycott of Jewish businesses, used his equipment to alter the date of the exit papers they'd received two years before and then been unable to use. "We're all learning tricks," Irma said in a whisper but a fully audible one, the muscles in her face visibly yielding to some new sense of safety. They would return to Frankfurt that evening after Liese's train left.

Neither the family furniture nor their savings had ever been returned, but their initial steps to reapply for a visa had been successful, Irma continued. As soon as the official paperwork arrived, they would come back to Luxembourg with Hedy to await final clearance to join their children in America. The greatest obstacle was that they must show the U.S. government that they had enough money to last twenty-four months. They didn't know how they would do it, but perhaps Uncle Hermann could be persuaded to take their promissory note. He was comfortably off and a good man. However, Albert—she looked at her husband and squeezed her daughter's hand—was adamant about not asking him. "You see, your father is as stubborn as ever!"

"I talked to someone at the American consulate in Luxembourg who is preparing our paperwork," Albert said. "I left him, I hope, with a good impression of me, which I believe has a lot of value."

"You make a wonderful impression, dear," Irma said, and leaning across Liese, she stretched upward to kiss him on the cheek.

"Mr. Roosevelt, on the other hand, looks upon us as too old to anticipate working in his country!"

"Father, you can find new clients in the U.S. I know that Ernie will want—"

Irma squeezed Liese's hand again, shaking her head almost imperceptibly. From the cryptic fragments in her mother's letters and from Ernie's reporting, Liese knew that her sixty-year-old father had been able to cope with everything until the salve of his work was taken from him.

"Please let's not talk about all this," Albert said, setting a brisker pace as they walked. "This is not the time to discuss such matters! Let it all come as it does. *Happy is one who forgets what cannot be changed.*" The latter was a line from the Johann Strauss opera *Die Fledermaus,* which Albert and Irma had attended every New Year's Eve at the Frankfurt Opera House since Liese was a small child.

Across the large tree-lined square fronting the train station, they found a wine bar that opened onto a spacious garden filled with the smells of plants and soil. Anything involving choices about food and wine had always filled Albert with a sense of satisfaction and completion—a fine wine, which, Irma always teased him, he invariably felt he could improve upon greatly, a well-seasoned soup, a beautiful vegetable, a warm loaf of bread, a square of bitter chocolate to top it all off. "After I've had my meal," he often said at family dinners, "I'm so happy that I momentarily lose my purpose in life!" As he examined the café's menu, the pink returned to his face.

"Now," Irma said, "the task of catching up with our well-educated daughter will require all our best energies." Her mother, Liese saw, had decided to be cheerful.

"A university unto herself!" Albert added, looking at Liese. "*To be a smart person is an incurable disease,* Goethe said! The best one can do is to come to terms with it!" he added, chuckling. Liese had never been able to tell when her father was being truly proud or when he was teasing her; she didn't know when to surrender to her desire to talk about the books she'd read, the ideas she'd had, or when to protect herself.

"Let's see if Father will think we have a useful opinion about what we should eat and drink," Irma said as the waiter brought them rolls and butter.

Liese's heart, quieting to a normal beat for the first time since she'd left Prague, was suddenly filled with simple wanting, whether a hot roll with butter or that nothing ever change again until she could catch up. She didn't want to let her parents out of her sight, wanted to fly them to safety like the goose that carried children high in the sky to a safe destination, in

Selma Lagerlöf's book *The Wonderful Adventures of Nils,* which she, Ille, and Lilo read aloud over and over again at their *Kränzchen* meetings long ago. Now she understood why such stories had been written.

In his best Luxembourgish, for he was gifted with languages, Albert ordered everything Luxembourgian: thinly sliced cured beef, turnovers filled with cheese, parsley, and onions, soup made of green beans floating in a rich chicken broth, and plum tart.

Once lunch was in front of them, Albert asked Liese about Erich Heller. "What are the gentleman's plans? Do you know if he will be able to come to the United States?"

"How is his mother?" Irma asked, stealing a sharp look at Albert and putting her hand on her daughter's in a way that Liese found both familiar and touching. Her mother had always known when to move to a new subject, ask a new question, in order to safeguard Liese from Albert's appraising gaze.

More than anything, Liese wanted to have the intimate conversation about these matters of the heart that, in all the years of their separation, they'd never been able to have. But with only hours left before her train, now wasn't the time. She made herself believe, as she had so many times before, that she would save the real conversation for a different kind of meeting. There would be a time when all the farewells would end. There *would* be. She endured the surface of casual conversation beneath which lived the words she most wanted to say. And so the time passed.

A few hours later, when Liese's train pulled out of Luxembourg station, her parents disappeared from view almost as quickly as they'd appeared, shrinking, old-fashioned dolls in the distance. When she set the bag of flowers and bread on the floor in front of her seat and lifted her suitcase (to which Irma, excusing herself to the ladies' room just before Liese boarded, had added the two cotton print dresses she'd worn under her own) onto the luggage rack, what Liese held in the privacy of her heart was still hers.

Throughout that September 1938, Paul worked at the medical school, completing the blood calcium experiments in Heinrich Waelsch's lab. Evenings, after a swim, he retreated to a back table at the Continental to study, giving himself practice tests in physiology, embryology, and pathology, timed to the waiters upending the chairs on the tables and sweeping the day's accumulation of newspapers and cigarette ends. Passing his second Rigorosum, scheduled for September 30, would mean he'd have only one more examination before receiving his medical degree. After five years of study, the "promised land" of professional life was inches away.

All the while, in order to hold his focus, he forced himself to resist being distracted by the political news, which changed with alarming frequency. Each evening, the boy who delivered the *Prager Tagblatt* to the kiosk outside the Continental faced a sea of coins and anxious hands before he could untie the first bundle of fresh papers. One day war was imminent, with reports of German troops taking positions at the border; the next came equally confident reports that a peaceful resolution to Hitler's "Czech question" was at hand. From Czechoslovakia's allies, England, France, and Russia, came their own ever changing reports. One day it seemed clear that the three countries would stand by Czechoslovakia if Hitler attacked, while the next report would have them waffling, with England's prime minister Chamberlain traveling several times to Germany to negotiate a compromise that would assure European peace. On none of those occasions was Czechoslovakia's president Beneš consulted.

On the Friday morning of his exam, which was to take eight hours, Paul willed himself not to look at the newspapers, listen to the radio, or engage in conversations with friends. He finished the exam a half hour ahead of schedule. He wanted to cheer as he left the examination hall, alert and confident. Within minutes of exiting the building, however, he was startled out of his happiness by the sight of students rushing, then running, out of classroom buildings, all of them heading in the direction of Wenceslaus Square. As he approached the intersection of Na Prikope and Vaclavske Namesti, near the Mayers' apartment, he spotted students he knew, his brother among them, standing at the edge of a crowd, some of them crying. Paul made his way toward them.

"That vulture Chamberlain!" Erich said, putting his arm through Paul's and leading his dazed brother through the growing throng of demonstrators. As they walked, Erich told him that while Paul was taking his exam, Britain's prime minister had returned to London after meeting again with Hitler and other world leaders, this time in Munich. His announcement to England of the signing of an agreement granting the Sudetenland to Hitler in exchange for peace was carried on Czech radio. President Beneš, who again had not been invited to the meeting, had just capitulated. The Nazi occupation of

Komotau and other towns of central and western Czechoslovakia was to begin in twenty-four hours. "Mother must be
frantic," Erich said. "I haven't tried to get through to her yet."

When they arrived at the Mayers', EP and Hans Posner,
Milena Jesenská, Paul Schülle, Egon and Karla Schwelb, and
others in their group of friends were already gathered around
the radio in the living room, listening for more news of the Munich agreement. " 'Let us prevent war'?" EP said, pacing and
imitating the voice of the British prime minister. "Is that mis-
guided missile of a man even remotely conscious? What he
does *not* say is 'Let us sacrifice Czechoslovakia to prevent war'!"

"Further, what he does not say is that it *won't* prevent war!"
Erich said, joining the group. Paul lowered himself onto the
Mayers' sofa, his hands shaking. Joszi hurried between the
kitchen and dining room, filling the table with sandwiches and
beer to feed the steady stream of students arriving from the
protest. Fredy, at the top of the stairs by the telephone, the
receiver wedged between his shoulder and cheek, ushered the
tired demonstrators into the living room. Standing by his side,
Hans Posner, pale and sweating, tried to keep count of those,
including EP and himself, who had family in the Sudetenland
who would need transportation to Prague and other safe loca-
tions that night. Each addition he made to the growing count
he communicated to Fredy, who was wielding the phone like a
weapon against chaos, ordering taxicabs and calling friends
who had extra rooms.

Erich joined his brother on the sofa. He started talking at a
rapid-fire pace, more, it seemed to Paul, to the center of the
room than to him. "I need to write about what is happening
while it is happening," he said, putting out one cigarette and

lighting a fresh one. "Who could have anticipated the likes of Chamberlain? Who could have anticipated what such a banal man could do? Reading *The Last Days of Mankind*, I didn't understand that Kraus actually predicted this, or if I did understand, I didn't believe it. Pauli, forgive me, please. Can I count on you to get Mother and Tante Ida? Writing an essay is all I can envision for myself tonight." He headed to the Mayers' back room before his brother could answer.

Paul couldn't keep himself from glaring at Erich, couldn't help but hope that his essay would be a disappointment. But he said nothing. He'd long ago made his accommodation to Erich's sense of entitlement. It wasn't worth doing battle with him over family responsibilities. He sat alone, trying to overcome his exhaustion and summon the strength to do the task he had just been handed. He left the Mayers' to join the long queue at a nearby pay phone, trying, as best he could, to keep his focus and not be affected by the panic-filled faces and voices of the other people waiting in line. Once inside the blessedly silent booth, in calls put through first to his mother and then to his aunt, he instructed them to be packed and ready by midnight. He then called his father's stepmother, Minna, who lived with Alfred's half brother, Walter, and his family in Vršovice, a southern district of Prague. They agreed to have a room ready for Else and Ida. Paul returned to the Mayers' apartment, downed several cups of coffee, and got into one of the taxis Fredy had ordered for the long drive to Komotau.

When Paul arrived at 16 Weltmühlstrasse just before midnight, the curtains of the Heller family apartment were drawn.

Else Heller was seated on the sofa in the front sitting room, which was lit by candles. There were rumors of bombings, she told Paul, and she'd been advised to turn off the electricity.

She was dressed formally, her long hair, still jet-black at fifty-four, gathered in a bun at the back of her neck. In front of her, the marble-topped coffee table was piled with books, clothes, and open boxes of photographs and letters. On the floor next to her sat her suitcase and handbag. She was clutching a small paper bowl, laminated with pictures of seabirds, that Erich had made for her when he was a boy. "You have to put candy in it in order for it to be balanced," she said as she looked up at Paul, her face ashen.

"Kind of like me," Paul said, trying to bring lightness to his voice, to avoid frightening his mother any further.

"I must tell you that cousin Fanny had yesterday, out of the blue, a tonsils operation," she went on, making conversation, as she always did when she was nervous or upset. "Lena and Karl came by and told me she was in hospital."

"The cab is waiting, Mother. We must go."

"Do you remember when Erich cut his finger making this bowl?" she asked, running her hand across its bumpy varnished edge. "He made a frightful fuss, a most terrible fuss. Do you remember that?" Else's eyes were cavernous.

"Mother, you'll feel better once you're in the cab."

"You must let me decide how I feel!" she said sharply. "I didn't have time to withdraw money. I haven't selected what I must take. I haven't sorted through Father's books. I cannot go! Perhaps tomorrow." She sat, stiff and delicate, her coat draped over her lap.

"Mother, we can do that from Prague. Anny [Else's house-keeper] can help us. She can send things."

Else's eyes roamed over the room, returning to the open boxes on the table. She fingered Erich's paper bowl again. "Have you eaten?"

Paul nodded.

"But you'll have a bite of something with me, no?"

"We haven't the time, Mother. We'll eat at Minna's." He stood motionless in front of her for several moments, then moved toward where she sat. "Mother, we must leave. We must go now! Please let me help you." He spoke in a stern and unequivocal tone he'd never used with her. He felt the blood go to the back of his neck. Else Heller was a tiny woman, standing under five feet, but over that height, she was solidly built. Paul put his hand under her forearm, but she rose on her own, went down the hall to the kitchen, and came back carrying the silver butter mold that Alfred's parents had given them at their wedding. She added it, along with the bowl, to one of the boxes, applied a few drops of cologne from a bottle in her handbag, and stooped to blow out the candles. Without looking at Paul, she laced her arm in his and let him lead her down the steps and out the door into the drizzly open night.

The street, which rarely saw traffic, was filled with cars and taxicabs. The route to Ida's apartment took them past Paul and Erich's gymnasium and the candlelit apartment where the parents of Paul's childhood friend, Camillo Fleischer, the only other Jewish boy in his gymnasium class, lived. He wondered what Camillo and his family were planning to do. The taxi climbed the hill past the Komotau Kino and the music hall where Paul and Erich had taken part in the children's theater and Dr. Fleischman had conducted the Komotau Orchestra, and continued past Bobby Komisch's haberdashery, Mendel's bookstore, then across the railroad bridge and past the old iron ore quarry, all, until that night, the unquestioned constants of Paul's life.

Tante Ida was waiting in the alcove doorway of her building, a small suitcase by her side. She was dressed warmly, the tight lace collar she always wore to Saturday services visible under her jacket. *"Du bist so tüchtig, Pauli,"* the diminutive sixty-eight-year-old said in the authoritative tone in which she issued all her judgments. It was the highest accolade one could receive from Tante Ida. *Tüchtig:* levelheaded, able to get things done.

Paul put her bag next to his mother's on the front seat. The two women sat in back on either side of Paul in their rain-moist fur jackets, their small spectacles glinting in all directions as the cab followed traffic toward the main road for what was usually a two-hour ride back to Prague but likely would take far longer tonight. The windows were opened just enough to let in the smells of exhaust and wet pavement. The honking and screeching of brakes in the middle of the night had a surreal quality. Else loosened the laces on her shoes. Through the rearview mirror, Paul could see in the distance the dim lights of other Sudetenland towns nestled at the foot of the mountains.

No one exhaled a normal breath. The only words came from the taxi driver, who talked about God. That day he'd become convinced for an absolute fact that there was none, he said. In the silence, he made weak, worried jokes. "How can anyone take the Nazis seriously? They march too much!"

Just before dawn, as the rain was ending, they arrived at Walter and Minna's apartment. Grandma Minna, whose sense of humor was legendary, poured hot coffee from a silver urn that sputtered more than flowed. "My ribald friends regard this coffeepot as having prostate trouble. It has a problem. It has a problem!" she declared with a great heave of a laugh, pretending, like the taxi driver and like Paul, to a sense of normalcy that she surely did not feel. She poured thick pulpy orange juice, which Paul, awakening to his body for the first time since he'd walked out of the examination hall over fifteen hours before, drank with such voraciousness that it dribbled over his chin.

As the sun came up, Minna enlisted Else and Ida's advice on the cooking of eggs for their breakfast, and a debate, led by Tante Ida, about the best way to fry them, followed.

That night, instead of returning to his dormitory, Paul collapsed on the sofa in the room that his mother and aunt now occupied, listening to their short, shallow breaths as they slept. The world, which for so long in his mind had looked one way, had begun to look totally different.

———

Erich cherished a line from Goethe's last published letter: *The best genius is that which absorbs and assimilates everything without doing the least violence to its fundamental destiny.* Recently, he'd typed it on a piece of bond paper and taped it to the wall above his desk next to favorite quotes from other writers. In the weeks since Liese had left Prague, he'd reached the conclusion once and for all that his destiny did not include her. He was relieved at how little he missed her.

He tried to sort out his feelings in a letter. Drinking copious amounts of wine, he wrote furiously over the course of several days, sometimes in his bedroom on Železná, sometimes at the Continental, sometimes in the Mayers' back room. He turned to Goethe, Hölderlin, Kant, Mann, even God, as he tried to explain to Liese that he would always feel love toward her, but it was a love that stood apart from what the world viewed as love, stood apart from what she needed. Summoning Kant's maxim that man can know only what he is equipped to know, he explained that now, since she'd left, he was equipped to know what he'd started to understand in Capri: that he could never make her happy. Filling page upon page, he turned the letter into a testament to his need to create something that was his alone to offer to the world, which he could accomplish only if completely free to follow his yearnings. "You would want that, wouldn't you?" he wrote, then surprised himself by asking a question he'd never asked: "Would not God want that?"

He assured Liese of his friendship, assured her that he regretted not a moment of their time together. He thanked her for her kindness, for being the conduit for his seeing what he now saw. After all, he wrote, taking a line from Hölderlin's *Life's Course*, one of the poems he'd given her the night of the Mayers' party, *All things man shall have proved, Heaven declares, and so / Strongly nourished, have learnt how to give thanks for all / How to cherish the freedom / Of departing for where he please.*

He ended with Thomas Mann's description of Tonio Kröger: *He stood there, his hands behind his back, in front of a window with the blind down. He never thought that one could not*

see through the blind and that it was absurd to stand there as
though one were looking out.

Until now, he thought, he'd been looking through a blind, not realizing that it was there. He didn't know what was on the other side. He knew only that he must free himself completely to see through to what it was.

He carried the letter folded in his breast pocket for weeks, adding and removing lines, changing syntax. When he was completely satisfied that he'd expressed what was true, he typed out a final copy, gave it the title "You My Life," and mailed it to Liese in New York City, though he realized by then that he'd written it as much for himself as for her.

By the time winter and the new year, 1939, came, Erich was spending virtually all his free time—when he wasn't working as a law apprentice—at the Mayers', often sleeping on their sofa instead of returning to his apartment at night. He ate Joszi's ever generous meals and sought Fredy's counsel, as well as that of Joszi's father, Rudolf Keller, the editor of the *Prager Tagblatt,* who now lived with them. Should he quit his job as an apprentice in law? Should he leave law entirely? Should he abandon his leadership in Freie Vereinigung and devote all his time to writing essays examining this time in Europe? Or should he give his energies entirely over to literature? After all, Schocken had just published his first book, *Escape from the Twentieth Century,* a collection of essays about Kraus and Mann, and more than anything else, he wanted to be a writer.

By midwinter, the devastating effects of the Munich agreement were multiplying. In the months since Germany had taken the Sudetenland, Czechoslovakia had virtually collapsed, a result, many believed, that Hitler had calculated carefully. Of the remaining Czech provinces, Slovakia, with Germany's support, would soon declare its independence; Moravia had assumed Nazi-dictated policies; and it was widely believed that Ruthenia, at Germany's behest, would be absorbed by Hungary, its ruler prior to 1918, weakening Czechoslovakia even further. Only Bohemia, with its cultural and political center, Prague, resisted Hitler's courtship.

Whenever the friends remaining in Prague gathered at the Mayers' apartment, conversations turned increasingly to how and when to leave. Every day there was another plan, another possibility. On one surreal day in late February, Erich and Paul Heller, along with Hans Posner, made three separate trips to Masaryk Station, first to say good-bye to Eve Adler, who'd obtained a visa to England; then to Kurt Plowitz, who'd received an affidavit from family in the United States; and finally, to EP and Paul Schülle, who left on separate evening trains. Paul had secured a visa to England, and EP would follow Franta Kraus and Eva Hirsch's route to Chile. For Hans, the farewell to his brother was harder than any, as he had rejected EP's plea to leave with him, having promised Erich that when the time was right, they would leave together.

Those who stayed grew closer. Paul Heller, for one, felt he had no choice but to wait. In the turmoil, all medical examinations had been canceled and not yet rescheduled. EP, Franta Kraus, and Franz Gollan had graduated a semester before and had their degrees in hand. For Paul, leaving Prague without his degree could mean his entire medical education would be

worthless abroad. In addition, he had his mother to consider.
Though Tante Ida had moved in with her oldest daughter,
Walter and Minna encouraged Else to continue to live with
them, and she was adjusting to life in Prague with surprising
vitality. Not having received any of the items she had asked
Anny to send from Komotau, she'd bought a gramophone and
several new recordings (among them Beethoven's *Kreutzer* Sonata) to make her life more pleasant. New books, which she
purchased on her weekly trips to central Prague to visit her
sons, lined the recesses of her window. She'd grown close to
Annerl Posner and other older Jewish refugees from the Sudetenland, who took solace from their belief that whatever was
to happen, Hitler seemed to have no interest in persecuting
Prague's older, nonpolitical Jews. Else's optimism—shared
by Annerl, Minna, and Tante Ida—that whatever Hitler's intentions, Prague would never succumb to Nazi domination,
added to Paul's determination to wait.

Then, on March 15, 1939, in the midst of one of Prague's
worst snowstorms in years, came the moment they'd been unable to imagine. Erich and Paul, along with Hans Posner, Egon
and Karla Schwelb, Rudolf Keller, and the Mayers, stood on
the balcony of the Mayers' apartment looking down as German troops, riding in snow-plastered tanks and armored cars,
and goose-stepping in neat rows, filled Wenceslaus Square. By
midmorning Nazi soldiers had occupied the Royal Palace. By
eight P.M., with the city under martial law, Staré Mesto and the
Malá Strana were ghostly still and silent. According to the rumors, Hitler himself had arrived in Prague to celebrate his
conquest.

The next morning, as Nazi soldiers fanned through the

city, posting maps representing the "New Reich" in store windows and on lampposts, Prague citizens filled the streets again, exhibiting that distinctly Czech brand of defiance and humor. "My God, what a miracle!" Erich and Paul overheard a group of Czech students say as they examined a new map displayed in the window of the toy store where Steffi used to work. "They've given us all of Germany!" But in spite of the Czech spirit, in spite of Hitler's promise that cultural and civic life would continue in Prague unimpeded, thousands more applied for the diminishing quota of visas, which now required the approval of the Nazi-directed government.

Egon Schwelb, an attorney who handled civil liberty cases and an outspoken anti-Nazi, was arrested the day after the invasion, and Fredy Mayer and Milena Jesenská were known to be on one of Hitler's lists. Erich tried to convince Paul that the case for leaving now, even if they did so illegally, was overwhelming. But Paul's last examination had just been rescheduled for the following month. Unlike Erich, whose presidency of Freie Vereinigung and involvement in *Die neue Weltbühne* made it dangerous for him to stay but nearly impossible for him to obtain an exit visa, Paul's politics had always been quietly held. The Freie Vereinigung meetings he had attended had been mainly to catch sight of Liese. He could safely apply for a visa. He planned to wait only long enough to take his exam and have his medical degree in hand.

CHAPTER EIGHT

Crossing Poland

May 1939–August 1939

Someone had heard that along the Polish border, four hours by train from Prague, was a series of abandoned coal mines rumored to be unguarded, through which Czech citizens unable to obtain visas were successfully crossing, unseen, into Poland. In May 1939, Erich Heller, Hans Posner, and Erich and Paul's cousin Karl Riemer began talking about making an escape from Czechoslovakia. Like Erich, Karl considered himself in danger, in his case because he was on record as one of the main financial supporters of *Die neue Weltbühne*. The three men held several meetings in Hans's apartment, above Erich's, with dance music from the BBC playing loudly on the radio to prevent them from being overheard. A well-traveled businessman with a wider circle of connections than his younger cousins, Karl had talked to a trustworthy friend who put Karl in touch with a reputable guide, a former miner, and assured him that the guide was honest.

Karl felt confident that he could negotiate a reasonable price. Once the guide had led them safely into Poland, the three men could make their way east to Katowice, then north to the Gulf of Danzig, travel the Baltic Sea to Denmark by ship, and then cross the North Sea to England, where Paul Schülle had written that he'd found work on a farm in Windsor and sent them his new address. Each time the three met to plan their escape, Karl filled them in on his progress.

As Italy had been for Goethe, Erich believed that England was the country where he might find his providence. In spite of his disdain for its prime minister, he'd always thought of England as a cosmopolitan country. Nowhere else, he thought, would it be more possible to remain European even if Europe went to war. Of all the English cities he'd seen in films and photographs, he was most drawn to Cambridge—to its rolling fields, its willow-lined river, and, of course, to its university, with the likes of Ludwig Wittgenstein and Bertrand Russell on its faculty. If he could study German literature in Cambridge and continue writing, he could keep the *real* Germany, the Germany of Goethe, Hölderlin, Kant, and Claudius, alive. That might be his destiny. Through his prose and intelligence, he could provide a counterforce to what Hitler was destroying.

On a cool overcast morning in late May, Erich closed the shades of his windows, locked the door, and walked the short distance to Masaryk Station. The afternoon before, he'd mailed his boxes to Paul Schülle's new address in Windsor. He included the tattered manuscript of his newly published collection of essays on Kraus and Mann, upon which his hopes for entrance into Cambridge University rested. He left his resignation letter under the door of the office of the lawyer for whom he worked. Inside the lining of his jacket, he carried an envelope of cash, several silver-wrapped biscuits from Stérba bakery, and a small pocketknife. His rucksack held no more than his passport, a carton of cigarettes, a change of clothing, and toiletries.

At the station, Erich found Karl and Hans. Their railroad passes were stamped for Ostrava, a heavily Nazified Moravian city about fifteen kilometers from the Polish border. Still part of Czechoslovakia, Ostrava remained a legal destination, though it was widely known that people prominent in anti-Nazi politics were routinely detained and arrested on any train that arrived there from Prague. As the men joined the line on the platform, Erich took great gulps of air. The conductor, consulting a clipboard bulging with official-looking forms, surveyed Erich and his companions, nodded, and, with an absence of expression, ushered them on. They found seats in the last car. The train stood idle as other passengers boarded. Doors opened and closed. A police siren wailed in the background. The train filled and lurched into motion.

Erich gathered his rucksack in front of him and began to smoke, promising himself he'd go through only one package of cigarettes on the train. He tried to read a newspaper but couldn't concentrate. They took breaks to buy beer, the froth spilling on their shirts and jackets as the train rattled on, passing the well-tended fields and pastures of Bohemia, and by afternoon entering the towns of eastern Moravia.

It was midafternoon when they arrived in Ostrava, a drab city full of desolate-looking factories. In the men's room of a café near the station, Karl cut the lining of his jacket and withdrew the rough map of the location where the guide was to meet them.

While the three men walked in that direction, between a

coal-processing factory and the abandoned mine, it happened. Erich heard the metronome-like clapping of boots, felt a hand on his shoulder, and froze midstep. He watched Karl shove the map back in his pocket before they turned to see two uniformed Gestapo officers, one perhaps forty years old, with a weathered, angular face, the other considerably younger, his face broad and open. They both wore revolver belts.

"You are from where?" the older officer asked, enunciating each word with chilling clarity.

"Prague," Karl and Hans said.

"Rakovnik," Erich said, giving the name of the town where the lawyer he worked for had a second office, and where he thought there might not be a record of his political activities.

"Rakovnik?"

"Yes."

"And you are going where?"

"Here. Moravska Ostrava," they said nearly in unison, standing in the broken light coming through a cluster of sickly-looking trees under which they stood.

"Your business here?" the older officer asked.

"Looking for work," Karl said.

"Coal industry," Erich added. "We're willing to take any job."

"And you believe you will find work here?" the older officer asked. "And who might you put out of work to accomplish that?" His voice was impatient.

The younger officer stepped aside to answer the radio stammering on his belt. Erich noticed his dimpled hands and the soft blond hair peeking from under his cap. He couldn't have been older than twenty, Erich thought.

The older officer carried a clipboard of forms similar to those of the train conductor, and he combed through them as he examined their passports. Turning back, the younger officer searched them, feeling inside their pockets and patting their jackets and pants, his eyes expressionless, showing no interest in Karl's map and giving no indication that he noticed Erich's knife. He requested their rucksacks and rifled through them. The radio stammered again. Erich couldn't make out the words. When it quieted, they were ordered to walk in single file toward a building several blocks away where the officers pointed. Once there, they were ordered to stand in the shadows of twilight traffic, arms by their sides. Several hours passed. People walked by them on the sidewalk, saying *"Heil, Hitler"* to the officers.

Once darkness fell, a police truck arrived, and they were pushed into the back. With each block, the truck accumulated speed. Sitting on the metal floor in the dark, Erich reached for Hans's hand, as clammy and slippery as his own. There was one small barred window, and through it, he tried to read the dark rain-faded signs along the road.

It was pitch-black, with no visible moon, when they arrived an hour later at a squat-looking building that stood amid a cluster of iron-colored factories. When they disembarked, Erich was so frightened that he expected his legs to give way. He grabbed Hans's arm as they walked, then thought better of it and let go. They were led into a building and down several flights of stairs to a jail cell that smelled of stale tobacco and mildew, empty except for a stack of newspapers and a pile of gray military blankets on the stone-paved floor. Gnats hummed around the bare ceiling bulb. In one corner was a washbasin and, next to it, a toilet with the brown stains of rusty water. The cell occupied about twelve square feet at the back of a dingy office. After closing the cell door, the night guard retreated to the desk and cleaned his revolver beneath a framed photograph of Hitler and a faded poster of a mining exhibition from years before.

Their rucksacks had been confiscated and were visible in a cubby next to the guard's desk, but they were allowed to remain in their street clothes. Erich put his hand over the lining, reassured by the pocketknife and the money. He was unbearably thirsty, and his fear was so great that he couldn't say a word.

Hans was silent, too. Goose bumps had risen over his neck. Karl talked quietly, determined to understand what had happened, whether it was his fault, whether the guide had given them up, and what to do now. His face was full of rational concentration. Erich began to admire Karl—his calm, his air of experience, his conviction that they could form a new plan and be able, somehow, to act on it. Erich withdrew one of his cigarettes, but he had no matches.

When they were silent, Erich believed that as long as they were silent, they would be all right. When they talked, he believed that as long as they talked, they would be all right. But exhaustion engulfed each of them at the same time. They took off their jackets to use as pillows, folded themselves into the scratchy blankets, lay newspaper over their faces to block out the harsh light, and fell asleep shoulder to shoulder.

In the morning a new guard, a bigger man, brought them bread, sausage, and watery coffee. They would be called out separately for questioning upstairs, he told them. He seemed to take pride in good form, calling them Mr. Heller, Mr. Posner, Mr. Riemer.

When Karl, the first to be called, returned from his interrogation, his face was drained of color. He said they'd asked whom he knew in anti-Nazi organizations—they wanted names, addresses, telephone numbers. He'd been handcuffed before entering the interrogation room. The officers were harsh and threatening and carried pistols. Karl told them nothing, sticking with their story of looking for work. He had no idea if they believed him. When they sent him back to the cell, they told him they were not done interviewing him, that next time they would be less patient.

Hans was called and led from their cell. While he was gone, Erich calmed himself by trying to remember aphorisms and phrases from the slips of paper above his desk on Železná.

When Hans returned, he looked as though he'd undergone the sort of disintegration Erich felt was about to overtake him. The guard left them no time to talk, immediately grabbing Erich's upper arm and leading him from the cell, the door slamming behind.

The interrogation room was smaller than the cell and had no windows. Three uniformed Nazi officers sat on one side of a metal table. One of them, his cheek covered by what looked to Erich like a dueling scar, motioned for him to sit, and he was handcuffed to the chair. The guard who had led Erich from his cell stood leaning against the door.

"You are from where, Mr. Heller?" the officer with the scar asked.

"Rakovnik."

Another of the officers offered him a cigarette from a tin

box and lit it. Erich inhaled so deeply, he felt as if the smoke drew down to his toes.

"And Mr. Erich Heller from Rakovnik, do you know an Erich Heller from Prague?" asked the officer with the scar. He played with the folder, keeping his eyes fastened on Erich, opening and closing it, pushing it toward Erich's side of the table, then pulling it back. "Mr. Heller from Rakovnik," the officer asked again, getting up from his chair and walking around to the side of the table where Erich sat. "Do you happen to know this namesake of yours from Prague who writes this petulant drivel?" He turned Erich's chair so that it faced him and leaned over him.

Erich felt nauseated, dizzy, almost drunk. He could smell the leather of the officer's broad revolver belt. Did they have his writings in the folder? Did they know who he was? "I don't know him," he said, his mind so paralyzed that he was uncertain if he'd spoken, if his lips had really moved.

The officer turned Erich's chair to face the table and walked back to his own seat on the other side. "Perhaps we'll have to speak with you again tomorrow," he said after sitting down. He nodded toward the guard at the door. "Good day, Mr. Heller."

The next six days followed much as the first one had, Erich, Hans, and Karl trying to pass the time in their cell, trying to ingratiate the guards. And each day they were taken upstairs separately to face more interrogations.

Then, during the seventh night, unwashed and unshaved, beer stains from the train ride from Prague still covering their jackets and shirts, they were awakened and taken out of the cell.

Along with other prisoners who appeared in the driveway from elsewhere in the building, they were hustled into the back of a truck. Rumors flew that they were being taken to a larger prison along the border. As the truck traveled at great speeds, the prisoners were jostled so hard on the crowded metal floor that Erich could practically feel his legs turning black and blue.

After about an hour, they arrived at a building that looked like the first one, but much larger and surrounded by tents. Again, there were no visible signs to tell them where they were. Hans and Karl were pushed into one line and Erich into another line moving toward the far side of the building.

With this sudden separation, Erich felt an agony he couldn't recall ever feeling in his life. He ended up in a cell with upward of eighty men. It smelled of a dizzying blend of sweat and urine and was cacophonous with a mixture of languages— dialects of Czech, Slovak, German, Hungarian—ever changing as more men arrived. The crowded conditions created a stultifying heat, unrelieved by the single barred window, too high to allow them to see outside.

In the next days came endless, exhausting waiting, for the one bowl of soup and piece of bread handed out at midday, for a chance to drink from the one water fountain, for a time to relieve one's bowels in the one toilet in the corner of the cell. Metal doors opened and closed as prisoners were taken out for interrogation. Some didn't return.

Days later, when Erich's name was finally called, he was escorted down a dank hall and pushed into one of the small interrogation rooms where officers with untroubled eyes asked more questions, endless questions, as they scratched their pens on papers and forms.

The prisoners were allowed two hours outside every day to exercise and work. The prison was near a coal-processing factory, and Erich's job was to sweep coal dust from the walkways of the yard. Though the dust filled his mouth and nostrils, these were the only hours he could breathe. He always looked toward the adjacent fenced-in work yard, searching for Hans and Karl, but never found them.

One afternoon after he had been there for almost a month, Erich could see a guard notice him, keep his eyes on him. Erich flashed glances over his shoulder as he swept. He straightened his back to appear more confident. He worried for the first time in weeks that he was unwashed, unshaved, the lining hanging loose from his jacket. The guard walked toward him, offered him a cigarette, and lit it for him.

When the other prisoners filed back to the cell, the guard motioned for Erich to follow him toward the tent area. Books were strewn on the floor and on his bedroll. The sight of the books—Nietzsche, Heidegger, Schopenhauer—thrilled Erich, brought him to life. There was vodka and gin and Moravian wine, which the guard offered him. The number of insignias on his SS uniform indicated a high rank, Erich thought. They concentrated on their drinks. The guard, a handsome man, had an elegance that Erich found compelling, and a sadness, if he read it right. They talked about books. They drank, the guard moving closer to Erich, then stroking his cheek. The guard told him he would see to it that Erich would not be missed from his cell. What was to happen became simple and clear.

That night, the guard escorted Erich a few hundred yards past the tents. "Now, out with you! Go! Go!" was all he said, and Erich ran. He ran in the direction the guard had pointed, spending the night in a gully under a few small trees, their branches creaking in the wind. He awoke with dirt and dead leaves and twigs ground into his hands and coat sleeves.

Polish police found him wandering just across the border and brought him by truck to a refugee camp in Bielsko.

With a large group of other refugees from the camp, Erich made the journey across Poland, sometimes working farm labor jobs along the way, to the port of Gdynia, where he boarded a ship to Denmark. From there, he got passage to England. En route he got word from Paul Schülle that Hans had arrived in England with another group of refugees and was staying with him in Windsor. Hans's wrists were bandaged when he arrived, Paul wrote, and he did not want to talk about his weeks in prison except to say that so far as he knew, Karl had not gotten out.

On August 1, 1939, after spending several days with Paul and Hans, Erich arrived alone in Cambridge, ready to embark on the next phase of his life, as he had envisioned. But he was no longer the same man who had made that plan. Though he tried to forget, the guard's tent became a vast space in his head, every remembered moment adding to its confused significance. He vowed to himself never to talk about it, so as never to let anyone turn it this way or that, to make it mean something other than what it had meant.

CHAPTER NINE

Away from All

Summer 1939

Liese had been walking for nearly an hour toward the White Plains train station when she spotted a handsome wooden building with a welcoming sign: LADIES' RESTROOM. *Ruhen.* After yet another discouraging job interview, finally, a place to retreat from the July heat, to sit in a soft chair, read the paper, and replenish herself before catching the train back to Manhattan. She couldn't wait to take off the dress shoes she'd worn for her interview, perhaps even have a cup of coffee. As she pulled open the door, her heart sank when she took in the heavy damp odor and the row of dripping sinks lining the cement floor across from the empty stalls. This fresh disappointment only added to the sense of defeat that had engulfed her during the hours just before.

For the interview, she'd sat across the table from the young, well-to-do Westchester County parents who had advertised for a nanny. At their request, she told them the story of her emigration, after which the wife came over to Liese's chair to hug her. The embrace felt so genuine and warm that she returned it almost too ardently, sending a plate of cookies to the floor and nearly knocking over a coffee cup. Trying to phrase her apology, she was surprised that instead of the English words she'd studied and practiced, she retrieved the Czech words she'd used so often at the Masaryk School of Social Work when she returned to the dormitory late: *"Lito, Strasne smitne!"*

When the cookies were picked up, fresh coffee poured, and Liese's composure recovered, the husband launched into the questions he'd prepared. "My wife and I entertain a great deal," he began. "Along with caring for our son, we'd like you to help out at parties. Do you mix drinks?"

"No, thank you," Liese replied, sensing immediately from his expression that it was not a winning answer. After the couple gave Liese a tour of their house, with its elegantly coordinated rooms (and not one bookshelf in sight, Liese recalled, telling herself she'd never work in a house with no books, anyway), she knew she wouldn't be hired. They would call her the next day and tell her, as had other potential employers, that they'd enjoyed meeting her and wished her well but needed someone with a stronger command of English and more experience with children.

She'd turned down their offer to drive her to the train station, preferring to gather herself by walking. She wanted to cancel the two remaining job interviews she'd scheduled for that week but knew her self-esteem would suffer more if she did.

Though Liese had been in New York for ten months, days like this made her feel as though she'd only just arrived. She knew perfectly well what a ladies' restroom was, of course. But her constant effort to make a good impression, to respond to what sometimes seemed like incomprehensible chatter, to make herself understood under the strain of not yet speaking fluent English, exhausted her to the point of disorientation. She felt ancient at twenty-five. At the end of such days, signs, crossways, streets, and buildings became indistinct in her mind—in the city, a mass of horns and bobbing hats and billowing skirts; and outside the city, arrows and signs that held no logic or association. She sometimes had to ask strangers to help her find her way home to the room on West Eleventh Street in Greenwich Village, where she'd moved that first winter when she felt she could no longer impose on Uncle Hermann and Aunt Sadie, paying for it out of the small sum that Ernie was able to send her each month.

Since her arrival, the greatest blow—greater even than receiving Erich's letter ending their relationship (which she'd found such a monumental act of egotism, such an entirely unsatisfactory farewell, that she swore she never wanted to see him again), greater than her growing estrangement from Steffi and Willi, who now lived in New York, over their sudden and inexplicable embrace of right-wing politics in the United States, greater than seeing the American Bund marching every Saturday in Central Park—was not having found a full-time job. It had come as a terrible surprise that no hospital or clinic in New York would honor her Prague social work degree, and though she'd applied to the New York School of Social Work to continue her studies, her English wasn't strong enough for her to master the content of American textbooks. Besides, she couldn't return to school without a scholarship, which had proved as hard to come by as a job.

After his own discouraging months of job hunting, Ernie

had been hired by a wine company in Wisconsin and had already moved to Milwaukee by the time Liese arrived in the United States. He was struggling himself, and Liese hated to have to turn to him. What little money she earned came from babysitting little Eddie, the child of Uncle Hermann's daughter, Adele, tending to Uncle Hermann's tiny back-porch garden, and translating letters at the offices of the *Aufbau*, the New York–based newspaper for German immigrants. She could now get through four or five such letters, exchanged between those trying to leave Germany and their English-speaking relatives in the United States, on a Saturday morning, when she worked side by side with Lilo.

Lilo Oshinsky, her childhood *Kränzchen* friend, had arrived in New York City a few months before Liese, lean and muscled from the factory job she'd taken in Venezuela after leaving Frankfurt. The afternoon Liese's ship arrived in New York harbor on September 9, 1938, Lilo was standing with Uncle Hermann and his family—Aunt Sadie, Adele, Adele's husband, Walter, and baby Eddie—holding up a homemade placard with the *Kränzchen* "battle cry" written out in bright blue and red letters: *And if all else breaks, our little wreath stays as one.* Liese dropped her suitcase and shouted Lilo's name with joy, blood rushing to her ears as she ran toward her friend, ignoring all the others for the first several minutes.

That same evening, after Liese had settled into Uncle Hermann's apartment on East Eighty-third Street, she and Lilo boarded a bus that took them across town to Riverside Drive, where they found an empty bench overlooking the Hudson River. Lilo had brought fried chicken from a cafeteria in Washington Heights near where she lived. Liese was ravenous after her journey and happy to discover that American chicken could taste so delicious. The two friends watched the fishing boats and inhaled the scents of the river while the sun went down over the Palisades. They imagined New Jersey was Germany and that one day they'd sail across the water and go home.

Lilo had found work in a button factory in the Garment District. Her job gave her confidence and an American boy-friend, a Southern boy named Richard, whose favorite description of foolish people was "nut bucket." Richard had helped her learn the subway and bus routes, showed her the paths and clearings of Fort Tryon Park, and introduced her to the cheapest cinemas and cafeterias. In the days that followed Liese's arrival in New York, Lilo made it her business to show all these to her friend.

In New York, Lilo had started to go by her birth name, Elizabeth, and advised Liese that her own birth name, Alice, sounded more American, a better name than Liese for job interviews. Only her teachers in Frankfurt had ever called her Alice, and then only on the rare occasions when she misbehaved. The distance Liese felt from her birth name, once she began using it, made her feel cut off from herself, and the way she associated Alice with being scolded only made it easier for her to blame herself when interviews didn't go well.

Lilo tried to breathe optimism into her friend, reminding her to insist upon happiness in the United States, to fight for it. The two met on the Hudson every Sunday evening during Liese's first months there. Lilo always brought chicken, Liese, a thermos of coffee and the book Eve Adler had given her at the good-bye party at the Mayers', *The Education of Hyman*

Kaplan. For Liese, her friend Lilo, a warm and matter-of-fact young woman, was the embodiment of her early life, of a time when she and her girlfriends had filled out each other's excited half-finished sentences, when it had taken almost nothing to send them into peals of laughter. While they ate, Liese and Lilo regaled each other with stories from their week and practiced their English by reading aloud from *Hyman Kaplan*. They copied lines into the notebooks they carried in their purses, increasingly satisfied with the full English sentences springing from their hands, their own accents perfectly imitating Kaplan's. "Avery day in de contry my vife vas gatink op six o'clock, no matter vat time it vas!" and "Ve all heaven a fine time!" The latter was the proud recitation of the fictional émigré Mr. Kaplan to his English teacher, when he was asked to use one of the week's new vocabulary words, "heaven," in a sentence. Liese and Lilo said it to each other as their reluctant good-bye every Sunday, followed by kisses on both cheeks, and then a few more Kaplan lines:

"I am glad I mat you."

"Mutual."

"Hau kay."

The two friends often met Saturday mornings as well, when they went to the *Aufbau* office at Seventy-fifth and Broadway to do their translations. In the afternoon, they spent what they earned—five cents a letter—on movies at the RKO Regent on Seventh Avenue, which featured successful young city women played by Betty Hutton, Barbara Stanwyck, Jean Arthur. Afterward, they walked down Fourth Avenue's "Book Row" to browse the discounted volumes displayed on carts.

On Saturday nights, Liese and Lilo spent their last nickels

on dinner at the Ladies' Grill in Times Square. "If you're going to be a vegetable, be a fucking vegetable!" Lilo said under her breath as she glanced at the soggy peas and carrots on her plate, proud of her growing command of the American profanities Richard had taught her. Liese studied the American waitresses—"For salad dressings I have . . . For vegetables I have . . . For desserts I have . . ."—admiring their crisp enunciation and envying their self-assurance and the world of choices over which they presided, as if asking, How can you not be happy when I am here to bring you exactly what you ask for?

After dinner they'd go to a bar, where Lilo met up with Richard and Liese allowed young American men to buy her gin with chilled olives and light her cigarettes. Lilo would size up the most fervent suitor and coax Liese away from going home with him. "Well, yes, there's an ache in your belly, and before you know it, you say, 'I love him,'" Lilo warned. "Come!"

Since she'd arrived in the United States, and all through the summer of 1939, Liese received a continuous stream of letters, sometimes four or five in a week, from EP—letters bearing return addresses like *Sometime and Somewhere at Sea, Middle of the Indian Ocean, Off the Coast of Africa*. Once he'd arrived in Chile, EP had taken a job as a ship's doctor and earned enough to get to England. In England he had joined the Merchant Marines, again as a ship's doctor. *I wonder what Georg would say if he would see this most faithful Café Continental regular rolling along on a British ship?* The letters were filled with tenderness and the sparks of romance EP more tentatively expressed in Prague: *My mind is crowded with questions and the usual prayer that the Bon Dieu will one day give us the money and time that we can meet again . . . as ever and forever.* The warmth of EP's words made Liese feel as though they were continuing their "spiritual sessions" at the Continental and almost made her forget his sloping shoulders and round stomach.

I listen to the ship's gramophone all night long . . . Without it I become too easily entangled into the jungle of political groups and differences that grow easily and quickly, even at sea . . .

I'm studying American newspapers; surprised at how much wishful thinking there is in the States. I hope everybody will realize the immense danger before it's too late. Excuse me these harsh words . . .

The efficient mail service of the British military allowed EP to be the hub of communication for their now widely scattered Prague friends.

Franta and Eva in Santiago . . .

Franz, Edith, with little Andy arrived in Cleveland. Trying to find way to get Werich and Voskovec to U.S. Exit permits seem impossible. Surely W & V are on Hitler's little list. But pray they succeed . . .

Eve in England. Rumors she is breaking hearts in London. Schülle in Windsor, working as farm trainee . . .

Egon Schwelb safe in London with Karla and little Frankie . . .

You may already have received the biggest news . . . Hans and Erich in England! They suffered enormously during their weeks in jail. Hans wants to join Royal Air Force. Erich hoping to study German literature in Cambridge. How anyone can continue to interest himself in German culture and language right now I am at a loss to understand. It will be worthwhile once again, but by God, it is not now . . .

By late July, his medical degree finally in hand and secure with the knowledge that Erich was safe, Paul had reason to believe that he would get a visa to England. A distant family friend, a Mr. Singer, had secured Paul an apprenticeship at a printing shop in London, the final requirement of his visa application. There were no medical job possibilities now, but perhaps, after his English improved, there would be. Else Heller, her leukemia still quiescent, had the means for a modest livelihood from Alfred's savings and pension from the years he was the physician for the Prague Railroad Union. Because the political air of Prague continued to indicate that older Czech Jews would not be in danger, Paul thought she could survive the troubled times, living quietly in Vršovice. She agreed that Paul should leave while he could, and she would follow if it became necessary. He purchased a ticket for September 4 for a flight to Belgium, the first leg of his trip, and that summer moved into Grandma Minna and Uncle Walter's apartment as he awaited the day of his departure.

My aim, Erich Heller wrote in his Cambridge University application, which he labored over for days, getting assistance from a university librarian who edited the text to convey a far more assured grasp of English than Erich had, *is to study the development of anti-humanistic tendencies in German literature in the 19th century. The question to be examined: whether pessimism about the essence of human life, which leads to negation of the individual and promotes readiness to accept anti-individualistic and anti-humanistic ideologies, is the foundation of anti-humanism. I shall review German literature with a view to discovering the*

sources which have nourished this pessimistic attitude, and discuss
from this basis, the humanistic optimism of the classical period of
German literature, the rational and optimistic philosophy of life it
represented.

As he had hoped, he was admitted as a Ph.D. student to
Cambridge on the merit of his little book on Kraus and Mann,
Escape from the Twentieth Century. He was to begin, under the
supervision of Professor R. A. Williams, in the fall 1939 term.
He was offered a scholarship allowance of fifty pounds annu-
ally.

Almost immediately, he fell in love—twice.

First, with the mind, voice, and mannerisms of Isaiah Berlin, renowned as a student in philosophy at Oxford for having
won every academic honor available. During Erich's first
month at Cambridge, he attended meetings of the Cambridge
Philosophical Society, where Berlin, now an Oxford don, came
to hear lectures by the new Cambridge professor Ludwig
Wittgenstein. Even more than watching Wittgenstein, Erich
watched and listened to Berlin in conversation afterward, not-
ing the Russian émigré's quick and assured command of English, the emphatic nods that accompanied his speech, the full
spoken paragraphs hurtling out of him one after the other, before he stopped for a breath and apologized for "going on so."
Berlin began to represent for Erich the embodiment of the hu-
manist academic that he saw himself becoming. He studied the
expressions Berlin used most often in conversation. "Tolerably well," he overheard him say several times when asked how
his day was going. The phrase soon became Erich's own answer to the polite English inquiries about how he was faring.
"Tolerably vell!" he'd offer with enthusiasm.

His second love was an eighteen-year-old student in law who asked Erich (shyly) if he could share Erich's table at the Corner House Café, a favorite gathering place for students. Over raspberry creams that arrived in frosty silver dishes, Erich and Graham Storey, from the nearby town of Meldreth, discovered an easy sociability and spent the afternoon talking about writers they admired in common. Soon Erich and Graham were taking walks along the Cam River, picnicking on bread, cheese, and wine on the campus green, and going to films at the Regal Cinema, where they shared their worries about the growing British nationalism so evident in the militaristic prefilm newsreels.

As the fall quarter approached, Graham's father, a prosperous dental surgeon, got to know his son's new friend and loaned him money for books and clothes, and at Burton's tailor shop on Market Hill, Erich was fitted with new flannel trousers, their cuffs breaking perfectly across the midstep, wool shirts in autumn colors, and dress shoes.

Erich taught Graham poems by Claudius and Goethe, insisting that every educated European, even the English, must be able to list every one of Goethe's love affairs. And Graham, who knew long passages from Dickens by heart, helped Erich master English by reading him chapters of *Bleak House*, stopping to analyze Dickens' vivid descriptions of life. "I can see it all," Erich said. "His words take me to every room in the house!"

Soon Graham entrusted Erich with his own stories, the first he had ever written.

The more I get acquainted with your story the more I like it, Erich wrote in a letter to Graham in late August 1939. Though they lived only a few miles apart, they had begun the practice of writing to each other so that Erich could practice his written English, which he mastered with astonishing speed. *There is something in* The Coal Miner *which exhales the enchanting scent of legitimate, genuine writing; a sort of gentle vigor and serene melancholy that fascinates me. Do carry on, Graham! There is but one thing I should like to recommend: "The hospital, quiet, like the very early morning before anything is awake." That's wrong, Graham, completely wrong. You can't compare the stuffy atmosphere, the oppressive silence, of a proletarian hospital with the purified air of an early morning. But you will find a remedy for this little atmospherical slip, and hopefully forgive me if my English is barely correct enough to help.*

Graham, awed by Erich's rapid mastery of a new language, assured him that whether his English was always correct or not, he never uttered or wrote a word that was not interesting. With his British good manners, he was careful not to intrude by asking Erich about the people in Prague he'd left behind.

"The afternoon we met, well, Graham, what made you choose my table here at the Corner House?" Erich asked, his eyes at first avoiding Graham's. It was one of the last days of August, and they were once again eating raspberry creams while seated at that very same table. Erich had never asked anyone this sort of question; nor had he ever longed to know the answer in the same way he wanted to know it from Graham.

"Well, *you*, I suppose!" Graham replied shyly.

"How wonderful! Isn't that wonderful! Isn't that remarkable!" Erich replied, now looking into his eyes. "Graham, one *can* know and read and write about darkness and yet be, oneself, happy, can one not?"

By late August 1939, just before her twenty-sixth birthday, and just as EP's letters were revealing ever greater concern about the plight of friends and family still in Prague, Liese's own life began to improve. At last she had received a refugee scholarship from the New York School of Social Work and soon would be taking classes with people whose names she'd heard in Prague: Erich Fromm, Frieda Fromm-Reichmann, Harry Stack Sullivan. Most important, she received the telegram she'd longed for since arriving in New York. Irma and Albert, along with Hedy, were in Luxembourg and would soon travel to Rotterdam, and from there, to New York.

The thought of her parents' arrival made everything about New York—the people, the buildings, the horses in Central Park—announce itself anew, and Liese allowed it to. For those few days in August, she felt almost young again.

Then, on Friday, September 1, Liese was alone in her apartment when she heard on the radio the news that Hitler had invaded Poland. On September 4, 1939, the day full-scale war was declared, a letter from EP to Liese from *Somewhere at Sea* brought news of friends still in Prague:

Mayers safe. No news of Tomas and Marietta, nor Milena. My mother is physically all right, but desperate. Most difficult news: Confirmation that Paul arrested. Else Heller in a desperate psychological state.

CHAPTER TEN

The War Years

September 1, 1939–April 16, 1945

Adjoining the sitting room of Minna and Walter's apartment in Vršovice was a little alcove that became Paul's bedroom when he moved in that summer. Minna hung pretty pictures of lilacs to make it more welcoming. He'd sent his most beloved books to Liese, paring his collection down to a few medical reference books and one Langenscheidt German-English dictionary that he studied in anticipation of his departure for England, still planned for September 4. The small apartment, filled at all hours with the scent of Grandma Minna's coffee, felt happy, which surprised Paul.

In the early morning of Friday, September 1, Paul was awakened by men's voices outside the apartment, followed by loud knocks on the front door. He heard his mother's footsteps heading from her bedroom to the sitting room near the door, her alarmed voice—"What is this all about?"—and their answer—"We just need some information. In a few days, you will have him back." He heard sharp words from Uncle Walter, demanding that the men leave. "Erich Heller does not live here," he said. "Please let us all go back to sleep." Not permitting himself to panic, Paul put on his robe and went to the door to help deal with the intruders.

By September 1939, Erich had moved into a second-floor apartment at 4 Saint Peter's Terrace, in Cambridge, which he shared with Paul Roubiczek, a history and philosophy professor at Cambridge, and Paul's wife, Hjordis, an actress. He continued his studies at Cambridge University, and continued to write letters to Graham Storey, first to Graham's new student address at Trinity Hall, Cambridge, and beginning in the winter of 1941, when Graham joined the British Royal Artillery, to his station with the Watson Unit in Shrivenham, Berk, UK.

That September, Liese began her studies at the New York School of Social Work and anxiously awaited her parents' arrival in the United States, which finally happened on New Year's Eve, 1939. Albert and Irma seemed to thrive during the first weeks, finding what they always called "creativity and concentration" from learning a new language. As often as she could, Liese went to Uncle Hermann's to have a late lunch with them between her classes. They spoke optimistically about finding purposeful activities once they settled in Milwaukee in the apartment Ernie had rented for the three of them to share.

After her parents moved to Milwaukee, Liese spoke with them by phone twice a week. Their first news was always that they were well, followed by the report that no one had been willing yet to hire a sixty-one-year-old man with limited English, not even on Ernie's recommendation.

Then, on February 15, six weeks after Albert and Irma's arrival in the United States, Ernie phoned Liese in New York. She should take the next possible train to Milwaukee. He'd wire her the money and explain everything when she arrived.

"Are you all right?" she asked. "Father? Mother? What is it?" Ernie insisted that she mustn't worry, repeating that he'd explain everything when he saw her. She stayed awake the whole night on the train, beside herself with worry about what she would find when she arrived.

Ernie was standing at the gate when her train pulled into the station. They walked together toward a line of taxis. Before they got in, Ernie took both her hands in his. "Father . . ." he said.

Father has finally found a job, Liese made herself think. He must have found a job in New York, and Ernie had asked her to travel to Milwaukee so she could accompany them on the train back to New York.

"Father hanged himself yesterday."

Liese heaved back and forth like a falling tree.

She sat shiva with her mother and brother and a small group of Ernie's colleagues at the Epstein Wine Company for the week following Albert's funeral. Each day Harry Epstein, Ernie's boss, brought sandwiches and hot dishes to the apartment.

Liese couldn't bear to leave her mother. She stayed on for several weeks, and she and Irma visited the cemetery each day, the ground brittle with frost.

Still in the depth of winter, she boarded the train back to

New York, forcing herself to return to school because Irma insisted that she must. "Suppress what draws you back," she'd said.

September 1, 1939, 3 A.M.—Two "friendly" Gestapo agents come. My anxious mother asks the agents, "What is this all about?" and receives the answer, "We just need some information. In a few days, you will have him back." I'm not permitted to take anything. I arrive at courtyard of Pankrac prison, then to window-less cell in the basement. On the eighth day we are brought by truck to the railroad yard. About 2,000 people are gathered. We stand for hours: the former mayor of Prague, Petr Zenkl; the novelist Joseph Čapek (brother of Karel); my medical professor, Kurt Sitte—before we are loaded on the train. The trip lasts 24 hours. In Dachau, we are ordered to undress and chased into showers. We receive uniforms with red-yellow Star of David. We stand for hours in the central square of the camp. One prisoner, a well-known manufacturer, who is obese, is pulled out to perform exercises to amuse SS. He collapses, is kicked by the SS, and carried away. We don't see him again. We sit in barracks. Boredom is inter-rupted by a loudspeaker bringing news of German military suc-cesses. After two weeks, the Czech prisoners are moved to Buchenwald; we are transported in cattle cars. We arrive two days later and learn there of surrender of Poland. Hitler's speech blares at us over loudspeaker.

November 9, 1939—A bomb explodes at Nazi headquarters in Munich. Five-day fast for Jewish prisoners is ordered. We're as-signed to work groups. I report to stone carriers. I'm ordered to run with stones in wheelbarrows. I wear wooden shoes and paper socks.

Worse than the cold is the mud. Prisoners around me collapse. They're carried to the infirmary and I never see them again. I work 7 A.M.–6 P.M. without purpose. Prisoners commit suicide by running into electrical fence. I become friend of political prisoner, Max Girnd, a former communist functionary, imprisoned since 1933. He has extra bread. Without his help I would become a "Muselmann," as the emaciated prisoners are called, very quickly.

Late November 1939—The central square of the camp is converted to a tent camp. Thousands of Jewish prisoners from Poland arrive. Most of them die of starvation and freezing temperatures. Tents are removed. Mass murder.

Cambridge, August 13, 1940—My dear Graham, Cambridge is lovely and quiet. And I am excessively in love with my writing desk . . . Yet there are lots of interviews, appointments, and other annoyances. The results are some vague but rather "promising" promises for next term. So let's hope and see . . . Erich

Cambridge, September 26, 1940—My dear Graham, There is a fine light in the fireplace, and the autumn's flowers on the table look pensive, deep, knowing, and resigned. One of these still and miraculous hours when the brain is on leave from its diplomatic duties and excessively receptive to the insinuations of the heart . . . music comes . . . What a great light from within. I had given up all hope that there could be again a summer and autumn like this.

At Sea, October 14, 1940—Dear Liese, . . . Like Old Vasco de Gama I round the Cape of Good Hope. Albatrosses, flying fishes, sunsets and sunrises; these wonders of nature transposed against

mood of melancholy when I think of Europe's horror . . . As ever,
EP

October 1940—SS are jubilant with German victories. The Kapo
selects me for a beating for not breaking stones fast enough. I can
hardly move.

 December 1940—Severe pain in back of neck. I remember from
medical school, "Shoveler's Fracture." It's risky to report to infir-
mary. Almost certain death. I am so weak and the pain is so severe
I do not care. Dr. Wagner's face lights up. My case interests him.
He orders my admission to the hospital. They apply body cast. I'm
here six weeks. I regain weight. I'm rarely visited by SS physician.
I'm reassigned to "light work" in builders' yard. I expect to be
reassigned back to stone quarry, but it does not happen—an over-
sight, I suspect, in bookkeeping at work office.

Cambridge, March 1941—My dear Graham, Alone with the
world, with the sun, the moon, the stars, the cosmic night. For the
first time in my life I am not frightened of solitude. There is no
fear, no childish curiosity which would interfere with the grim and
blessed lucidity of my wandering, seeing, listening. I am not afraid
of life, not afraid of death, not too proud and not too humble. If the
trumpets of doom were blown just now they could not break my
stillness.

 Cambridge, July 31, 1941—Dearest Graham, I was in bed,
very bad need of talking to you, seeing you. One of my officer pu-
pils, one of the nicest of all the lot, was killed, shot by a sentry
when walking with a girl on absurdly forbidden grounds near

Cambridge. I cannot free myself of this awful feeling of life dying, of an absurd death, of all life dying, of an all-absurd death. There lies on my writing table a yet uncorrected translation of his, and will remain uncorrected for all time to come . . . How can eternity begin with a piece of Swift, translated into German, and full of mistakes? Graham, Du, let's work hard, live hard, feel, feel, feel. Do take care of yourself. I think we live on friendlier terms with eternity; sometimes I know that we have even fallen in love with it; let's never fall out of love with it.

Somewhere at Sea, August 1, 1941—Dearest Liese, During the long and monotonous weeks at sea, I am reading and remembering like an old man . . . I am a Central European, not to be altered, and won't be happy if I cannot see all that again. As ever yours, EP.

Cambridge, November 17, 1941—Dearest Graham, Tomorrow night I am going to read to the joint German courses and many people from the faculty and the joint refugees. I shall read German poetry, mainly Claudius and Goethe . . . The simplicity I seek is not the abolition of it all, but its gentle, gently preserving conquest, not its clumsy sum, but its delicate balance and synthesis . . .

Cambridge, November 18, 1941—I can't possibly go to bed without talking to you, Graham. I miss you for I am unspeakably happy tonight. What an evening it was! . . . Goethe and Claudius and Schubert. The Music Room in St. John's, a very beautiful, intimate architecture, some hundred people in it . . . and you feel in your fingertips that they obey you, they cannot help following you,

you could do with them what you like, and you feel like doing exactly what you are doing: to kidnap their souls for an hour or so (and what a variety of souls: British officers and German refugees and Cambridge undergraduates) and to "lead them astray" from the path they are forced and willing to go every day, and to lead them somewhere where the unaltered heart of humanity beats as if it were its first hour of life, its first and its last and its ever-lasting hour.

January 1942—There are days, Graham, where all my life reverberates the emptiness of a million human hearts. I understand best the temptation to ease this burden by activity and events . . . I don't know why: I am permanently tired and exhausted now. I suspect it is the war and this world so absurdly alien to the pattern of my heart and brain and nerves.

April 14, 1942—At Sunday morning assembly, the loudspeaker orders Jewish prisoners to stay standing. We are surrounded by guards and marched to quarry. We're ordered to load stones into handbarrows and carry stones while running. My partner is a sturdy 35-year-old physician. We have to pass a row of SS guards with whips. After an hour or so prisoners start to collapse and are carried away. Fortunately, we two are strong enough to bear it without collapsing. We have no idea what caused this episode. We surmise it was a celebration of a victory on the Russian front.

April 1942—The date of this cruel interlude remains in my memory, but my recollection is vague of other happenings and the dates during the summer and fall of 1942. This is the approximate time when letters from my mother stop coming. Until now, we are permitted to write home once a month, and can receive mail as often, which, of course, undergoes strict censorship. Before correspondence stops, Mother hints to me in carefully camouflaged language she is moving from Vršovice to Terezín.

Cambridge, May 4, 1942—Dearest Graham, I have read The Brothers Karamazov *twice, and each time found it more depressing because, more true to life. I still see a trifle of cynical-satirical showing-off. But under that, I hear the final and unanswerable criticism of Christ. And it is a deadly, devastating summing up. It is reality versus illusion, and the illusion was Jesus . . . The opinion is, baldly, this: Jesus, you are inadequate . . .*

Cambridge, May 11, 1942—Dearest Graham, If life—yes, "just to live"—is senseless, it cannot borrow sense (but only a surreptitious and ephemeral pleasure) from its own achievements. "To be or not to be" is no real question: language is wise and the sense and meaning of "not being" stands and falls with the sense and meaning of "being." . . . Illusion? Well then, there is more reality in certain illusions than in all the facts of our cosmos.

June 1942—At least half of the Jewish prisoners went on a "transport," the official term for removal to another camp, usually Auschwitz. This transport led to reassignments of the remaining prisoners and I lost my job at the builders' yard and became again a carrier of stones.

———

Cambridge, June 16, 1942—Dearest Graham, I have been feeling very lonely and homesick lately, that's all. It has nothing whatever to do with any "real" home. It's like a yearning for something where it is equally painful to penetrate as not to penetrate. Like a pain in a limb that does not belong to one's body. There is still the absence of any news from Mother and Paul.

Cambridge, July 15, 1942—Graham, I feel for certain that this world is in itself but an experiment of God's unharassed curiosity. The idea does not at all seem absurd to me that its success depends on us. Thus our cruel and blessed task would be: to make God happy. I am not very helpful, am I?

Somewhere at Sea, November 29, 1942—Dearest Liese, Mother and Aunt Aninka deported. Nothing has been heard of them. Grandmother, 87, separated from Mother and put into Terezín, conditions said worse than Poland, if such is possible. Franz Gollan's parents and sister, and Else Heller there, too. Hans has joined RAF and made up his mind to drop bombs on Germans and I cannot blame him. He has changed; nothing left of youth . . . As ever, EP.

April 17, 1943—Every week two Czech-Jewish prisoners are called to the gate. These people are transported to Auschwitz to be killed. On April 17, my name is called, along with Max Bitterman, a former official in office of the prime minister of Czechoslovakia. He is a pillar of strength. We are brought to the railroad station under heavy guard. We spend nights in prisons along the way: Gera, Dresden, Breslau, Görlitz. During the night in Görlitz, a uniformed man with kind face asks us not to be afraid. He's an old social democrat and tells us he will help us by keeping us in Görlitz another night so we arrive in Auschwitz on Sunday morning when chances are good the SS officers are tired after Saturday night drinking. Miraculously, he is right. When we arrived Sunday morning, the officer in charge is disinterested, and after a superficial look at us, we are not selected for oven. The processing con-

sisted of the usual shower and something new, the tattooing of a number into the left forearm (my number is 119581). For several days, we carry stones and bricks. Then, for the first time since our imprisonment we are asked about our civilian work. Bitterman says, "Farmer." I am called to infirmary and am asked by the Kapo of the infirmary whether I have experience as doctor. He is friendly. Before I answer he tells me I am assigned to mining camp in Jaworzno, a sub-camp of Auschwitz, on the road between Kattowitz and Krakau. After four years in Buchenwald, I am not prepared for this announcement and am not sure whether I should be jubilant or fearful. We travel thirty miles by truck with guards. Approximately 200 Polish prisoners in the camp are busy building barracks to house expected 2,000 Jewish prisoners to work in two coal mines near the camp. I see up to 100 patients each evening. Injuries, exhaustion, respiratory diseases. Twenty beds, which are soon fully occupied. We manage to have a low death rate and the SS officer in charge is cooperative and supportive. He seems mainly interested to restore sick prisoners to work capacity and less eager to organize selections for transport back to Auschwitz. Nevertheless, we cannot avoid that after the arrival of new prisoners he orders a few of the older ones to return to Auschwitz. Sometimes I can prevent such an event. For some unknown reasons, the SS officer is replaced by another one. He turns out to be most cooperative and even helps us hide sick prisoners when inspections are announced.

Cambridge, July 13, 1943—Dearest Graham, Last week in Cambridge I heard a lovely concert, given by the New London Orchestra . . . the 4th Piano Concerto by Beethoven, 5th Brandenburg concerto, and Mozart's Linz Symphony. It is so important to realize

that this world still is! No, Graham, you must not be frightened.
There are no demands, no claims, only the wish that you should
not lose yourself, that you should become what you are—for what
is our own we must strive for even harder than for anything that lies
outside ourselves.

Spring, 1944—Polish prisoners working in the mine in Jaworzno
are ordered back to Auschwitz for a trial, accused of preparing to
escape. Gallows for multiple simultaneous hangings are erected.
Prisoners have to do the ghastly work. The next day, the order is
given for the early return of all prisoners from work. They have to
assemble on the central square to witness the executions. A few mo-
ment later, a truck arrives with condemned prisoners. The SS com-
mander of Auschwitz soon appears, delivers short speech, and then
the hanging takes place. It is horrible. I am ordered to pronounce
the executed prisoners dead, whereupon the bodies are removed by
other prisoners ordered to do so, and loaded on the same truck that
brought them. SS officers assemble near kitchen and drink. I am
ordered to report to them. I, of course, am terribly fearful of their
intentions with me. When I arrive some of them are obviously
drunk and all they want is assurance that the executed prisoners
are dead. It is a terrible experience.

At Sea, August 23, 1944—Dearest Liese, My mother gave her
last sign of life in April. Today, the Soviets are only 50-60 kilome-
ters from the camp in which she was reported. You can imagine
how we count every kilometer of the Russian advance . . . As ever
and forever, EP

January 17, 1945—Jaworzno bombed. Three killed. Work all night to care for injured. Noon, bell sounds. Ordered to assemble in camp square with blankets and ration for day. News of advancing Russians. No time for orderly evacuation. Sick ordered to stay in infirmary. Only the hope that the SS will have no time to kill the sick prisoners relieves my guilt. Camp commander orders me to take charge of cart loaded with boxes. Threatens to blow up infirmary if I'm not in convoy. Leave camp 11 P.M., westward toward Kattowitz. 3,200 prisoners, 300 SS. 2 A.M. older prisoners collapse and are shot. Next morning, ordered to run into a courtyard of foundry in Laurahuette.

January 18, 1945—Laurahuette: huge iron factory with working camp. Yard small. Stand in freezing temperature, hardly room to move feet. No food. No water. Stench of urine and feces. Aged prisoners die; bodies remain upright. Relief when gates opened. Shadows of high houses like giant ghosts. Feverish. Afraid houses will collapse and bury us. SS open fire at prisoners. Arrive in forested area. Sky full of stars, snow glistening in moonlight, crunches under steps. Remember such nights beautiful many years ago.

January 19, 1945—walk in trance obeying unknown hypnotizing power. Unbearable thirst. Swallow snow. Head hurts. Thoughts in turmoil. Incapable of putting order into them. Associations fall apart. Past, present, future, chaotic mixture. Strong enough to become my own observer. Organization of soul and mind disintegrating. See all trouble, but cannot avert it. Must collect strength; if I fall, SS will kill me. I know I am not yet completely demented because I know where danger lies. Must go on because next to me is rifle of an SS. Fever. Talk nonsense, as if purgation of the brain. Like drunkard, babble irrationally, saying I am going home.

January 20, 1945—121 prisoners die during night. Hundreds

injured and receive coup de grâce by SS, among them, my best friends. Commander tells us we will get something to eat. Fighting among prisoners. Some have madness on faces, fall over each other, trampled. SS smile. Wail of sirens. Witness battle between Russian and German planes, crash few hundred meters from us. March continues westward. Next to me, friend collapses. Try to pull him along. Walk up to the knees in snow. SS shoot everybody who stays behind. Temperature below zero. Limbs dead. See electrical fence of concentration camp Blechhammer. Chased into camp, running.

January 21, 1945—Enter camp, feeling we are saved. Counted by SS officers. 1,000 from march killed. Other prisoners in camp. Situation confused. SS guards come and go. A few prisoners separate from the crowd and run to barracks. I join them. Find empty mattress. Fall asleep.

January 22, 1945—Think SS have gone. We seek our way to kitchen. Suddenly SS run into camp with battle cry, "Prisoners rebel!" Bloodbath. Hundreds die. I and other prisoners withdraw into the barracks and stay motionless on floor. Crying of sick and injured for help in many languages. One SS, couldn't be older than eighteen, brutal face, points finger at my group. Orders us behind him. Some try to get back to barrack. They are shot. Seventeen selected. Ordered to run in unison to a cart loaded with boxes. Get cart moving, accompanied by SS. Darkness falls. In addition to ammunition are bags. I help myself to cubes of sugar. What strength-giving food. Pass long columns of prisoners of war— French, Russians, British, evacuated west. Torn shoes. Nothing between my feet and snowy ground. Fingers stiff.

January 23, 1945—I thought we were doing something urgent by pulling cart. Turns out to be only whim of SS. Another torture instrument. SS has whip. Snowing. Sun invisible all day. No direction. March in aimlessness.

January 24, 1945—Every 100 meters a corpse, a prisoner stumbling along. SS approaches him and says, "Can't you walk faster and longer, poor Itzig?" Stays behind with him. We hear shot that puts another German milestone on this road of desolation.

January 25, 1945—First time in four days, given food. Then, marching again. Walking guided by mechanical principle, as if each prisoner receives signal from comrade in front and next to him, passing it on to the man behind. Universe of prisoners moves. Arrive in Neustadt. Remain standing on the street, one, two, three hours, and on and on. Many collapse. Walk for another hour. Find a sleeping place in barn, let go and fall asleep in straw. Farmer's calendar with pencil. I take it. Paper freezing cold. I write fragments of memory.

January 26, 1945—Dark when SS open barn and chase us out. Some trampled. Others unconscious or too weak, waiting to be killed. Cannot find two friends. My shoes, gloves, earmuffs so severely torn, driving me to despair. Begin to wish I joined my friends. Play with thought about best way of dying. Beautiful to lie down tonight in the straw and arrive dreaming in other world. Other world visible. Am called before judge, asked about pluses and minuses of my life. I am sure only of not really having lived. I must ask judge to be returned to earth to wait for real life. Passages from Goethe I keep reciting: "I feel powers clearer, I glow as drunk with new-made wine."

January 30, 1945—Determination to stay alive remains. Life that of marching ghosts. Our number is 600-700.

February 6, 1945—Will to live leaving. Hardly any food. No water. Full of lice. People die like flies, precursors to my fate, un-

less we are moved into other camps. Rumors that Russians should reach us soon. We have become phlegmatic. I picture myself liberated into better world.

February 7, 1945—SS announces transport by train to Buchenwald. Buchenwald. As cruel as my remembrances are, I left friends behind. Perhaps they will still be alive. Loaded on train.

February 9, 1945—Unloaded at station in Weimar, sirens sound. Station hit by bombs. Crawl beneath wagons. High fever. I am an automaton when we march up road to Ettersburg (often in Goethe's diary) and camp. I separate myself to infirmary, where I had friends two years ago. Within minutes, in shower, deloused. SS select prisoners for death transport. I escape selections.

April 11, 1945—SS flee, soldiers of Sixth Armored Division of American Third Army arrive. Liberated prisoners take over the well-equipped SS hospital, first building of camp complex on road from Weimar. I fluoroscope prisoners for tuberculosis, which has reached epidemic. They must be isolated. Fluoroscopy room close to building entrance. Man in uniform with label "War Correspondent," who arrived with American soldiers, comes to entrance. Asks American guard if he could meet a former prisoner. I am called out. Agree to his request to guide him through camp. Several other former prisoners join us on the way. He is deeply impressed with what we made him see. He promises to return. He introduces himself, Edward R. Murrow.

CHAPTER ELEVEN

Reunions

April 1945–August 1946

During the years Graham was stationed with the Royal Artillery, Erich began the habit of having early Sunday dinner with Eve Adler and her new English-born husband, Sinclair Road, at their apartment in Cambridge, and after they moved to London, at their place in Pembroke Court, Kensington. Eve served their meal on trays so they could eat in the living room close to the radio, on which they listened to the BBC news. On Sunday evening, April 15, 1945, as they started to take their dishes back to the kitchen, they kept the radio on for the *Evening Postscript*.

"Permit me to tell you what you would have seen, and heard, had you been with me on Thursday," Edward R. Murrow began. "It will not be pleasant listening. If you are at lunch, or if you have no appetite to hear what Germans have done, now is a good time to switch off the radio, for I propose to tell you of Buchenwald . . . Men and boys reached out to touch me; they were in rags and the remnants of uniform . . . I asked to see one of the barracks. It happened to be occupied by Czechoslovakians . . . I was told that this building had once stabled eighty horses. There were twelve hundred men in it, five to a bunk." Murrow reported, giving listeners all over Europe and the United States a glimpse of conditions in the concentration camps for the very first time. He enunciated each word with deliberation as Erich, Eve, and Sinclair stood, silent and stunned.

"The stink was beyond all description," Murrow continued. "I asked how many had died in that building during the last month. They called the doctor; we inspected his records . . . Behind the names of those who had died there was a cross. I counted them. They totaled two hundred and forty-two. Two hundred and forty-two out of twelve hundred in one month . . . As I walked down to the end of the barracks, there was applause from men too weak to get out of bed. It sounded like the hand clapping of babies . . .

"The doctor's name was Paul Heller . . ."

Erich collapsed into a chair, letting out a low penetrating sound like that of an animal, a shocked sound of joy. They knew that U.S. troops had liberated Buchenwald five days earlier, but since summer 1942, when Else Heller's letters had stopped arriving in Cambridge, Erich had gotten no information about Paul. He'd obtained unconfirmed news that his mother had died in Terezín, and for years, like everyone, he had been sure that Paul could not possibly be alive.

In the hours that followed the broadcast, Eve and Sinclair's telephone rang constantly. The entire group of Prague friends who were now in England had heard the *Postscript* that evening—Paul Schülle in Windsor; Hans Posner and his new English-born wife, Polly, in Essex; Karla and Egon Schwelb in London—all beside themselves with joy.

EP had heard the broadcast at sea:

April 16, 1945

My Dear Liese, Last night Edward Murrow broadcasted from Germany about Buchenwald. The first name he mentioned was a doctor, Paul Heller, who has been in the camp since 1939. There seems little doubt that it is our Paul. He is only 30. Maybe that is not too late to be born again. Yours, EP.

Erich slept at the Roads' apartment that night and took the underground early the next morning to the Columbia Broadcasting System headquarters near Trafalgar Square. Though all of Erich's friends were convinced that the Czech doctor mentioned in the broadcast was their Paul, Erich became terrified en route that he might not be. Heller was a common name in Czechoslovakia, after all. But a Paul Heller who had been imprisoned for nearly six years? A young Czech doctor?

He found the office of Edward Murrow, which on this day was occupied only by his secretary, who introduced herself as Rose Campbell. Mr. Murrow had not yet returned from Germany, she told Erich. She was cordial and kind, offering him tea, taking his telephone number, promising she would call him the moment Mr. Murrow arrived. She suggested that before he left the office, he write a message to the Paul Heller mentioned in the broadcast.

"But how will it get to him?" Erich asked.

"That will be my business!" she said in an assured tone that made Erich immediately adore her.

A week later, Rose Campbell phoned Erich at his apartment on Saint Peter's Terrace in Cambridge. Edward Murrow had returned from Germany and had with him a bundle of letters and a diary, now safely locked in a drawer of her desk. They were from Paul Heller—from his brother, Paul.

During the chaotic days after the liberation of Buchenwald, when it was nearly impossible for displaced persons to reach the outside world, Rose Campbell and Edward R. Murrow continued to facilitate the exchange of letters between Paul and Erich, as well as efforts to get Paul a visa to England.

Tuberculosis was epidemic among the liberated prisoners in Buchenwald. Paul, along with another former prisoner, Willy Jelinek, who'd survived Buchenwald as a carrier of dead bodies, persuaded the chief medical officer of the Sixth Armored Division, Colonel Abner Zehm, to requisition a castle called Blankenheim, once used as an SS training school, for use as a long-term TB hospital. Colonel Zehm gave Willy and Paul use of a military car to accompany patient transports the fifteen miles between Buchenwald and Blankenheim. While driving back to Buchenwald after transporting a patient to the new hospital, Willy missed a curve, and in the rollover, Paul's hip was fractured. Righting the jeep, Willy drove twenty miles south to Jena, the nearest city with a hospital providing orthopedic surgery.

During Paul's recovery came news that within days, Jena and the surrounding area would be turned over to the Russians. Fearing that once this happened, Paul would not be allowed to leave, Willy stole an ambulance, making the entire process appear legal and official, with hospital orderlies bringing Paul out on a stretcher, though enough time had passed since his accident and surgery that he was able to walk haltingly. They drove south to Bayreuth, Germany, which was to remain under American control, and for several more days Paul continued his recuperation at a hospital there.

Colonel Zehm and other soldiers familiar to Paul from the days of Buchenwald's liberation were also in Bayreuth, preparing to convoy west. Though it was illegal to do so—the war was not officially over—Zehm agreed to take Paul with them, provided that he hid under blankets during the military inspections along the way. The ride lasted several hours before the soldiers let him off at an isolated railroad station a few miles from the French border, gifting him with a knapsack packed with clothing, food, and a wallet filled with slips of paper containing the soldiers' names and addresses, as well as enough money to last Paul several months.

He waited there through the night for the first morning train to Paris, his certificate of liberation from Buchenwald his only identification. Sitting on a bench on the station platform, surrounded by sleeping forests and fields, he was alone, his surroundings still, for the first time in nearly six years. Also for the first time in as many years, he wept, making no sounds, tears flowing in torrents down his cheeks and onto his neck.

In Paris, Paul went directly to Hotel Scribe, hoping to find Edward Murrow there, for Murrow had mentioned the Scribe as the French headquarters of the Columbia Broadcasting System. Unable to find him that first day, he rented a room nearby. When he located Murrow several days later, Murrow promised to help him obtain a visa for England. Erich, Eve and Sinclair, Hans and Polly, the Schwelbs, and EP, who kept Liese informed of their progress, all tried to help as well, but the British consulate hadn't received authority to issue travel permits to Czechs yet, and the Czech consulate could only issue Paul a passport to return to Czechoslovakia. Each day he walked the blocks between the consulates, hoping to move the bureaucracy and get information about the fate of his mother and other family members. In hushed voices, officials warned him that the takeover of his home country by the Communists was inevitable, and with his German accent, Paul would not be welcomed back.

As he waited for the moment when the evolving visa regulations would change in his favor, Paul wandered Paris's parks and galleries, unable to comprehend his freedom to do so.

At night in his hotel room, he continued to study English and tried to remember chemistry formulas from his medical school classes, which he'd jot down among the names, addresses, and telephone numbers of Willy Jelinek, Murrow, Zehm, and the soldiers who had taken him to the border. He scribbled vocabulary words and tiny diagrams of chemical interactions onto the pages of the pocket-sized notebook he bought at a Paris stationer, trying to convince himself that the neural pathways of his mind were alive and fully at his disposal.

Finally, on October 9, 1945, six months after the liberation of Buchenwald, and with continued help from Murrow, Paul received a British visa. Carrying the knapsack Zehm and his soldiers had given him five months before, he left Paris for Dieppe, where he boarded a ferry for England.

His brother was standing on the pier. As Paul walked toward him, he saw Erich's lips tremble on the formation of Paul's name. Erich took him in his arms, then held him at arm's length as their eyes toured each other. Awkwardly, wordlessly, they ascended the worn stone steps to the landing above, where they took a cab to the train that brought them to Cambridge.

No one in Erich's crowd had met a camp survivor. He looked so normal, Paul overheard them say, so little like what they'd expected.

He stayed in an extra room in the apartment at 4 Saint Peter's Terrace that Erich shared with the Roubiczeks. Erich now held a faculty position in German, and his Cambridge University friends gathered at the apartment many evenings. The men wore tweed jackets, drank Algerian wine, smoked pipes, critiqued lectures they'd attended, and discussed their almost finished novels and plays, bending toward Paul with their desire to communicate.

Paul wanted only to get away. He didn't want to wear the authority of what they couldn't understand. He felt the weight of his brother's empathic gaze, of Erich's sense of responsibility for his well-being, and it oppressed him. He felt comfortable only alone or in the company of EP, who had returned from sea, Sinclair and Eve, or Hans and Polly and their toddler son, Ricky, the first child born after the diaspora of his prewar Prague circle of friends.

In his back pocket Paul carried a small German-English dictionary that Eve and Sinclair gave him, and he spent hours

walking alone along the river Cam, practicing English by reciting German lines from his favorite Morgenstern nonsense
poems, then making the lines rhyme again in English.

A pair of pine roots
old and dark
make conversation in the park
The whispers where the top leaves grow
are echoed in the roots below.

An aged squirrel sitting there
is knitting stockings for the pair
The one says squeak; The other, squawk
that is enough for one day's talk.

At night, in his room, and unbeknownst to Erich, Paul
wrote to Liese Florsheim in New York, drafting his letters in a
notebook, writing the initial ones in German but translating
the later ones slowly into English, then painstakingly revising
before copying them onto light blue letter paper.

Cambridge, October 19, 1945

Dear Liese,
*After accumulation of incidents over the past days that kept
me confusedly busy, my inner balance slowly returns. I feel
like a Heimkehrer after all that I cannot explain, but I also
feel at battle with the soul. My energies impatiently wait to
become active. It becomes clear to me that it will be America
and I prepare for this, internally and externally, so grateful*

for your help. At the consulate they pushed a questionnaire into my hand with no explanations for the confusing questions. I filled it out, thanks to the helpfulness of Ed Murrow. I believe that my urge for activity, which couldn't be killed, can be fulfilled best in medical work.

Could you write me something about the American examinations? Which books do I need? Here, I am confused and still don't have the calmness I need. Murrow pushes me to write something about Konzentrationslager, which I cannot yet do.

Did you keep the books I sent you? Could they be useful to you?

Please write soon.

Be from the heart greeted.

Paul

Cambridge, November 3, 1945

My dear Liese,

A mail harvest today! A letter from Heinrich Waelsch, a letter from Edith and Franz Gollan, and most important, your letter. My last doubts regarding my decision to come to America disappear, due to my hopes and because of the evil that permanently turns Europe into a field of guilt. The historians are happy that Germany gets to feel its own weapons on its body, that the mass migrations are now forced upon the Germans themselves. That the collective defamation of a people has now been adopted by the world in regard to the evaluation of Germans. That philosophers of "dialectic" invent formulas, thesis/anti-thesis systems, makes me realize that people don't want to understand that there was something human that led to the hopeless system that brought Hitler, and there is really no rescuing anti-thesis free of its own potential for evil.

I realize that what I just wrote doesn't belong into my letter and I ask you to excuse me.

And I thank you from my whole heart for the touching help of all of you and the wonderful things you sent to Cambridge. I delight in the chocolate. Just now it is the inner pendant of my dearest gratefulness.

I wait for the day when I can start my life afresh. I have nearly lost all doubts that America will give me hope. You are there.

I am with all cordiality for you, yours,
Paul

Cambridge, November 23, 1945

My dear Liese,
I just received the information that it is not possible to get a place on a boat before twelve months have passed and on a plane before six months, unless I receive a priority right from somewhere. "Somewhere" was not specified. Apparently it doesn't exist for ordinary people, and an ordinary person I have—thanks to God—luckily and finally become.

I am in London since a few days to observe English practice of medicine. I realize that I have lost little of my basic medical knowledge, but unfortunately my position is affected by my difficulty in the English language and my lack of knowledge of the practical side of medicine. I wish the state of my being a foreigner everywhere would be over! I long for feeling of belonging to people—the absence of a condition puts the condition I long for into the right level of appreciation. Happiness: the simple absence of disaster.

I would like to get rid of the feeling that I am passive and let things happen to me instead of regaining my inner sovereignty. This feeling contains the sadness of the lost years, my difficulty turning my painful introversion to the outside. I only wish it were as simple as intention. It simply is that I will only be freed from the impacts of solitude if I somehow become creatively active.

I believe that only in this way will the tensions I feel come to a liberating solution, the mix-up of feelings and thoughts, triggered in me with every opening of my eyes and every look into this world, be brought into healing order. I continuously suppress the intention or urge to deal with my experience because I believe that my reaction could desensitize me from the beauty and charm which survived it. But the opposite seems to be the case. The more I postpone the less I am able to recognize who I am.

All I know is that I want to stick to the work that gave me satisfaction when I was at the threshold to life. Forgive me. I didn't intend to write you about my Magic Mountain thoughts, about what life gains through closeness to death. It is too much to say, to think.

I am anxious that after I get to America, I may be overwhelmed by the hyperactive sense of medicine as business, which I don't have any talent for and which seems to be the basis for commonality among Americans—at least as I imagine them. My elbows have never been a strong part of my body and furthermore, they have been used up.

I am not able to think all my thoughts in English words. But maybe I have learned enough and now I can finally live? It might be that this sounds arrogant—but I do not mean it in this way—I hope you understand.

Thank you for sending my anatomy book. You will excuse me if I put it on the shelf for the time being. I don't want to have to study anatomy again! I feel that before I am able to remember all branches of the arteries, I will go to a mental home.

I am, in all heartedness,

yours,

Paul

Ps. Please excuse my handwriting. My fountain pen has its problems.

Cambridge, December 14, 1945

My dear Liese,

It is not only a great happiness by which I was moved when I read your letter, but also anger at myself that a certain tone smuggled itself into my letter. It seems that my sense of proportions has been ruled out by the past years and instead of having a more objective perspective, I simply see the world the way I see it. Please forgive me that the immediacy of sorrow appears so huge. I wish that I could gain more distance to it. A part of my life was so incommensurable with my hopes and intentions that I need to learn again to connect where my life stopped. I feel that every step is hindered by thick fog. And to be a fog breaker I have just as little talent as to be a sleepwalker. It is still inside me, dear Liese. It is surprising to me that I am able to act it out and observe it at the same time. I will try to speak of other things, to think of other things.

Unfortunately, the weeks I got to experience English medicine in London are coming to an end and I go back to Cambridge soon. "Unfortunately" refers to my lack of independence in regard to Erich. He has suffered from the knowledge of my imprisonment and seems to have projected losing me onto losing this world. His feeling of guilt somehow remains alert and complicates his understanding that the reason I want to leave Cambridge is that I won't be able to reach an everyday existence here. He believes that he has to make something new and good for me, to make up for something, and therefore would love to keep me as long as possible in his sphere of influence. The force of this resistance is so great that rational insight into my inner and outer necessities is forced out of Erich's consciousness.

But I don't want to speak about it anymore and will wait until the "pathos of distance" (my most enduring learning from Nietzsche) will enable me to find the right and real spoken words.

Here, there is no opportunity to do real work. Even the well-meaning Labor Government has a hard time fighting discrimination toward foreigners exhibited by the British Medical Association. Brits are fond of foreigners when they admire how nicely they have advanced their country, but this kindness turns into a hostile attitude as soon as they get a scent of competition.

*In this country the New Year's Eve is not being cele-
brated. I will do so though. It shall be the day to remind me
to let the past be the past and to give the future full rights
over me.*

I am in all heartfulness, as ever
yours,
Paul

Cambridge, January 3, 1946

My dear Liese,
*Now there is not even the smallest doubt that it will work
out and I am full of hope that I will be able to leave the UK
and come to the U.S. Murrow is expected back during the
next days and I hope that his attempt to help will have an
impact. A few days ago I got the affidavit of a friend of
Franz and Edith Gollan so that now, with Heinrich Waelsch's and Benno Baecher's, I have three. Just to ponder
over the imagination of all the possibilities gives me pleasure.*

*I was surprised that your telegrams came from New York
and am worried that you didn't put your plans into practice
to go to Milwaukee to be with Ernie and your mother over
holidays. I hope that your holiday and New Year were as
wonderful as you wished for and as wonderful as I wish for
you. These days, I thought about you full of gratitude and I
hope that you could feel these thoughts. EP and Hans and
Eve Adler, who, as you know, is now happily Eve Road,
with husband Sinclair, Paul Schülle, and of course, my
brother, send their love.*

The constant rush inside me, I know from where, but not where to—is now slowly coming more under my control. I know that if the inner impetus doesn't soon get me where I belong, then my fortwürschteln is soothed by writing to you. I know that for some time my restlessness nearly helplessly pushed me along, but it got its impulse, its reason, from somewhere. It isn't enough to reason, as if it were true, that some psychological explanation of what happened could bring healing. It only brings exhaustion. There are people— certainly incomprehensible and strange—who live on as if the world before now had never existed. I almost admire everyone who can get away with a cheap black and white painting, who can oversimplify, who can say, here is the good, there is the evil, here the imprisonment, there the freedom, here nonsense, there sense. I admire such a person because I know how easily misfortune can be distinguished from happiness in such a projected worldview. I know this type of person who looks at the world in this way as well as I know myself, and I know that only a few months ago I was able to gain quite a bit of truth from this deception. But I believe now that contradictions—sense and nonsense, lies and truths, moral and amoral, freedom and imprisonment, human will and causality, misfortune and fortune, sickness and health, birth and death, love and hate—are not as separable as we like to think, and must come together for a rendezvous in this dying world, rather than in an endless fight. God knows this fight cannot end in reconciliation.

I know, dear Liese, this has been thought hundreds of times, thousand times before, as many times as there are living beings on earth. How easily it is thought, but how

difficult to make expressible as an experience. Only Dos-
toyevsky and Shakespeare and Tolstoy knew how to do this.
I believe my inner restlessness is due to having experience
and wanting to bring it from inside to outside. There is the
unbridgeable wall of inadequacy of expression: one should
be an artist, but one is not. This unveils the agonizing para-
dox of having experienced something without being able to
measure up to it. If one is forced in this way to deal with the
experience on a different level, it unveils itself in its imme-
diacy as a longing and as a guilt: the guilt to have saved my
own life while thousands died all around. The guilt that
during the months when I thought I was a doctor I wasn't
able to save everyone from the gas and that I was among
those I managed to save. Nothing helps against the pene-
trating power of the eyes of the dead, my bond to the dead.
My own experience feels like having died every day over
many years. Only one thing might help: to experience life in
its fullness and its contradictions and at the same time exert
some control over it. But to do so, I would have to be an art-
ist or a magician. And this is where the circle closes.

But I will talk about all this another time. It is 1:30 A.M.
That is what happens if one writes in the middle of the night.

Good night, with gratitude and heartfulness,
your Paul

Cambridge, March 18, 1946

My dear Liese,
So far I wasn't able to understand the practice of the Ameri-
can consul. For two hours I am attacked with courtesies so

that my mouth is watered for a country that has such wonderful officials, so that my heart happily beats faster, excited to soon get the American visa, and with each heartbeat my mood is better. But at the end of such a promising morning the consul presents the folder and says my number is not there. Which number? This morning I permitted myself the inquiry. The Oracle of Delphi was an exact mathematical equation compared to this mysterious number. As much as I could figure out, it seems to be that the quota number of doctors has been reached. In the meantime several boats left without me. But I am still hoping that the parlor game—if I have a visa, I have no boat, and if I have a boat, I have no visa—won't provoke my grim sense of humor for much longer.

   Yours,

   Paul

Cambridge, April 3, 1946

Dear Liese,

Yesterday, I was at the consulate for my last rites—but they didn't come. I wandered from one station to the next, to the doctor, to the X-rays. My fingerprints were taken. I pledged my word that I would never become a member of Parliament, and assured them that I am neither insane nor leprous. Everyone gave me congratulations, even the vice consul—more vice than consul—wanted to give me his congratulations, when he suddenly discovered that he again ran out of the Czech numbers and I could not leave. Again, a magician's trick.

But oh what a bad-mannered rascal I am. I have so far not mentioned a single word to ask how you are, although my thoughts are with you all the time and the words are hanging in the pen.

Please do not postpone your trip to be with your mother and brother so that you can greet me if I am able to get on a boat this month. Please forgive me if my advice sounds a bit grandmother-like, but one realizes more and more that the advice of grandmothers is not such bad advice after all.

Erich sends loving and warm greetings, which contain the best wishes for you. Not any less from your Paul

All my thanks and my dearest wishes,

always yours,

Paul

Ps. Ed Murrow went to New York a few days ago to take over his post and should have arrived by now. He has a note in his copybook to remind him of his offer to animate the State Department to send new numbers.

On April 12, 1946, a year and a day after the liberation of Buchenwald, Paul boarded *Cape Igvak*, a small Merchant Marine boat accommodating twelve passengers.

There was an air of intimacy and privacy . . . so intimate was it that the strip of water which grew and grew seemed to grow just between him and me, Erich wrote in a letter to Liese after seeing his brother off at the harbor of Liverpool. Erich and Liese had communicated little during the war years. After Liese had received his letter in late September 1938 ending their relationship, she rarely answered his later letters that inquired how she was. But during Paul's months in Paris, she'd corresponded with Erich more often, wanting to contribute to the efforts to get Paul a visa to England. Erich knew almost from the moment Paul arrived in England that he was intent on getting to the United States. He sensed, too, how much Liese's presence there affected his brother's determination to go.

I want to thank you very, very much for everything you have done for Paul, for everything you will do. I am deeply ashamed that I didn't say it earlier. But you will know what it has been like while Paul was with me. It is only now that I realize how little I was prepared to acknowledge the fact that he was to leave me again. Oh, these separations of which one's lives seem to consist. It was this profound disinclination to deal with his going that stopped me from writing . . . All I can do now is pray that Paul should be happy over there, as happy as he deserves to be. I love and admire him as much as I shall ever be able to love and to admire . . . If only I could be with you when he arrives. Thank you so much for giving him a bit of my love as well when he comes. Excuse this disjointed letter. It has been a strange and strenuous day. God bless you and him.

Ever yours, Erich

———

When *Cape Igvak* entered the harbor of New York, Liese, Edith Gollan, and Paul's cousin Benno Baecher were waiting on the pier.

The wind kicked up and carried the sea smell as the four walked to Liese's apartment on East Fortieth Street, where she now lived. She wanted to show Paul that the books he'd sent six and a half years before, which she'd reboxed after reading several of them, were safe and sound. They all had dinner at a midtown diner, where Paul ate slowly, reluctant to finish, for he didn't want the evening in Liese's company to end.

That evening Benno, carrying Paul's suitcase, and Paul, carrying the books, took a taxi to West Seventy-second, where Paul moved into his room in the Baecher family apartment.

In the days that followed, Paul called Liese almost every evening, hoping she would meet him for dinner, and most of the time she said yes.

In outward ways, Liese might have seemed unchanged to anyone who didn't know her well. Drawing on the fragile yet surviving hope in her mother's eyes when Irma saw her off at the Milwaukee train station after Albert's death, Liese had tried to go forward with her life. She finished her degree and took her first full-time social work position at Montefiore Hospital in the Bronx. But during those years she'd felt her spirit diminishing, her soul shrinking, her heart buried in protective layers.

Lilo, hardly able to recognize her once vibrant best friend, noticed these changes most of all. All those weekends after Liese had arrived in the United States, those Saturday evenings when she and Lilo had rendezvoused at the bar on Broadway, Liese had made herself turn down the men who'd complimented her beauty and wanted to buy her drinks. But after her father's death, she began to accept their advances, looking for mind-numbing comfort with men she barely knew, even those who invited her to their apartment while their wife was away. As long as they didn't ask her questions, as long as they didn't make her think. Anything not to think.

That was where she was in her life when she'd gotten word from EP that Paul Heller was still alive. When she saw Paul disembark *Cape Igvak,* it felt to her for a brief moment like his miraculous survival was her own.

NY, May 10th, 1946, 2 A.M.

My dear Liese,
The moment passes and the thoughts continue to flood over me, demanding that I communicate to you what is inside.

How can I make myself understandable and how can I prevent to appear like a bold intruder and only increase your loneliness instead of turning it into calmness that releases sorrows? I can only call on my feelings as witness to prove what is true. If all that I am saying seems not enough, my feelings are pure. They are pure, but not free of guilt.

I feel guilty because for the years you were in Prague I silenced the voice of my heart. And even now, I increase this guilt with every day that I am silent, just like back then, when out of a painful confusion of feelings I refused to be happy. Today, when I tried to speak, your rational statement that our meeting again now must be called healing and nothing else, stopped me. But my own rationality, which in the past has so fatefully fooled me, no longer has hold over me. There is only one certainty for me: that my love for you is so big that I constantly, whatever I do, live with you.

Please excuse this confession, which I wasn't able to postpone any longer. Please forgive me, but I would only be able to restrain my feelings if I still had the strength to set back my own happiness in order to not endanger the happiness of someone else. I fear that the morning will bring me back to the cool-headed deliberation of my former "Do I have a right?" and that I won't give you this letter and in this way will cause myself miserable hours. But what kind of a sin is it to speak about "right" if love with its cleansing force gives me nothing but right?

Let me tell you, dear Liese, on the Sunday in 1933 when you appeared to me for the first time, the fact that I couldn't speak led me into my loneliness and taciturnity. I didn't allow myself to tell you. What kind of a sin has that been! Maybe everything would have been different. However it may have been, the loneliness and closeness to death have made of me the person I am, full of longing, with a pure heart to love you and—if God gave it—to be loved back.

Please excuse this force of the heart. I pray that you will understand it in the same pure way I feel it. I pray that the soberness of what may be your words in response won't paralyze my tongue again and make my love impossible to express.

Be embraced in my thoughts,
Your Paul

June 1, 1946

My dearest of all Liese,
How wonderful and soothing your letter would be, if the word, "doubt" wouldn't exist in it. "Doubt about myself," you call it. But can you really limit and isolate yourself and can you keep the doubt, which you believe you are carrying

inside you, away from the "us"? Doubt about yourself,
which means doubt about everything which means the world
to me and of which I am only a part, but not separable from
anymore. If you doubt yourself, and you are everything to
me, then you doubt my world.

My dear Liese, I am happy about your hope that all this
doubt will fall away from you. I would be happier, though,
if it sounded more convincing. Your opinion of yourself
makes me so sad. The blame falls back to me. Why can I not
help you believe that you are yourself, the yourself I see, the
yourself I know?

Don't make a decision out of what you describe in your-
self as tiredness and softness. Don't make a decision in the
presence of gnawing doubts. I couldn't bear knowing you in
doubt and unhappiness. I cannot take away your freedom to
have doubt. I only ask you for one thing: don't put upon me
the anguish of uncertainty. You write that our past will
make our lives together complicated. But it is not the past
itself that we carry, but our interpretation of it.

I am with you, with all my heart.
Your Paul

Liese asked Paul to give her two weeks to consider his proposal of marriage, requesting that during those days he not
call or write to her. How much doubt she pushed through before she could say yes to him was something she shared only
with her mother and Lilo. In the end, it was a leap of faith,
guided by her mother's admonition, *suppress what draws you*
back, that persuaded Liese that their reunion was not mere

"healing and nothing else." Meaning and continuity, she made herself believe, were resident in Paul's reappearance in her life, in the extraordinary intimacy of his words, in his need for her. She convinced herself finally that whether she had the capacity to open her heart to him was the only question worth asking.

In early July, in response to Erich's letter of congratulations, Paul wrote to his brother, including in the envelope a photograph of Liese and himself leaning against a stone wall in Central Park.

My dearest Erich,

I feel trepidation as I search for words. In the end I may not be able to bring my words into tune with their proper melody. I count on your loving understanding that my heart is filled to the brim, just short of overflowing. I know that my mere notifying you about my love for Liese means a lot to you and that all words that I want to say may be superfluous. I thank you from my whole heart for your words about Liese and your good wishes. Only one more thing I want: that our human relations not become a sphere of guilt. I hold to it that all that has happened appears as it should have happened in order to bring me here.

Be embraced.

Your Paul

CHAPTER TWELVE

Manifold Homeland

Liese and Paul were married at New York City Hall on August 3, 1946. Lisa Ertl Plowitz, an old friend from Prague, and Fredy Mayer (who, with Joszi, their daughter, Ina, and Joszi's father, Rudolf Keller, had made it safely to New York in 1940) served as witnesses. Liese wore a blue suit and matching wide-brimmed summer hat; Paul, a gray linen suit borrowed from his cousin Benno. While they were being married, Joszi prepared a party for them at the Mayers' small apartment on East Ninety-eighth Street.

Though Liese had seen the Mayers frequently in NYC and Paul had spent time with them since his arrival, their marriage celebration was the first intimate get-together this group of friends had shared since Liese's farewell to Prague. Steffi Schlamm came bearing a cake and her embrace, after years of semi-estrangement caused by political differences, felt like friendship's return.

From Milwaukee, Irma and Ernie sent peach-colored roses, accompanied by a check covering a weekend honeymoon for the newlyweds in the Adirondacks.

From London, Eve Road wrote: *My very dear Paul and Liese, I simply cannot tell you how happy I am to hear of your marriage. And now I can admit it: I have always hoped it would happen, although it seemed at times to be a bit fairy-tale-like. Thank you also for the beautifully colored picture postcard you sent, saying "This is America" (I would have been a very bad psychologist if I had not put two and two together then!). Well, if this is what America looks like to you, you must be seeing things through rainbow-colored spectacles and that, after all the gray and black, must be viewed as a great achievement! As ever, Eve.*

A letter from EP, who had returned to sea, read: *Feeling for him as I do, it is a very good and reassuring thought for me that you will be with him now and no doubt you will feel yourself grateful that the best of our old company takes the very tender strings of continuity back to you. Hans will write separately and sends all his love as well. Yours as ever, EP.*

And from Cambridge, Erich Heller, who asked the Mayers to recommend the finest New York florist, sent a spectacular summer bouquet along with congratulations: *What a stimulant was this splendid photograph of you; a thousand thanks for sending it and a thousand good wishes to both of you. As ever and always, Erich.*

Paul and Liese's first home as a married couple was Liese's one-room apartment at 139 East Fortieth Street, where, after their honeymoon, Paul often worked into the night, writing job inquiry letters and studying for the state medical board exam scheduled for that October.

On the little table by her side of their pull-down bed, Liese kept the family book of Claudius poems that Ernie had carried with him to Prague twelve years before, and an ever changing stack of library books checked out during her frequent trips to the New York Public Library. On his side, Paul kept the stack of medical books he'd sent to Liese before the war, a bottle of antacid, and several flashlights (Liese teased him for always carrying one in his pocket when they went out in the evening, since the streets of New York were so brightly lit).

Each day before Liese got home from her job at Montefiore, Paul recorded in his notebook the number of hours he'd studied, the number of job inquiries he'd mailed out, the number of dictionary words and English grammar rules from *Fowler's* he'd mastered. He turned these daily reports into weekly reckonings in which he described the conditions that would allow him to accomplish even more.

"I think I can report some preliminary thriving," he'd often say upon Liese's arrival from work each evening, and then read from his list as though she'd requested him to, which she never did, for she preferred that Paul take everything at a slower pace than he was inclined to do. At the end of his recitation, he'd conclude that he hadn't done enough. Making up for "lost time" in his professional life became his most overwhelming concern, and though he shared this preoccupation with few people, he poured out his heart to Liese. Only after hearing her encouragement about the strength of his accomplishments was he able to ask her about her own day—*Wie ist der Mikrokosmos?*—though by the time he asked, he rarely had the patience to listen, and preferred to keep working.

Liese increasingly devoted herself to providing the conditions Paul requested: trying to fall asleep with the lights on when he studied into the night, reading at the twenty-four-hour café near the apartment if he needed to sleep, protecting him as well as she possibly could from the tides of daily life so that he could live at last with a rested mind. This she saw as her duty to him, and it became second nature.

Though she put in long days at work and far preferred cold cuts and rolls to her own cooking, when she got home (always with sweets for Paul and herself wrapped in a napkin from the cafeteria), she prepared dinners on their rickety stove—the simple beef or chicken dishes with potatoes that Paul requested, with neither spices nor fat because his years in the camps had wreaked havoc on his liver. On weekends, she tried, usually unsuccessfully, to make his favorite potato dumplings, which Joszi taught her to prepare after their marriage. And she took pleasure from the knowledge that her presence, her willingness to respond to his needs, seemed so fully to affect Paul's sense of well-being. When he awakened from nightmares, his face and hair drenched in sweat and for several moments not knowing where he was, he found her face and looked at her as though she were his only port, and they held each other through the night. Only then, in the dark, and never for long, did he talk about the camps.

They had quarrels—about spending money (Liese feeling that they could occasionally treat themselves to dinner out, while Paul worried about every penny they spent); about which routes to take through the city (Paul studying maps and timetables with the same seriousness with which he studied for the medical boards, while Liese preferred to meander with book in hand and plenty of places to stop for coffee along the way). And tensions filled their apartment when letters from Erich Heller, addressed to them both, arrived. They were filled with news of his successes—that one or another of his essays had appeared in *The Times Literary Supplement* and *The Cambridge Journal. The reception,* he wrote in one letter, *has been extraordinarily good! Suhrkamp seems to want to publish a collection; the best letter came from T. S. Eliot, in which he announced that my essay on Mann was the best he'd ever read!* He never failed to mention his growing list of famous acquaintances, such as W. H. Auden, Werner Heisenberg, Graham Greene, and E. M. Forster. Liese kept her eyes closed when Paul read the letters aloud, but even then she could sense the moments when he looked up at her, and she knew that he was studying her face for every sign of what she felt. She rarely knew how to tell him that, other than anger, she herself struggled to identify what it was.

But each lived with a deep sense of gratitude for the other during those early months in New York. Saturdays they took the bus to Fort Tryon Park, Paul's rucksack and pockets crammed with maps and nature guides. On Sunday afternoons they met the Mayers, the Schwelbs, the Plowitzes, and sometimes the Schlamms (though the whole group found it a struggle to deal with Willi's new right-wing politics) at the free chamber concerts held in the Frick Collection. And there were always Sunday dinners at the Mayers' apartment to look forward to. In the company of Ina and Joszi's father, the old friends huddled close together around the small dining table, Paul's hand on Liese's knee.

Their streams of conversation carried them from memories of Prague to their present lives and plans for their future, which, neither Paul nor Liese questioned, would include children.

By the summer of 1947, Paul had passed the state medical

board, completed an internship at Beth Israel hospital (where, in his surgical scrubs, he'd seen his supervisors curiously eyeing the number tattooed on his left forearm), and secured a residency at the tuberculosis sanitorium at Montefiore Hospital. The next spring, Paul accepted his first post-residency position at the new Group Health Association in Washington, D.C.— $5,800 per annum, plus the use of a 1942 Plymouth for making weekend house calls to patients. Liese stayed in New York while he searched for an apartment on the southeast side of Washington, near Saint Elizabeth's Hospital. The day before he returned to New York, anticipating the beginning of the next chapter of his life, he had his concentration camp number surgically removed.

On August 3, 1948, two years to the day after they were married, Liese and Paul's first child, my brother, Thomas Allen Heller, was born. There may well have been other little Thomases born at George Washington University Hospital in Washington, D.C., on that day, but I suspect my brother was the only one who was named after Thomas Mann.

They began life as a family in a small apartment at 4302 Third Street, S.E., which Paul and Liese furnished with a mattress, a cradle, a Philco radio cabinet (a present from the Mayers), and a bookshelf filled with their old books, as well as three new volumes of Goethe, gifts from EP, who, since their wedding, had sent them one volume of the *Complete Works of Goethe* every August. On the bare walls Liese hung her old print of Van Gogh's rush chair, along with two prints she and Paul bought on their last Sunday trip to the Frick—Van

Gogh's *The Peasant* and Cézanne's *The Card Players*. Irma Florsheim arrived from Milwaukee to help care for Tommy and stayed on when Liese accepted a social work position at Saint Elizabeth's.

I was born in Washington, D.C., two years later, named after my maternal great-grandmothers, Caroline and Elizabeth. In the family lore I was the sprite, the *Mumpitz* (silly one), while my brother was more earnest and serious.

Paul responded to the births of his son and daughter in a way not unlike the way his brother responded to poetry—as confirmation of the existence of a meaningful world. Every day when he got home from work, he held each of us close to his face as though reading us, and at night he bent over our cribs, studying our features while we slept. But if anything, our births only increased his impatience to make up for the lost years of his professional life. Liese, with two small children, a job as a social worker at a nearby hospital, and an increasingly frail mother, continued to devote herself to providing quiet order to Paul's world.

Perhaps during those early years of her life as a wife and mother, she didn't even view it as a sacrifice. Tommy and I—precocious, keen observers, both of us with our mother's dark curls and brown eyes—must have given her something that nothing since she'd left Frankfurt in 1933 had thus far provided: I am here. I am here with them. This is me.

PART II

The Unthought Known

CHAPTER THIRTEEN

Riverside

1955–1968

At the beginning of his memoir, *Naturalist,* the biologist E. O. Wilson wrote, *What happened, what we think happened in distant memory, is built around a small collection of dominating images.*

What I *think* happened during the earliest years of our life as a family comes largely from what my parents told me and from what I've seen in photographs—the four of us at the Washington Zoo, me feeding Bau peanuts from a crumpled bag; Tommy and me asleep on my mother's lap; my grandmother Irma, looking frail—she would soon be diagnosed with the cancer that would kill her—pushing Tommy on a swing in a park in Washington; Uncle Erich holding Tommy and me in his arms the first time he met us, in Omaha, when I was three years old. But from the time we moved to Chicago when I was four, and most of all, to Riverside when I was five, I can tell the story of our family life based on my own images, which rise up with an intensity of detail: our special walks in the forest preserves; Bau reading to us from *Doctor Zhivago,*

Tom and me perched on either side of him eating our Christmas cookies; Mr. Dombrowski asking a perilous question.

And others, so vivid and distinct that time seems to vanish
as I write.

Herrick Road

Our parents bought a two-story brick house on Herrick Road
in Riverside, Illinois, the summer before I entered kindergarten and Tom began second grade. Unlike the cramped apartments we'd lived in while my father ascended through the
ranks of medicine—in Washington; in Omaha, where he finished a second residency; and on the west side of Chicago—
our new house was big enough for Tom and me to have our
own bedrooms on the second floor and for Bau to have a study
down the hall. There was an alcove off the living room where
Bau kept his collection of classical records and my parents
kept their oldest books on a special glass-enclosed bookshelf.
There were other suburbs that would have fulfilled my parents' criteria of good schools and an easy train connection to
Bau's job at the Veterans' hospital and the new University of
Illinois Medical Center on the west side of Chicago, but Riverside, designed by Frederick Law Olmsted, with its streets
radiating from the banks of the Des Plaines River in soft
winding patterns, reminded them of neighborhoods in
Prague. In addition to its river and gently winding roads, Riverside had old-fashioned gas streetlamps lit at dusk each evening by two men riding on a ladder truck. It had a village
square with a Victorian water tower, a vine-covered sand-

stone public library with a steep gabled roof, and a quaint railroad station.

My parents bought our house in this picturesque suburb at the height of the McCarthy era. It was only a few miles from downtown Chicago, but the town, which at first they didn't realize was a bastion of Christian conservatism, drew into itself in a way that made it seem hundreds of miles from anywhere else. The golf course was "restricted"—a code word meaning that Jews and other minority groups were not welcomed—as were many of the resort communities that lined the southern shore of Lake Michigan, nearby. Although Riverside, along with the neighboring suburbs of Berwyn and Cicero, had a large Czech population going back several generations, there were virtually no Jews or members of any other minority group.

We continued to attend the Third Unitarian Church in our old west side Chicago neighborhood, but we were school age now, and my parents turned to our Herrick Road neighbors for ideas about how to raise children in suburban America— how we should look and who we should be. They sent us to a popular Lutheran day camp in Berwyn with the Dahlgren boys, who lived across the street; before lunch each day, we sat with Lutheran children, praying in the church sanctuary. They enrolled me at Blythe Park Elementary School as "Carol," believing that it sounded more American than my given name. My mother brushed my hair until my curls grew limp, and my brother, though far more interested in reading books than playing baseball, was encouraged to achieve the athletic walk of the neighborhood boys. In a photograph taken at Christmas by my kindergarten teacher, Mrs. Kirby, I'm posed, a solemn look on my face, holding a paper banner decorated with snow-flakes on which, in carefully formed letters, I'd printed *Merry Christmas, Daddy.* I pasted the photo on the back of a plywood facsimile of Santa's face and gave it to my father as a holiday gift. For my mother's holiday gift, I sculpted out of modeling clay a figure of the baby Jesus in his manger.

Perhaps most important, just when we might have been old enough to learn something about the events that had shaped our parents' lives before we were born, their quest to provide a sense of belonging for us in this postwar suburbia kept them largely silent about the past. We were told that Bau had been a prisoner of war, implying that he'd been a soldier. We frequently saw our uncle Ernie and his family, who lived in Milwaukee, and were told that we had an uncle Erich, who lived in Great Britain and was a writer. We had vague memories of our maternal grandmother, who died the year we'd lived in Omaha. But as for other family, we were told only that our grandfathers and our other grandmother had died of illnesses in Europe long before we were born.

Our living room contained none of the family photographs that decorated my schoolmates' living rooms—pictures of smiling grandparents holding new babies. On the wall above our mantel hung a painting of a desolate forest. On another wall hung the dark print of *The Card Players,* in which four men wearing long plush coats and sad faces are seated at a table bent over their cards. Across from them the tired, watchful eyes, protected under a straw hat, of *The Peasant* seemed to be in conversation with the somber cardplayers. These pictures, along with the faded wood-framed print of Van Gogh's yellow rush chair and several charcoals of Prague, lived in my imagination like old photographs we lacked, the people in them fiercely alive, each looking like someone I should know. I thought of the old man in the straw hat as one of my grandfathers and the cardplayer wearing the thickest blue coat and black hat as my other grandfather. They, like the books in the glass-enclosed shelf, evoked in me some sense of memory, not quite mine, but not quite not mine.

Unlike my schoolmates' seemingly imperturbable and chirpy mothers, my mother, though emanating kindness, seemed sad and restless. Unlike my schoolmates' fathers, who seemed brimful with ease and confidence, my father seemed like a man in a race he was sure he couldn't win. On weekdays, when Bau came home from work, he went straight to his study. He kept a broom handle by his desk, pounding it on the floor if Tom and I disturbed his work with our playing in the rooms below. My mother frequently dispatched me to Bau's study to cheer him up before dinner, and there I saw such quantities of medical books and scribbled-on pads of lined paper filling his desk and the floor around him that he looked buried. Bau often had a crusty white film around the edges of his mouth from the Gelusil (an early form of Maalox) that he drank from brown glass bottles that arrived in cartons in the mail. Along with an assortment of sedatives, which both my parents took every night, the Gelusil bottles covered his nightstand and dresser.

More than associating family meals with food or casual conversation about the events of the day, I associated them with Bau's chronic sense of pending disaster. My shoulders would tense when he spilled his worries about money (he always feared we were on the verge of poverty), about whether his medical research would be successful (much later, I would

learn that he won many awards for it), and about his colleagues' opinion of him (even then I sensed enough to know
that he was widely admired). More than anything else, Bau
wanted to make up for what he always described as "lost time,"
which meant that nothing should interfere with his freedom to
work. My mother was ever solicitous of him, but she was never
able to praise him enough to relieve his self-doubt. By the time
the meal was over, she looked like she carried the weight of his
worries, while he, having been relieved of just enough of that
weight to go on, returned to his study, where he would work
into the night.

Occasionally, Bau would interrupt his work before my
bedtime, and I'd watch him tread softly down the stairs and
make his way toward the kitchen, his head lowered as though
he were trying not to be seen. "I have just one slice of bread,"
he'd whisper to himself. I'd sometimes follow him into the
kitchen, walking a few steps behind him with a more emphatic
gait than his. He was hyper-focused on his mission and didn't
ever seem to notice me following him. "I will have ten pieces
of bread! The whole loaf!" I'd say under my own breath, but
with vigor, as if trying to correct the tentativeness of Bau's approach with my own. I was upset and confused that this same
man who ruled over our house would think he could have only
one slice of bread.

Odyssey

The summer that we moved to Riverside, my parents gave my
brother *The Children's Homer: The Adventures of Odysseus and*

the Tale of Troy for his birthday. He printed his name in pen on the title page and permitted me to print mine in pencil underneath, allowing that his full rights of ownership would not begin until after we finished reading it to each other. More than anything else about this book, I remember how deeply the characters' names, which our mother helped us to pronounce by writing them out phonetically, appealed to me: *Resourceful Odysseus of Ithaca, son of Laertes and Anticlea, grandson of Arcesius and Autolyceus; Brave Telemachus of Ithaca, son of Odysseus and Penelope; Faithful Penelope of Sparta, daughter of Icarus and the nymph Periboea.* The fact that everyone had a definite place in the world and parents and forebears to whom they forever belonged, even after they left home, held enormous reassurance, particularly as the beginning of my first year of school in Riverside approached.

Throughout that summer, the mere mention of the word "kindergarten" had filled me with such foreboding and sadness that I felt as if my shoulders would rise up to cover my ears. I couldn't have described it this way then, but some necessary part of myself seemed to disappear whenever I was away from my parents and brother, especially from my mother, even for a few hours. It felt like something essential had been ruptured.

By the time I was to begin kindergarten, I was already a worry to my parents, particularly my father, for my unwillingness to leave their side. "Carrroline," my father reminded me in his rather grave Bau-like way, for he had reason to know I needed a push, "it vill be goot for you to go to school. It vill be fun for you to meet ze other children!" Bau even promised that if I didn't cry, he would take a *Müssestunde* with us at our favorite nature preserve on the outskirts of Chicago the Sunday after the first week.

When I was three, the year my grandmother died, I'd (unsuccessfully) protested going to nursery school after a Christmas pageant in which I was among the preschoolers chosen to portray angels in the upper school's performance of *The Little Match Girl*. The story of a child who sells matches in the street in order to buy food for her family, it ends with the little girl ascending to heaven in the arms of her grandmother. When the holidays ended and it was time to go back to school, my parents had to bribe me with sweets and promises of extra *Müssestunden*. I had convinced myself that the Little Match Girl's ghost would still be wandering the halls or waiting for me in my classroom.

The next year, after we'd moved from Omaha to the west side of Chicago, I hadn't wanted to attend Sunday school at the Third Unitarian Church because it meant I couldn't sit with my parents in the sanctuary for the adult service. That time I succeeded in my protests and was permitted to stay by my mother's side, the only small child among the adults listening to E. T. Buehrer's sermons. And that same fall, when my parents enrolled me in prekindergarten at Emmett School, I became so bereft that they pulled me out after the first month.

During the first weeks of kindergarten in Riverside, it happened again. While my classmates seemed eager to say goodbye to their mothers in the cubby area outside the classroom door, I couldn't stop myself from crying when mine let go of my hand. An almost unbearable ache filled the pit of my stomach, and nothing—not my brother's reminder that he was in a classroom just down the hall, not Jocelyn Gunnar and Debbie

Tompkins's invitation to join them in play, not my nightly promise to my parents that I would behave in a manner becoming of kindergarteners—could prevent my tears or assuage my grief. For several weeks, when the other children had already taken their places on the rug in the middle of the classroom, waiting to begin the morning song, my teacher, Mrs. Kirby, came out to the cubby area to encourage my mother to leave and to coax me into the classroom herself, holding my hand tightly to keep me from running after my mother. She then led me, still sobbing, to the windows that lined one wall of the classroom, through which I could catch another glimpse of my mother waving to me from outside the school building. Mrs. Kirby must have thought another good-bye would help, but the sight of my mother growing smaller and smaller before disappearing into the parking lot only deepened my pain.

I'm told that in the ensuing weeks, Mrs. Kirby arranged for my parents to meet with Dr. Augusta Jameson, the school district psychologist, not just because I seemed so unhappy but because I didn't dress appropriately. Each morning I refused the dresses my mother laid out for me, insisting on wearing the western shirt, the corduroy pants with white fringe, and the boots embossed with stars and horseshoes that had been my Halloween costume in Chicago the year before. What one could accomplish by virtue of one's appearance, including not drawing attention to oneself by being seen as different, was vitally important to my parents, especially my father. But knowing I'd be without my mother, I felt I needed this outfit—the perfect weight of the boots, the softness of the long sleeves and pant legs against my skin, the bold feeling that the outfit inspired in me—to restore my courage. I remember my mother defending my choice of clothing against my father's insistence that I wear a dress. She must have laundered the outfit repeatedly, for it was the only thing that got me out the door and on my way to school without tears, at least until I got close to the schoolroom.

As the school year progressed, I grew very fond of Mrs. Kirby, who turned out to be infinitely kind and tender and always brought special books from home for me to read. I soon wore dresses and skirts without making a fuss.

The painful beginning to my life as a schoolgirl might not hold such a vivid place in my memory were it not for the fact that this sense of utter desolation would return many more times in my life, always provoked by the thought of having to launch myself into the world and away from my family.

The Conductor

I was seven years old and recovering from encephalitis, a sudden acute infection of the brain, the first time I remember being left alone in Bau's care. My mother, who rarely left my side during my illness, had to accompany Tom to a school event. I sat on the living room sofa adjacent to Bau's chair, where he sat reading the newspaper. The day I'd been diagnosed and admitted to the hospital, I'd witnessed my father weeping in worry over me; on the day I came home, I witnessed him looking happier than I'd ever seen him. Now I wanted to seize the rare opportunity to have an important conversation with him about *something*, *anything*, but he sat silently in his chair, absorbed in his reading, and didn't peer above his newspaper at me. Sometimes, when my mother dispatched me to his study to bring him down to dinner and I'd see the side of his mouth encrusted with his white stomach medicine and could detect behind his glasses his pained expression, I'd reach my hand up to his back and try to hug him. Mostly, when I did, Bau didn't bend toward me but remained stiff and frozen. On those occasions, I'd feel so alone and embarrassed by my unsatisfactory offering that I'd freeze, too, the hug hanging somewhere in the air between us. At those times I always had Tom or my mother to return to. Tonight Bau seemed to be in that distant mood and I had no one. Then, quite suddenly and still without a word, he jumped up, went to the alcove adjoining the living room, put on Beethoven's Seventh Symphony, which he'd played repeatedly when I came home from the hospital, and started to conduct, gesturing to me to join him. "Carrroline," he said, turning toward me, his entire bearing relaxing as he bounced to the runs and turns of the music, his puffy bluish hands (my mother told Tom and me that his fingers had frozen when he'd been a prisoner of war) swooping the air, "Vizout us, zey vill make too many miztakes!" I, too, jumped up and, following his movements, conducted the music with him, grateful, fortified even, that with our invisible batons, we were linked together in this important undertaking.

The Brick

I became a Shark in the summer of 1957, just months after I'd been sick. I'd begun that summer as a Minnow, and then, along

with another seven-year-old girl having made the most progress in the Riverside summer swimming program, was pro-
moted to the rank of Shark. I walked through the corridor of
mandatory showers, my bare feet slapping the puddles gathering on the tiles, and stood for a moment in the arched entrance
to the pool where the still water and clean cold air felt other-
worldly. Today, the last day of the summer season, my mother
would be in the bleachers watching me.

After the Minnows, Fish, and Flying Fish performed their
kicks and strokes, wrapped themselves in towels, and joined
their families in the bleachers, the Sharks lined up along the
deep end and dived in, swimming two lengths of the pool. In
the hushed peacefulness of the water, the feel and sound of my
sturdy, rhythmic strokes filled me with joy.

At the end of our laps, the athletic director, Mr. Perkins, his
sports medallions shimmering in his dark chest hair, grabbed
the microphone he used for just this day, and announced my
name and that of the other little girl whose swimming had
most improved. He knelt down between us as he explained,
the words amplified through his microphone, that both of us
would dive into the deep end, and whoever retrieved the three-
pound rubber brick from the bottom of the pool would be the
1957 summer champion and receive a trophy. After that moment I have no memory of the other little girl.

I dived in, the cold water seeping under the edge of my
bathing cap as my arms and hands pulled my body down
toward the shadowy dark object below. I took firm hold of the
brick in my left hand, allowing my stronger arm and hand to
power me to the surface of the pool and my triumph. Mr. Perkins pulled me from the water and held up the black rubber

brick to the audience as the emblem of my victory. To a loud current of applause coming from the bleachers, he then presented me with a trophy, a small golden girl with a tiny face of barely discernible features, standing on a vanilla-white pedestal, poised to dive. My pride was so great it was almost painful.

Scrunching my eyes against the light coming through the windows above the bleachers, I found my mother's face. She was glancing right, then left, as if seeking confirmation from the mothers sitting around her that this great event had really happened. When she looked toward me, her face was awash in tears. Even as, in a separate corner of my mind, I replayed every thrilling stroke that had propelled me from the bottom of the pool, now, seeing my mother's face, I could scarcely breathe. Her tears seemed earthshaking, as if my performance had represented the clear condition of everything she needed. Before my dive, I hadn't known that I possessed the strength that had won me this prize, and now, in a flash, I felt my own realization taken from me, engulfed by the intensity of my mother's emotion before I could claim it as my own.

Trying to hold myself tall, to step back into the exaltation I'd felt a moment before, I smiled at her, but what I'd felt was gone. Replacing my pride came an anguish deeper than anything I had words for. Achingly devoted to her, I did not have it in my power to think, much less to say, I am not really this strong; I will not always be able to do this; I will disappoint you. It was the first time I remember wanting to grow backward into tininess, into invisibility.

On the drive home, my thighs damp against the hot vinyl car seat, my trophy lying on the seat between my mother and me, the responsibility I felt to make her happy, to make both my parents proud, was too great for my body to hold. I started to cry so hard that my nose began to bleed.

Uncle Erich

I was in fourth grade, and Tom in sixth, when Uncle Erich moved from England to the United States to take a faculty position at Northwestern University in Evanston, a suburb just north of Chicago and thirty miles from Riverside. His writings had given him some renown in academic circles, and Northwestern had succeeded in luring him away from Europe. Though I was told and can see from earlier photographs that he visited us once in Omaha, my first memory of him is of an immense man with a large pink face, bushy eyebrows, a tweed jacket, and a deep lyrical voice, standing in the doorway of our house on Herrick Road.

From the time Uncle Erich arrived in the United States, we saw him almost every weekend. He came to dinner on Sundays smelling of sweet tobacco and sherry and often accompanied by young men who seemed like his assistants—Peter, who had a woebegone face and thinning blond hair; then Joachim, a beautiful man with boyish features and a scar under his eye who wore leather sandals that reminded me of those worn by Odysseus in my brother's illustrated *Homer;* then Barton, a gentle-seeming, quiet man with curly red hair. Occasionally, Erich arrived with Hannah Arendt, who was clearly *not* his assistant. She smoked cigarettes from an ivory holder and spoke in a husky, commanding voice so in contrast to my mother's, which was in a higher register than usual when Erich visited, her face tighter than at other times. If Erich was present, my mother gave me none of the warm glances that she offered at other times, and I felt that she was in a world I could not hope to reach.

Uncle Erich always brought *"Mitbringen,"* a telescope for Tom, a piggy-bank globe attached to a plastic pencil sharpener for me, flowers for the table, a copy of his most recent book or article and "clippings from ze reviews!," which he paperclipped to the book's cover or the article's first page. "Tolerably perceptive," he'd say to my parents about the review even before he walked through the front door.

Though much of the time our house was in a state of disarray (my mother hated housework), on days Erich came to dinner, my mother attended to domestic chores with a vengeance, straightening cushions, putting out bowls of salted nuts and plates of rye bread with thinly sliced cold cuts, her face red and hot. She drove to the Czech bakeries in Cicero to buy apple strudel and frozen bread dumplings, then spent more hours preparing elaborate dishes of beef in sour cream sauce or veal coated in soggy bread crumbs, dishes we never ate at other times because of my father's bad digestion and my mother's lack of interest in cooking. Before Erich arrived, while Bau got out the bottles of red wine and the Black & White whiskey Erich loved, my mother, wearing her best dress, sat at the kitchen table eating squares of the bittersweet chocolate she always kept in the cupboard, looking unable to rouse herself from somewhere far away.

When speaking to "ze children," Erich addressed most of his comments and attention to my brother. "Toe-mahs," he would say, making the O sound rounder than when anyone else said his name, "what a fine collection of little biographies you have. And what a handsome pullover you're wearing!" He'd wave his thick, expressive hands, which were always stained yellow and blue from tobacco and ink. Everything about Uncle Erich—his height, the cascade of names and quotations that poured from him, the booming lilt of his voice, the way my parents lowered their voices and exchanged glances when he was there—made it seem as if he carried incomparable authority. When he spoke, it was as though all of Europe were talking, the words carrying my parents away, blotting out our Riverside world and leaving Tom and me alone with only each other. In Uncle Erich's presence, I found it nearly impossible to speak. I felt that I should be doing something elevated and serious—reading important stories or at least taking brisk walks in the fresh air. Uncle Erich said "quohtah" instead of quarter, "wohk" instead of walk. "Ah yes, I believe you took yourself for a wohk," he'd say if, instead of greeting him at the door, I came in from playing outside after he'd arrived. "Yes, my darling! How was your wohk?" Though I longed for his approval and hoped he would look at me in the same way that he looked at my brother, his gaze always traveled well above my head, as though I were still on my wohk.

Once, when I was in fifth grade, Uncle Erich came to dinner on Halloween and I greeted him dressed as Casper the Friendly Ghost, my favorite Halloween costume since second grade and by then rather threadbare. He stared at me when I entered the living room, throwing his hands up in surprise. *"Ich wehr verückt!"* he bellowed with delighted incomprehension. It was a phrase my parents also used when they were happily surprised. My costume, which smelled of oil and plastic, had a hood that covered my head, with holes for my eyes and nose. Wearing it, feeling my own moist warm breath on my face, and knowing I couldn't be seen, I imagined that Uncle Erich and I suddenly shared an almost childlike friendship. Under the protective layer of my costume as a little ghost, not a little girl, I thought of myself as someone he could love.

When Uncle Erich visited, my parents spoke German and Czech, which they rarely spoke at other times. As more wine and whiskey were poured, our living room became more and more crowded with the specters of people I'd never met but whose features I'd piece together in my imagination from movie and television characters I knew. Goethe, of course, was Jingles from *Wild Bill Hickok;* Nietzsche was the Scarecrow from *The Wizard of Oz;* Thomas Mann was Walt Disney; EP was Big Tim Champion from my favorite television program, *Circus Boy,* and on and on.

It wasn't only their world of Prague and books that they discussed. Many times the conversation turned to the war and things I couldn't follow and believed I shouldn't try to understand. When the tone in the room changed, Tom and I were sent to bed.

Alone upstairs, I fell asleep to the muffled rise and fall of the voices in the living room, frequently crescendoing into loud argument. I wondered if I should hear such things, which sounded at once intimate and terrible. "Where were *you* during the war?" I once heard my father ask, his voice heated, breaking, before the sounds grew distant and muted.

The American Revolution

Each year, the fifth-graders at Blythe Park school put on a play during the last weeks of school. The year I was in fifth grade, our play was focusing on the American Revolution. When my teacher, Mrs. Slanec, whom I loved, announced the list of characters, I raised my hand for the role of Ben Franklin and was given the part.

Still affected by having been summoned by the school psychologist when I wore my cowboy outfit to kindergarten, my parents had become more concerned than ever that Tom and I fit in with the norms of Riverside. I'm sure it added to their worries that Uncle Erich teased me about my "bouncy walk" and referred to me as a tomboy; I overheard him on several occasions and knew from his tone that it was not a compliment. My parents winced at the news that I was to play Ben. They urged me toward the role of Betsy Ross or a soldier's wife—which, to my relief, other girls in my class had already spoken for. Late at night, I overheard my parents in worried conversation about me. My father was unbendable, but when I implored my mother to let me keep the part of Franklin, she agreed. She rarely challenged Bau's wishes, but just as when I began kindergarten she'd hand-washed the playground dirt out of my cowboy pants almost every night so that I could wear them during the first days of school, she stood her ground on my behalf. Not confident with a needle and thread, she nonetheless spent hours designing a wig for my character, carefully threading tufts of gray yarn onto a piece of thin pink rubber that she molded into a domelike shape. When I wore it, my head looked bald at the top, with long wisps of gray hair falling down the sides and back, like Ben's.

Just as my pessimistic, distant father could suddenly exude ardor and tenderness when conditions (such as Goethe's poetry and Beethoven's symphonies) momentarily released him from his worries, my cautious, deferential mother could spring forth to defend the freedoms of her daughter. On these occasions, my parents seemed to transform into their opposites, as if reunited with some other self.

Dr. Futterman

Though I had strength and fortitude, as well as a lighthearted, impish side, my main currency as a child was worried sadness. Sadness delivered me to my parents and they to me. A slender pale boy lived on Addison Road, the block behind ours. Afternoons, he sat on his porch under blankets. When I was about ten years old, I felt compelled to stand at a spot across the street from his house almost every day after school. Though I worried I'd catch his illness (Bau told me he was very sick), I stood there, watching him, monitoring his decline. When I talked to my parents about my vigil, my mother gathered me in with hugs, and my father tried to comfort me with books from the glass-enclosed shelf—most often poems from Goethe or Claudius that I could barely understand—*See in each beginning, ending, double aspects of the one*—or passages from *Tonio Kröger,* equally opaque—*He stood there, his hands behind his back, in front of a window with the blind down. He never thought that one could not see through the blind and that it was absurd to stand there as though one were looking out*—using their words to try to explain our limited capacity to understand the workings of the world, his tenderness and concern, mostly hidden behind his dark moods and urgency toward his work, pouring forth.

My brother's currency was goodness, though I was also very good, and he, I think now, was also very sad. Tom gave himself over to people in need, and I was one of those Tom gave himself to. My mother, always concerned for our safety, preferred it when we were together, so Tom took me with him everywhere, a protective look on his alert, intelligent face. I sometimes squelched my own vivacity in order to secure his caretaking and thus our bond, just as, I believe now, he squelched his need to be cared for and protected.

We both did well in school; our parents seemed to take our academic accomplishments as a given. Tom was the greater achiever, the doer in the world, auditioning for Chicago Public Television's re-creation of *The Whiz Kids,* signing on with the Unitarian youth group to take Chicago housing project children to museums and the zoo, elected president of the Unitarian youth group, then president of the high school student council. And in high school he dated, if somewhat shyly, taking Amy Wood, whom he met through the Unitarian youth group, to the high school prom.

After the brick, I'd become cautious not to overreach. My parents worried that so many occasions still prompted my anxiety. They also worried that I took little joy in growing up, showing none of the euphoria other girls seemed to feel as they sprouted into their womanly bodies. All of these signs of distress drove my parents to consult with more child psychologists.

By the time I was in high school, while Tom was winning more honors and heading off to Yale, I was spending most Saturday mornings at the Marshall Field Building in downtown Chicago, sitting on a slippery leather chair, my hands folded in my lap, across from Dr. Edward Futterman, an earnest, chain-smoking child psychiatrist. My mother would wait for me at Kroch's and Brentano's bookstore while I tried to give the right answers to Dr. Futterman's questions so that I wouldn't have to come back. Sometimes, when Uncle Erich came for dinner and when the adults thought I was out of earshot, I'd overhear Erich, fueled by whiskey and red wine, say to my parents, "Zis girl is costing you so much money!" in the same disdainful tone he used when he teased me about my bouncy walk or said "Lieeese." I felt deeply ashamed to be such a source of worry and burden to my parents, but I had little idea how to change.

CHAPTER FOURTEEN

A Home in the World

1968–1985

I started college at Grinnell, in the heart of Iowa, feeling confident after several years with Dr. Futterman that I was ready to master life away from my family. But a feeling of desolation returned with a vengeance, and throughout my first semester, it rarely let up. Though I made friends and was courted by boys, an experience new to me, I spent almost all my waking hours studying. Assigned to a noisy dormitory, I searched for quiet places so I could be alone and think, studying in empty classrooms late into the night in order to feel my own mind, hear my own thoughts, as if creating my own contained world like the one I'd witnessed Bau create. Only when I was alone with my books and my mind could I quell my anxiety.

By the end of the semester, I'd so exhausted myself that I wanted to take a break from college altogether, move back home, and get a job. But Bau was upset at the thought of his daughter "losing time," the very feeling that so dominated his sense of life. "Postponement too often means that it does not happen at all," he argued. My mother, this time, agreed with him. There was to be no interruption to college.

Thinking that if only I were closer in proximity to my parents I would feel happier, I applied to the University of Chicago and was accepted for my sophomore year. Under different circumstances, this storied place, with its Gothic buildings, famed professors, and existentially anguished students trying to make sense of the world at the height of the war in Vietnam, might have filled me with a sense of new freedom and possibility. But once again, despite my intentions to swim and play sports and be part of the campus political life, I couldn't seem to vault myself into the heart of anything besides studying. I sought out places where I could be alone with my books, trying to absorb and assimilate everything from them, drawing lines and double lines under the text, bearing down on my pencil as if trying to scrape the meaning off the pages. My favorite building was Judd Hall, connected to the University of Chicago Laboratory School, where children's drawings covered the walls of the hallways. It was a perfect place to exercise my solitary study habits but also to be surrounded by images of childhood, which comforted me.

I wrote letters to my parents and brother, several of which I found in my father's files many years later:

October 12, 1969

Dear Bau and Mama,
Everything is so overwhelming. I am thinking about you and Tom so often. I wonder sometimes if you are thinking about me at the same moment, but I hardly think your lonely thoughts for me can compare with mine for you. I

read now in The Iliad *for my humanities class. The family is so important to the ancient people. It's so wonderful. I wish we could stick together always. As Athena runs to Zeus and Telemachus to Odysseus, I wish to be with my own father and mother. I wish I could grow up and be a college girl graciously. I always have to make a big fumble of things. Well, I'd better get to work, I'm afraid. I hope I will one moment soon see my feet right there firmly on the ground instead of high in the branches of a faraway tree, reaching for some faraway commodity—like a mama or a daddy or a brother. I love you. Caroline*

Soon I all but stopped eating, taking just enough nourishment to keep myself alert and functioning but never enough to feel warmth or satisfaction. Years later, anorexia would become a much discussed and researched illness, but at the time it was far less known. There's little doubt that I had some form of it, but looking back, I find it nearly impossible to fit all that was going on inside me into so cramped a category. My mission, though it lived in me as instinct more than thought, was to develop my mind and disavow my body. Becoming an impeccably learned person was, I sensed, the only reliable ballast available, the only route that could deliver me into adulthood as the daughter my parents needed me to be, the niece that my uncle, still holding ultimate familial authority, might finally admire, even love. Being hungry, I thought, would help me to study harder, fulfill my goal more effectively. Hunger would outwit the other longings in my body that I wanted so desperately to contain, longings that I must have feared could forever undermine my capacity to make my parents proud and happy.

My mother sent me care packages containing Sara Lee cakes and bars of dark chocolate, which I left in the lounge of my dormitory for others to eat. And Bau, who'd written cards to me when I was at Grinnell, started writing longer letters, though I frequently took the train home on weekends and might have seen him only days before. I read them over and over, used them as bookmarks so I'd have them with me while I studied. He'd offer up Tante Ida–isms—*Fortgewürschteln*—to encourage me on, as if he knew something that I didn't yet. Sometimes, in rare revelations of inner feelings, he'd superimpose his own journey onto mine.

April 14, 1970

Dearest Caroline,

I just arrived in New York and have to rush to catch a train to New Haven. It took me two hours to get here from the airport. The congestion of traffic, I think, so defeats the purpose of the city as a citadel of culture! Caroline, I miss you already. You will get through this stressful phase. I know it. I can see the light on the other side of the tunnel—your inside-looking eyes might not have caught the glimpse of it as yet, but they will, they will, they will, because the light is there. Vaihinger, whom I always read in Komotau as a boy, had the great theory of "as if." You act "as if" it will turn out well, "as if" the world were a sensible place. How I wish I could talk to you more about the complicated roads feelings sometimes have to go through before they appear on the surface, simple and shining and true.

Be embraced.

Your Bau

November 17, 1971

Dearest Caroline,

This is Thanksgiving time and soon you will be home with us and we will remember everything for which we feel grateful. With a sense of humor and a sense of reality we might also think of the things for which we have no good reason for gratitude, but, nevertheless, even that seems to deserve recognition as part of life. As we had to sing in the war (the song was by Fritz Lehmann, who had written all the libretti for Franz Lehár's operettas): "We want to say 'yes' to life, because better days are ahead." That I know that day will come for my Caroline is reason for rejoicing. I know the feeling of sadness, which is sometimes so irresistible. Chase it away with the certain feeling of pride of yourself, my Caroline.

Be embraced.

Your Bau

Dr. Futterman had been the first person to use the word "homosexual" with me. "You mean your parents never told you that your uncle is a homosexual?" he once asked me rather matter-of-factly, and not in an unkind way. It was a word I only dimly understood, for it wasn't part of the common parlance of suburban teenagers of that time. My parents had never talked about Uncle Erich's sexual orientation; nor had Tom or I ever asked questions about who the attractive younger men he brought to our home really were to him, beyond friends or assistants or protégés. By the time Uncle Erich had entered our lives, Tom and I were already well versed in the art of not asking. Now, when Dr. Futterman uttered the word, a feeling came over me not unlike what I'd felt earlier that year when my American history teacher, Mr. Dombrowski, had asked if anyone in the class was Jewish. Each of these words drew me toward some ellipsis of personal meaning that had a confusing finality and weight. This time, instead of seeing myself on the ceiling looking down, I felt myself going pale and silent. I don't remember what we talked about in the moments that followed. I do remember that by the time I left his office, I felt a new swirl of my own disorder and peril, an "unthought known."

It would take me years to acknowledge, much less embrace, my sexuality and put those feelings to rest.

I left Chicago in the late summer of 1973, August 19, to be exact, after accepting my parents' gift of a week's holiday on the West Coast. I'd graduated from the University of Chicago and had a teaching job in a Head Start Program on the south side of Chicago to return to right after Labor Day.

I boarded the plane on that hot summer morning wearing a blue denim dress and carrying a yellow backpack filled with clothes and guidebooks, including a map of Bay Area youth hostels where I'd made reservations to stay. I was particularly drawn to one about forty miles north of San Francisco, on the edge of the Point Reyes National Seashore.

When I got on the plane that morning, I didn't know how unspeakably beautiful the beach and the surrounding national park was—that I would see all manner of seals, birds, sea lions, and even an occasional gray whale in the distance. Nor did I know that the hostel managers would be looking for helpers to paint and renovate the buildings after the summer season. I didn't know that Inverness and Point Reyes Station, the towns closest to the hostel, were ebullient, fascinating communities of artists, musicians, farmers, ranchers, and young East Coast and Midwest expatriates who saw in the rolling hills and jagged shoreline some promise of their own new home in the world.

Most of all, I didn't know that my instincts for a full, unimpeded run at life would emerge sturdy and clear, and that in Inverness, where I settled, and in Oakland/Berkeley, where I moved a few years later, I'd find mentors, friends, and loves; that I'd learn to trust anew the rhythms of my heart as well as my mind; and that I'd begin to tiptoe toward unearthing the structure of my parents' past and the ways it had shaped me.

All I knew when I boarded the plane that morning—once again, not a fully thought-out "known"—was that I had to do something dramatic in order to fully inhabit my own life. For the moment, hard as I knew it would be on my parents, hiding my return ticket to Chicago in the bottom of my backpack, not to be used for many months, was a fine beginning.

———

I had wanted to take literature classes when I was at the University of Chicago. I'd often stood in the student bookstore in front of the shelves where the books for the literature classes were stacked, longing for the peace of mind to read them, know them. But beyond my required humanities sequence— and influenced by my feeling that literature was somehow Uncle Erich's province and could never belong to me— I didn't pursue it. Looking back, I see it was probably a very good idea not to bring something so precious into the whirring motor of my psyche during those years. I majored in the social sciences in part because I must have known that Durkheim and Parsons and even Margaret Mead could better yield meaning to my frantic underlinings than Emily Dickinson or Jane Austen or James Joyce would have at the time.

In Inverness, where there weren't enough hours in the day to do all the things I wanted to do—be with my new friends, hike the beaches and trails, learn to make a living, if meager, in all manner of ways (shucking oysters, assembling dried-flower mobiles on an assembly line, selling Fuller brushes in a nearby valley cluster of villages, dishwashing in every restaurant that would have me)—I began to read books that drew me in, allowing myself a turtle-slow, luxurious pace. One of the first I checked out of the Inverness Library was Frederick Exley's *A Fan's Notes: A Fictional Memoir*, about a young man trying to find his way back into the world after a breakdown. *If I went wrong*, Exley wrote toward the end of his story as he tried to understand the trajectory of his life, to acknowledge the mystery and nonmystery of why things had come to be exactly the way they'd come to be, *it was because, like Tonio Kröger, there was no right way*. I found it almost shocking for the hero of my parents' favorite story to show up in the pages of so American a novel, checked out from this tiny rural library. It was as if Tonio, via Exley, had traveled across the country to find me.

After *A Fan's Notes,* and on Exley's implicit recommendation, I bought a used paperback of Thomas Mann's novellas
and read *Tonio Kröger* for the first time—taking in the meaning of that line I'd always heard my parents quote—*He never
thought that one could not see through the blind and that it was
absurd to stand there as though one were looking out*—in new
ways. Then came more Thomas Mann: *Buddenbrooks, The
Magic Mountain, Joseph in Egypt, Death in Venice, Disorder
and Early Sorrow.* After that came Rilke and Kafka, along with
an assortment of books of my own time and place, my American generation—*Zen and the Art of Motorcycle Maintenance,
Stranger in a Strange Land,* among many others—that I added
to my growing library.

April 24, 1974

Dearest Caroline,

*I am bursting with my bad conscience for my writing inertia.
It is absolutely terrible that during the last few weeks I was
so overwhelmed by my own work life and fatigue that I
could not get myself to write. Now it is much better and your
letter today has given me an enormous lift. I much enjoyed
your description of the people in your little town of Inverness.
It is proof to me that I am—in my heart—a small-towner
from Komotau who enjoyed walking around on the "Büm-
mel" and gossiping with Bobby Komisch about the newest
stories of the vices and virtues of our co-citizens. It is a fact
that I feel very much part of the lonely crowd of Chicago,
whose main attachment, too often, is going to and from
work. I still feel sometimes like a visitor here. So, I look*

forward to the enjoyment of reading about your new friends. Last night we had an evening with Erich (that was somehow, for once, enjoyable). We talked mainly about Komotau and old friends. Otherwise, nothing new here. Your mother is fine and told me wonderful things about her visit with you. As you know, Mayor Daley is sick and most people feel that this is rather decisive for his final retirement. In the meantime, his close associates keep getting indicted for corruption and his sons pass examinations because the examiner corrects the answers they give. What crazy times.

Once more, be embraced.

Bau

There was no clear moment when the prohibition against asking my parents questions about the past simply came to an end. Just as the silence likely began more as a surrender to habit than thought or plan, in the years after I left home, a new family agreement began to forge itself.

During the last two years when I lived in West Marin, I worked as a teaching assistant at Davidson Middle School in San Rafael. Davidson was a rough school by Marin County standards, many of its students the children of San Quentin prison guards and most of its teachers longtime locals. In April 1978, my first year at Davidson, a miniseries starring Meryl Streep and James Woods aired on national television. Called *Holocaust*, it focused on a family of German Jews trying to retain normalcy during the years of Hitler's rise to power. My parents watched it, Tom watched it, I watched it. The teachers' lounge at Davidson school was abuzz with conversation about what the television series depicted. "Was it true?" several of my colleagues, few of them Jewish or emigrant, asked. "Could this have happened?" With a sense of ownership and honor that I took note of, I identified my parents as Holocaust survivors and promised I would call them and relay to them my colleagues' questions. At first Bau and Mama answered in a highly compressed form, in blunt diction that lacked texture, color, detail. But there was a naturalness to our conversation, an invitation, if not an ease. If I were pressed to name a time when the new family agreement made itself known to me, it might be then. But only if pressed. More truthful is that the passage of time itself became an instrument of seeing and communicating. Perhaps that is what Nietzsche really meant when he wrote about the "pathos of distance."

When I'd first told my parents that I was staying in California, they reacted in a fashion similar to the response they had years later when I told them I was gay—with shock, dismay, then acceptance, and always love. The one-week trip that transformed into nineteen years was an utterly formative time, not only bringing me a sense of who I could become but *that* I could become—apart from my family.

My parents and Tom (who moved to Seattle shortly after I arrived in Inverness) visited me frequently during those early years in California, and I visited them. Once, for Bau's birthday, I sent him a whimsical picture of an orchestra conductor wearing a blue cutaway coat and red-and-white-striped pants that I'd spotted at an Inverness crafts fair. Several years after moving from Inverness to Berkeley, I sent as a Father's Day gift an art photograph that an Inverness friend had taken of a

Norman Rockwell–like dentist. The picture reminded me of Bau's description of his own childhood dentist, which he'd shared in a letter to me while I was in college. On the card accompanying my gift, which I found in Bau's files years later, was a picture of a fierce-looking horseman carrying a banner declaring that we should all recognize our strengths and live by them.

June 21, 1982

Dearest Caroline,

What a very nice Father's Day present, with the attached good wishes transmitted by the muscular horseman with the angry face. Looking admiringly and smilingly at your dentist certainly led to "remembrances of things past," and to an incredible connection (almost ESP) with another favorite gift you sent: The Conductor! You know that our family dentist in Komotau, Dr. Fleischman, did not do his own work except for occasionally looking into somebody's mouth, but let his associates, all non-doctors, Hans Schneider, Fran Wagner, and Herr Morovec, spoil my teeth! Dr. Fleischman was always sitting at his desk and while the others drilled, he studied the music of symphonies and he had a good reason for doing this—because he was the conductor of—YES!—it existed!—the Philharmonic Orchestra of Komotau! Suddenly, when I looked from the picture of the dentist to the blue and red conductor hanging on my wall, here he was, Dr. Fleischman! Bald, potato-nose, mustache, long neck and cutaway jacket. Incredible similarity! I nostalgically exclaimed, "Ah, Dr. Fleischman! How I have missed you!" And how could I have missed the similarity with the conductor earlier? Your good dentist brought it all back. The other message your messenger brought with the admonition for celebration of our strengths is certainly true. We all should do a little more of it.

Be embraced.

Bau

CHAPTER FIFTEEN

Reading Claudius

Summer 1985–Early Winter 1987

It was in the spring of 1985 that my mother, who was put off by answering machines, and if she spoke to one always got straight to the point, began to leave long, rambling messages that started in mid-thought.

"It wasn't a real accident," began the message I remember most vividly. She repeated the words several times, speaking so breathlessly and in a voice so raw that I couldn't tell if she was crying. "I have little sense directions suddenly. Does one say little? Little directions? *Orientierungssinn?*"

By that time, I was studying for a doctorate in education, teaching, and waitressing evening shifts at the Rockridge Café in Oakland. I got home too late to call her back. When I reached Mama the next morning, she continued, again as though in mid-thought. "The fish needed *eine Zitrone. Zitrone,*" she said, as if this were the crucial information I needed to understand. *"Zitrone."*

After a lengthy struggle to convey the story, she was able to explain that she had been cooking dinner when she realized she didn't have lemons, a key ingredient. Driving to the grocery store, which was just blocks away from the house in Evanston where my parents had moved shortly after I started college, she'd ended up in a part of Chicago she didn't recognize. She had no idea how she'd gotten there. Trying to right herself, she'd backed into a parked taxi, leaving her fender bashed in and a taillight dangling from its socket.

In a voice conveying a child's sense of helplessness, she asked me to promise that I wouldn't tell Bau. She felt too fragile to contend with his being upset. She'd already spoken with my brother, and she repeated his advice like a schoolgirl reciting steps for a fire drill: She'd give the insurance company her work number so they wouldn't call the house. Until her Dodge Colt was fixed, she'd park across the street, the mangled taillight facing away from Bau's view. She'd open her own checking account, transfer savings, and pay for the damage without his ever finding out. It was settled.

Then, a few days later, another message, another car accident—this time on her way to work—another late-night plea to her children to help her figure out what to do while subverting Bau's knowledge of the event. Tom and I talked to each other almost every day by phone, comparing notes on how she'd sounded, what she'd said.

In each message, my mother's voice sounded desperate, as though she'd been wandering alone for days until these moments of shelter in her children's answering machines. There was also something resolute in her tone that conveyed an absolute instinct for self-protection resembling nothing we'd ever seen in her. Tom and I must shield her from Bau's dark moods and critical judgment, she cried, her voice protesting something horrible happening inside her that she couldn't understand or explain. She described how the association between movement and direction would slip away from her as abruptly as it would reappear. The purpose of her everyday activities would suddenly elude her. English words she'd used for almost fifty years would evaporate, while long-lost German words would spring from her unbidden. Sometimes she didn't know for a moment who was saying them.

For weeks Tom and I kept our word to say nothing to Bau, Mama's need for protection seeming to come from such an unsoundable depth that we somehow lost our capacity to fully evaluate or question what was going on—just like when we were children, we unquestioningly behaved in ways that shielded Bau from disruptions to his work. When we spoke with Bau, who was preoccupied with a deadline for a grant proposal he was writing, we tried to get a sense of how he thought Mama was without telling him about the accidents. Immediately afterward, Tom and I would call each other to share reports. Tom consulted doctors in Seattle, who suggested her symptoms could indicate early Alzheimer's. I consulted with medical friends in the Bay Area who guessed similarly. In the meantime, Mama continued to call us with descriptions of new mishaps. She walked to her colleague and friend Marie Burnett's house in the pouring rain, but at the door, she had no idea how or why she'd arrived there. She was presenting an intake case to her social work colleagues at Saint Francis Hospital in Evanston, where she'd worked since 1969, and though part of her knew that she was going on too long, she couldn't stop talking. She burned her hand badly—picking up the teakettle, she thought—but didn't notice the wound until it was swollen and blistered.

In early July came a frantic late-night call from Bau. My parents had been on their way to the symphony, where they'd gone one Thursday night a month since I'd been in kindergarten. My mother had stepped out of her shoe as she got out of the car and didn't notice its absence until Bau did. Suddenly, a neurological detail—a shoe falling from a foot with no feeling—went directly to a doctor's diagnostic instincts, bypassing a husband's nearly-forty-year expectation that his wife provide quiet order in his life. He helped her back into the car and rushed her to Evanston Hospital.

Tom and I flew to Chicago the next day, planning our flights to arrive at the airport within minutes of each other so that we would have time together to prepare for the ordeal we knew awaited. I carried my lucky pen, lucky pebble, lucky feather, lucky penny. As he enveloped me in a hug, my brother began, "Be . . ." and I hoped he wouldn't say "brave." "Embraced," he said, never impressing me more than at that moment.

By the time we arrived at the hospital, my mother had already been put on massive doses of steroids to shrink the cancer that was rapidly crushing her brain stem. Bau berated us for not telling him about her calls and berated himself for his lack of doctorly perception in the weeks leading to her diagnosis, his need for her steady willingness to make life work for him having overwhelmed his capacity to observe her, attend to her.

I waited outside the door of my mother's room in the ICU while Bau and Tom spoke authoritatively, doctor to doctor, to the specialists charged with her care. Once when I entered and bent over her narrow gurney-like bed to kiss her, I thought I saw blackness behind her eyes. The steroids and the size and position of the tumor in her right temporal lobe had distorted the familiar planes and angles of my mother's face. While Bau and Tom continued to talk to the surgeon about the all-day operation she would undergo the next morning, I sat by her bed, willing my presence—as I always had with her and she always had with me—to loan her authority, to mold something, anything, in her favor.

"I'm right here, Mama."

"Zis is altogether my nicest blouse," she said in a strained whisper, lifting a limp hand and, with the smallest movement, leading my eyes to the rust-colored silk blouse that had been my birthday present to her the previous summer, folded, with the rest of her clothing, in a plastic hospital bag at the foot of the bed. *"Hübschtest Bluse."*

She asked me the age of my dog, Harpo, of whom she was very fond.

"He's three, Mama."

"Zis is a nice age for a grandson," she said.

As we spoke, technicians drew blood and inserted IVs, scurrying around her at a bewildering tempo. At regular intervals, one neurology resident or another—none seeming any older than a teenager and all of them looking at her with indifferent eyes—bent over her to ask her name and who the president was: questions of choice, I'd learn, for patients with head traumas. I wished I had brought something for her that belonged to her real life—one of the Van Goghs or the Cézanne in the living room, or the Claudius book from her bedside table—anything to grant her identity in this hard-surfaced room where she was surrounded by preoccupied strangers.

"Ronald Reagan, unfortunately," she responded, as she would say each of the many times she was asked, in what would become her trademark comeback to the indignities of hospital life. I thought I could see a brief look of triumph in her eyes. In the weeks before her diagnosis, she told me, she'd been reading a biography of Albert Einstein that Bau had brought home from Kroch's and Brentano's, and impressions from it now pushed through. "I wish it were Albert Einstein instead," she added, then looked at me quizzically. "Wasn't his first name Albert? And he wore a leather jacket?" (He did in a photograph in the book.) Crystal-clear lucidity alternated with words that had no apparent relevance, mislaid images and fragments, lines of poems she'd memorized as a child, which sprang from her mind like drops of water looking for their way back to the current of a river.

"Perhaps it is beautiful elsewhere, but I am here anyway," she announced to the resident as he was leaving. "Okay, good," he said absently before she continued with another poem: *Hurrah hurrah / the little white tooth is there. / Mother, come, and everyone in the house / grown-ups and children / look inside and see the bright white gleam! / The tooth shall be called Alexander the Conquerer! / Dear child, God preserve it for you / and give you more teeth in your little mouth / and always something for them to bite on!*

"Who knows why I think of this now?" she said. "I can't explain everything. It made me think of this old Claudius poem. The molecules in my brain get all mixed up! It just occurred to me lately . . . One more I want to say . . ." But she drifted off to sleep before it came out.

While my mother was in surgery, Bau, Tom, and I walked

along Lake Michigan near the hospital. Everything smelled damp, of limey cement, oil, fish, life—adamant life.

Bau and Tom talked like the doctors they were, explaining to me the histology of the tumor, a glioblastoma, its relentlessness, the certainty that it would grow back. I needed more air, needed something to unzip or unbutton. A woman and a little girl jogged by in matching pink running suits, and I suddenly felt as if I were the little pink girl. A dog on a leash barking at a jutting rock reminded me of my childhood dog, Sam. An old man pushing an infant in a stroller looked like my uncle Ernie. Everyone suddenly resembled someone from the past or someone I knew long ago or someone who'd died or someone I once was.

That night I dreamed that my mother was sleeping in the tiny post office box that I'd rented in Inverness when I first arrived there, but in my dream, Inverness was an unknown village that now I couldn't find. In later dreams, Mama would be hidden in a drawer in an attic, or under a rickety porch, or sitting on a roof in a thunderstorm. In every dream, I was culpable for having left her somewhere she was in danger and then having forgotten her. And yet in my dreams, she made no effort to let me know how to find her.

When I saw her the next morning in her seventh-floor post-op room, her face was swollen, warm, and pink. The muscles of her mouth and cheeks, always so disciplined to her desire to please, were slack and relaxed. She greeted each nurse who came into her room with confirmation of Reagan's presidency. "Reagan, still Reagan," she said. With a slightly trembling hand, she picked a mint meltaway from the array of treats that filled her tray table—Pepperidge Farm chessman cookies,

Lindt bittersweet chocolate that Uncle Ernie had sent, truffles dusted with cocoa powder brought by Uncle Erich, who, my father told me, had visited while she was still sleeping. With oratorical flourishes, Bau, fresh from the barber and wearing his nicest linen suit and striped tie, was reading the hospital menu to her, making her available dessert choices sound rarified and European.

We were all in a new rhythm.

When the bandages came off ten days later, my mother had a crater covered with purple smears on the right side of her skull, and an openness and vulnerability that was like that of a young animal.

In the weeks and months that followed, the effects of the tumor and the surgery to excise it—affecting the right cortex of her brain where adult censors prevail—brought out a quality in her I'd never witnessed, seeming to rise up from a place that she hadn't opened in my lifetime. Always soft-spoken and cautious, except in defense of my own choices when I was a little girl, she was now forcefully direct and far less willing to observe social protocols. Ask her a question and she responded in English, in German, going on so long that one might be tempted to interrupt. But one mustn't. She wasn't done yet. When she was, she'd rest her hand on the bed rail or on her stomach, or lay her head on Tom's shoulder, and close her eyes.

Just when I thought she'd finally fallen asleep, she'd open her eyes and catch my sleeve. "Lately, I always want fun and cheerful things. That's how I used to get so carried away with the *Fledermaus: Happy is one who forgets what cannot be changed*," and she'd offer a plot synopsis of her favorite opera, the one her parents had attended every New Year's Eve in Germany. "Just masterfully written," she'd say, and recite another poem, and then another.

She had comments about everything around her: the perfect weight of the quilt Tom and I brought her when no hospital blanket felt right on her body; the pleasing sight of a rich sweet dessert, particularly chocolate cake, which she ate with exuberance; and again and again, the indignities of Ronald Reagan's presidency and the degree to which the leadership of Albert Einstein would be preferable.

She took off her glasses when she spoke; she put on her glasses when she listened. "You might have noticed this. I've been wondering about it myself. I can't hear without them," she announced. "I can't explain everything," she'd say frequently, as if wanting to convince herself that she could stop trying to.

Apropos of nothing, she wanted to tell the story of her name, a story I hadn't heard since I was a little girl. "In Frankfurt, I was Liesel. But in Prague, I wanted to be only Liese! Then I was suddenly Alice!"

"We meet again!" she said whenever Bau, Tom, or I entered her hospital room, even if we'd been gone for just a few minutes. "I'm so glad you were available."

In one of my first outings with my mother after she left the hospital, we visited friends who served us a spread of pastries. As we were leaving, they asked if we wanted one more cookie. We both declined. As we rode the elevator down to the apartment lobby, Mama seemed to be deep in thought. We were already out the door and on the sidewalk, heading to a cab, when she stopped and grabbed my arm as though an incredible idea had struck her. "I do want another cookie," she told me. We promptly went back.

This was how it was as fall approached, then Thanksgiving, then my birthday, then spring, summer, and early the next fall. Uncle Ernie drove most weekends from Milwaukee. Tom and I alternated flying to Chicago from the West Coast so that she'd see one of us each month.

When we weren't there, Bau phoned us with updates and wrote us brief report-like letters: *I would have to be a talented novelist in order to describe the picture adequately,* began one. *In the foreground is fatigue and overall slowness, impairment of co-ordination of purposeful complex actions which depend on memory of immediately preceding events. Memory of the past is remark-ably sharpened, including poetry and literature. Her sense of humor is uninhibited and often exhilarating and her intelligence and judgment, whenever expressed, unimpaired . . .*

When I visited, I brought a tape recorder, having asked if she would let me record her stories about the past. When we recorded, she wanted to talk privately, out of earshot of Bau, in the small basement room that had been Tom's bedroom during the summers of our college years. She slipped her arm through mine, and we took the stairs slowly. We descended the steps together several times during those visits, and she talked for hours about her early life, as if making up for all the years she hadn't allowed herself to tell the whole story. After each taping, she handed me folders of crumpled letters—one labeled *P* for Bau's early letters, another *V (Vater)* for those her father and mother had sent to her long ago, another with letters from EP, another with early letters from Uncle Erich— asking me to keep them for her.

Just before Thanksgiving 1986, the tumor, silent for sixteen months, reappeared, not at its previous site but in my mother's spinal cord. She was rushed to Evanston Hospital with paralysis of her lower extremities and abdomen. She was operated on again, but the tumor could not be removed. Tom visited as often as he could, and I arranged to stay in Evanston the six weeks before her death—ever grateful to my employers and doctoral adviser, who kept a place for me while I was away. I cooked for my father and spent hours by my mother's bedside, moistening her lips with a small pink sponge on a stick.

Uncle Erich visited her hospital room almost every day, never staying longer than twenty minutes. In my entire life, I'd never seen the two of them alone. Sitting beside her bed, wearing shirts of different autumnal browns and matching wool vests, he picked up her old gray book of Claudius poems, which I'd brought to her hospital room, and read to her. *The moon has risen / the golden starlets sparkle / brightly and clearly in the heavens / the wood stands black and silent / and from the meadows rises / the white fog wondrously.*

At seventy-five, Uncle Erich looked like an aging actor. In his deep, semi-operatic voice, he made the poems come to life while my mother lay perfectly still, her eyes closed, her lips forming the words as he read.

At some point during those last weeks, my mother told Bau that she wanted to speak with a rabbi. Bau joined a synagogue for the first time in his life in the United States in order to fulfill her wish. Rabbi Arnold Rachlis visited my mother's hospital room frequently during those last days. I never learned what they discussed, but each time he stayed by her bedside for several hours. Rabbi Rachlis officiated at my mother's memorial service, which we held at the synagogue, speaking about her in ways that made me feel he knew her. I spoke on behalf of my father and brother, never feeling more transcendent than I did that day.

Bau seemed helpless in the months after her death. Tom and I alternated our trips home so one of us would be with him every month. At Christmastime, almost a year after my mother died, Bau invited me to accompany him on a Charles Dickens tour of London, the first trip he planned, other than visiting Tom and me on the West Coast, since Mama's death. Anna Novak, a widowed social worker from Chicago and a survivor of the Kraków ghetto, just a few years younger than Bau, was on that tour.

Anna and my father married in July 1989, Bau's life renewed one more time.

CHAPTER SIXTEEN

At the Archives

Fall 1999

I last saw my uncle Erich in the spring of 1990, during one of my frequent trips from California to Evanston to visit Bau. On that day Erich wore a tweed jacket with a bright plaid shirt in the colors he favored—rusts and reds and browns—underneath. His top button was buttoned, but as had become his custom, he wore no tie. He still had those big hands, always stained with bits of ink, and so accustomed to dangling a cigarette or holding a handful of cocktail nuts. From the very first day I remember meeting him, he always positioned himself for debate behind a dish of nuts, depositing handfuls in his mouth while he listened intently to the issue of the moment, shooting back at whomever he disagreed with, his voice filled with the pure delight of verbal combat. "Have you not read the original in Freud?" "Do you not remember the Goethe poem?" If you had not, his face always flushed with indignation; honest amazement shone in his eyes. "But then this conversation is idiotic!" he would bellow.

During all the years I'd known him, whenever I watched Uncle Erich hold forth on European literature, philosophy, and the state of world politics, nearly bringing himself to tears with the force of his own beliefs, my hope was that I would not be found out for my lack of intellectual acumen, for all that I hadn't read and didn't know. In his presence, obliterated by the sea of his words and the intensity of his passions, unable to retrieve or express what I felt or thought, I surrendered to what I assumed was Erich's verdict of me—the most dismissable Heller, the one who interested him least.

However, that last time I saw Erich, his appetite for all of this had faded. His hands lay folded in his lap. He was seventy-nine, and emphysema from his years of heavy smoking had left him stooped and drained, his face colorless against the vibrant plaid of his shirt, his eyes milky and distant. Every so often he pushed himself up and out to enter a conversation, but mostly he hunched into himself, even bringing his lunch plate from the table to his lap to hold. George and Connie Cohen, to whose house Erich, my father, and I had come for lunch that day, wanted to discuss an article they'd read in *The New Yorker*. My father and I had read it too, but Erich hadn't. "I will soon give up my subscription to *The New Yorker*," he said. "I no longer understand the cartoons!" He looked at me in a way he hadn't since I'd worn my Casper costume in his presence—without a trace of derision, but instead, I thought, with pure kindness. "No, my darling, I do not find them funny." Then he returned his gaze to the plate in his lap.

Among all that was changed about him were his feelings toward me. When I visited from California in the last couple of years before his death, he frequently asked me to take him shopping. After we unpacked the groceries, he poured each of us a glass of sherry, wanting me to stay with him. Now, when my father and I drove him back to his assisted living residence after lunch with the Cohens, I walked him to the door of his apartment and skirted the ceremonial touch of my cheek that he always offered as good-bye, instead wrapping my arms around him and pressing my cheek to his chest.

The next time I flew to Chicago, it was to attend Erich's memorial service. He'd committed suicide by taking an overdose of sleeping pills. Bau found Erich's body and the hand-written note he'd left: *Those who are close and dear to me will understand. I wish it were only from myself that I am absenting myself. I do not wish to destroy their memories of times when, perhaps, I caused them pleasure. Forgive the inevitable trouble I am giving you now. Bless you all—Erich.*

In the days that followed, Bau, Tom, and I packed his letters and papers into boxes but didn't have the heart or the attention to read through them. Erich's spirit still presided over the emptying rooms. It wasn't the time.

Those letters and papers now live in thirteen meticulously organized archival boxes at the Northwestern University Archives, a tiny underground wing of NU's Deering Library. If one calls ahead of time, a staff member will retrieve the boxes requested from the temperature- and humidity-controlled quarters and have them waiting on a metal trolley next to the nutwood table that occupies most of the archive's reading room. When I moved back to Chicago in 1993 to become a professor myself, I became an Erich Heller sleuth, spending hours at that table, poring through the contents of those boxes, hoping to wander into every available corridor of my uncle's life, career, and character—perhaps, too, to discover docu-

ments that would give me more understanding of his relationship with my parents.

Among the treasures I found in the archival boxes were
thick folders of letters from Werner Heisenberg, whom Erich
had gotten to know toward the end of the war when Heisenberg, along with other German scientists, was kept under
house arrest in England. Occasionally, he'd been permitted to
practice piano in the music room of Peterhouse, Erich's college at Cambridge University. Though I hadn't known about
the correspondence, I often heard Erich tell the story of first
hearing Heisenberg play a Beethoven sonata and then delight-
ing in the words that followed his impromptu performance.
"Now I can tell you more clearly what the difference is between the arts and the sciences," Heisenberg had announced
as he turned from the keys to the little audience gathered in the
oak-paneled music room. "I am convinced that if I had never
lived, somebody would have discovered the uncertainty principle. But I can assure you that if Beethoven had never lived,
this sonata would never have been composed!"

In another box I discovered handwritten notes from
Thomas Mann, addressed to Erich's apartment in Cambridge
from Mann's last home in exile in Pacific Palisades, California.
"I don't really understand Kierkegaard. Never have," he declares in one. Finally, a full-fledged German grown-up who
will admit to such a failing, I thought. And Thomas Mann, of
all people. "What you say about my *Buddenbrooks* being influenced by Schopenhauer is not quite right," he writes in another. "My pessimism is all my own!"

Alongside folders of these letters, I found typed ones from
T. S. Eliot, Stephen Spender, and Iris Murdoch, all with re-

sponses to Erich's early essays. There were handwritten, gossip-filled letters from E. M. Forster—*Yes, it did get into the* Times, he writes about one of his own recently published articles, *and it is very much to the credit of the country, don't you think?;* Hannah Arendt—*Where are you?? Where have you gone?? This is a fan letter. I read the Kafka essay, and bestow superlatives upon you! . . . New Year's Day without you was entirely wrong.* And among correspondence from W. H. Auden was a poem entitled "A Gobble Poem." Two memorable stanzas read:

> I glanced as I advanced. The clean white T-shirt outlined
> A forceful torso; the light-blue denims divulged
> Much. I observed the snug curves where they hugged the
>   behind,
> I watched the crotch where the cloth intriguingly bulged
>
> I produced some beer and we talked. Like a little boy
> He told me his story. Present address: next door.
> Half Polish, half Irish. The youngest. From Illinois.
> Profession: mechanic. Name: Bud. Age: twenty-four

With Auden and that vast secret society of gay men coming of age after Wilde's era and before Stonewall, Erich must have shared another life altogether from the one he revealed to his family—one that likely had shaped his personality and choices more than I would ever know. Erich had never talked about his sexuality with my parents; nor, I learned later, had he ever talked about it with his dearest friends, the Cohens, or with others of his closest friends, including Eve and Sinclair Road, to whom he'd been so close during his years in Cambridge. Perhaps if he were still alive or I had fully understood my own sexuality earlier than I did, Erich and I, the least likely Hellers to be close, might have talked about matters that would have bonded us.

Or perhaps, even with such knowledge, we couldn't have, wouldn't have.

There were Erich's datebooks and diaries, and in one box, occupying a folder all by itself, a handwritten fairy tale with a note, *copy for the children*, about a strawberry named Irene who befriends a bilberry named Berta, which Erich had composed in 1945 for Hans Posner's little boy, Ricky.

The folders contained pieces of the towering uncle who had intimidated me all my life, but they also held an Erich far more tender, loving, and in search of love than the man whom, until his very last days, I had known—or, according to all I'd observed or been told, the brother my father had known and the lover my mother had known. I wanted my father to see them.

With thick reading glasses, good light, and occasional help from the little magnifying glass he now carried in his breast pocket with his notebook and pencil, Bau still read voraciously. He'd reluctantly retired from medicine a few years before, at age eighty. Even in retirement, he continued to keep up with medical journals, continued advising the team of medical researchers he'd trained, even editing the papers they submitted to research journals. But his macular degeneration was worsening, and I knew that the disease, although unpredictable, eventually made many blind. This was the fall of 1999, several years after I'd moved back to Chicago, a period in our lives when Bau hungered for time with his children and we with him. One rainy morning, I convinced Bau to be my co-sleuth at the archives. We'd go out for lunch afterward. Maybe we'd even have time to visit the Shakespeare Garden on the Northwestern campus, where almost thirteen years before, along the tidy rows of spring flowers, we'd scattered my mother's ashes.

All my life, Bau had admired practical skills—*Tüchtig*-ness. It was not simply handiness he held in such high regard but the ability to make things happen. In his later years, as his own capacity to navigate the world diminished, his eye for *Tüchtig*-ness grew so keen and generous that he began to see this quality in me. When I found an inexpensive ticket for an airline flight; when, contrary to his expectation, I found a parking space in front of a restaurant where we planned to have dinner; when, after my mother's death, I set up his first answering machine ("At ze sound of ze beep, leave a message and I vill come to you" was his ambitious first greeting); when I arrived at his door carrying a compact handbag rather than my usual overstuffed backpack: These were achievements that made his world, at least for a brief moment, turn exactly right. "Ach, Caroline!" He would beam at me with such breathtaking pride that I'd get goose bumps. "Zis is so *tüchtig*!" It was rare for me to feel that I possessed such mysterious authority over the concrete matters of daily life, rarer still to feel that Bau viewed me with such boundless confidence.

When I pulled up in front of the redbrick house on Dobson

Street in Evanston that once was my parents' and that he'd shared since his marriage in 1989 with my stepmother, Anna, my father's admiration for my on-time arrival and my freshly washed, well-running car was large enough to inspire him to quote Tante Ida, who, he'd often told me, had been the highest arbiter of excellence: *"Mit gesundere Haut!"* With healthy skin . . . with healthy rings and valves!

The massive white complex of Deering Library sits at the center of the Evanston campus of Northwestern University. Uncle Erich had loathed its fortress-like architecture. He'd much preferred the earlier building, nestled between Lake Michigan and a meadow behind his campus office, whose architecture had been inspired by the classical and Gothic buildings of Cambridge, forever his spiritual academic home.

As Bau and I approached the campus that morning, the sky above the lake turned battleship gray. High waves pounded the rocks separating the campus from the lake, and the rain started to fall in sheets. I suggested to my father that I drop him off as close to the library's entrance as cars were permitted, sparing him the trek from the distant parking lot. *"Ja,* vell, *hast tu ka leid, mast tu ka leid"* (If you don't already have trouble, don't cause yourself trouble), he said, quoting Tante Ida again with a gentle, almost apologetic smile. He zipped his blue windbreaker high, adjusted his sailcloth cap, and raised his umbrella. Through my rearview mirror, I tracked him as he walked off, the tip of his flashlight peeking out of his side pocket, one hand holding the umbrella, the other waving.

When I returned some fifteen minutes later, I spotted Bau

far in the distance, at the top of the tiers of building-wide steps that led to the library's doors—one small bright blue dot against the white bulk of the building. Northwestern students full of muscle and spunk trotted past his motionless, stooped figure. His eyes searched over my head, as if waiting for further information and instruction. When he spotted me, that look of his reappeared—the one that said the world had become right once more.

The route to the archives winds through several cavernous reference rooms with dark polished floors. An archway just past them leads to a twisting, gently sloping hallway with walls lined in framed photographs of illustrious alumni. Voices grew louder as we reached the end of the ramp and entered the archive's reading room, a cramped space with barely room to maneuver between the reading table, the staff desk in one corner, and the bookshelves lining the walls. On this day, it was also filled with bright overhead floodlights and commotion from a film crew.

"Try to look like you're talking about a book," an officious-sounding, middle-aged woman instructed two impeccably dressed young people, a boy and a girl, with handsome, unblemished faces. Each wore a purple-and-white NU baseball cap and appeared about eighteen. "Let's have you lean back against the bookshelf close together," the woman continued, taking each by an arm and positioning them a few feet from where they'd been standing. She handed the boy a book she'd pulled from the shelf behind them. Whispering to each other and giggling, the two huddled behind the book's open cover, peeking up occasionally to receive further direction. "Perfect! But give me a bit of your faces now, and a look of excitement, please," the woman added.

The two young people chatted while a photographer positioned himself in front of them and punctuated the air with clicks. Lights flashed as the woman in charge backed up toward Bau and me, almost trapping Bau against the bookshelf by the door. "Stay right there! This is perfect! You guys are awesome!" she boomed to the young people.

"Vhat? Vhat did she say?" Bau asked in a panicked voice as I tried to usher him past them to the main desk. There, as my father signed his name in the open visitors' book, the archivist informed us that a shoot for the alumni magazine was in progress. My uncle's boxes had been brought up and were waiting on the trolley at the far end of the table, but would we possibly consider coming back another time? It might be noisy, and there was so little room. The crew had been setting up all morning. He'd forgotten to mention it when I called, he apologized. Bau stood enveloped in the dustlike haze of the lights. "Vhat does he say?" he asked me as I tried to explain.

"Do you vont to leave?" I asked, suddenly speaking in his accent, which I'd done before on chaotic occasions. "Is kind of crazy here today. Zhould ve just go have lunch?"

My father had taken off his rain hat and was tapping on his hearing aid. "Hello, hello, hello," he said softly, his first line of defense in unfamiliar situations—a signal that he was momentarily oblivious to everything except the worry that his hearing aid battery had failed. "Hello, hello, hello," he repeated, tapping at his ear again as I turned back to the archivist.

"This is my father, Erich Heller's brother," I explained in a voice tight and defensive. "He's eighty-five," I went on, "and not seeing or hearing well. It wouldn't be a simple matter to return." We'd stay.

While the photography crew took a break, Bau and I worked our way toward the wooden chairs at the far end of the reading table, next to the trolley containing Erich's boxes. My clothes were clammy, my hair wet and dangling in my face. Bau's shoes and pants were a bit muddy, but he looked peaceful as he set his hat and umbrella on the table by his side, laid his magnifying glass and flashlight in front of him, and pulled off his windbreaker. "I hope you won't catch a cold," I said.

"I'm an old tree, I don't get sick," he replied matter-of-factly as he tapped on his hearing aid again, removed it from his ear to study it, then pronounced it, too, in good health.

I searched for the folders I'd flagged with Post-it notes the last time I'd visited, slid the little pile toward my father, and watched as his thick fingers sifted through before opening a folder containing his brother's handwritten journal from 1936–37. "Ah, one of ze famous quote notebooks," he said. Bau filed many memories of his early life under the heading "ze famous." Lately, he'd attached these words to more recent memories as well: ze famous coffee shop near Chicago's Orchestra Hall, where he and my mother often had dinner before going to the symphony; ze famous Botanical Gardens near his house, where Anna took her hikes; ze famous Tony and Markos, my brother's best friends; ze famous Mandelbrot, Anna's ever-present homemade cookies. Now he sat for several minutes, leafing through his brother's quote journal, holding his magnifying glass close to the thin brown paper.

"Karl Kraus!" he said as he examined the opening words from the Viennese satirist that Erich had jotted down fifty-three years before: *Language is the divining rod which discovers wells of thought.*

"He was Erich's favorite of them all—at least of the modern writers," my father explained. "He came to Prague every few months to put on Shakespeare or little operettas by Offenbach, who set Goethe's poems to music. I can't think of the name of the hotel where he performed. Kraus even sang. He translated Shakespeare's sonnets into German. Ze famous translations!"

He read aloud another quote: *There are writers who can express in a mere twenty pages things I sometimes need two whole lines for.* "Always zese wonderful wisecracks!" Bau laughed, borne forward in his wooden chair as he continued to read from the threadbare little notebook.

"Ach, I still can't think of the name of the hotel where Karl Kraus performed!" he repeated, looking up after several minutes of reading silently. "It had a coffeehouse on the ground floor. I could see it when I was arrested," he added quietly before reading aloud the next quote, this one from Rilke. Erich had copied it in August 1936, when neither he nor my father or my mother was fully aware of the forces about to be unleashed on their world.

He who has no home can construct nothing else.

"Ve knew many of zese sayings by heart," my father said as he set down the magnifying glass, closed his eyes, then opened them a moment later as if rousing himself from deep thought, and returned to the notebook.

Across the room, the photography crew had resumed their work, and the woman in charge of the shoot walked toward our end of the table and asked if we'd mind if they took some shots where we were sitting. "It looks so authentic," she added. My father, reading aloud to himself with growing absorption, seemed not to hear her and waved me away when I tapped his shoulder. I nodded to her, pleased that we might go home with a photograph of my father reading—a gift to make up for the disruption of the quiet morning we'd anticipated.

A moment later, the young people arrived at Uncle Erich's trolley and pulled a folder from an opened box. Standing just a few feet from where we sat, they began, in mock German accents, to read from the pages inside—an essay Erich had written about the intellectual relationship between Nietzsche and Rilke. "Awesome! Neet-shee!" the young man exclaimed. "Oh boy!" he repeated while the director coaxed him into various positions of reading. "Go-ee-thee! I just love Go-ee-thee," the young man said as he and the young woman leafed through another folder, this one containing one of Erich's essays on Goethe. "Please!" I shouted, and stood up, intending to complain to the director, but stopped in a corner as a new set of floodlights went on and another volley of flashes burst into the air. I couldn't tell if the young people were poking fun at Goethe, Nietzsche, or Erich, or responding to the false postures they were being asked to assume. Whatever their meaning, a familiar feeling overcame me, the longing to explain to the world, to myself, and now to these young strangers the very thing I so incompletely understood—the magnitude and substance of this river made of books and words and separations and secrets from which I'd been formed. I longed to believe that however much the world would keep turning, this, all that was left of this, was still worth having.

My attention returned to where Bau sat holding his magnifying glass over his reading, oblivious to the crew's dominion over the table, oblivious to my yearning to ford the river, as

Tonio Kröger described, *between a world without knowledge and knowledge without a world*. Each time the camera flashed and the lights were changed to a new angle or intensity, it took a few seconds for my eyes to adjust and locate him.

"Sorry," the director called to me. "We'll be finished here in a minute."

My face grew hot. I pictured myself wresting the folders from the young people's hands, scolding them for taking Uncle Erich from my father and me. "Look at him," I'd shout, pointing to my father. "He's the real thing!"

I said and did none of this. Instead, I returned to the chair next to Bau and whispered into his better ear that I thought it was time to go. The breakfast menu at the Original Pancake House on Green Bay Road, his favorite, ended at two o'clock, I told him. If the rain had subsided, we could visit the Shakespeare Garden and still make it for pancakes. He didn't argue.

Reequipping himself for the rain, my father signed out at the front desk. His was the lone signature for that day. Once out the door, I left him holding the handrail while I returned to the reading room. "Did you get any shots of my father?" I asked the photographer, who was setting up for another shoot. He looked confused, as though he didn't remember who I was. "Oh, the old man!" he said after several seconds. "I'm sorry. No—you guys were just background."

On the way out, Bau said his mind was filled with pictures from reading. "But only snapshots," he added. "Nothing quite comes together. Disconnected snapshots."

"What of?" I asked. He didn't answer. I asked again, but again he didn't respond. For the first time all morning, he seemed exasperated.

"Fortgewürschteln!" he declared. A Tante Ida–ism I knew well.

The rain had turned to drizzle as we walked arm in arm to the parking lot, both of us silent, and from there drove to the Shakespeare Garden on the far side of the campus, tucked between a tiny stone chapel, a modern building of science labs, and a parking area. A small wooden sign at the garden entrance reads: LEAVE THIS CHAPEL GARDEN RENEWED IN ALL THY STRENGTH——TO SERVE THE PRESENT AGE.

A bust of Shakespeare looks out over one end of the rectangular garden, while at the other end a curved cement bench invites visitors to rest and take in the beauty. This bench once was a favorite destination for my mother and me. In the first few years after she died, I visited here often, either alone or with Bau or Tom, but I hadn't been back in quite a while. Though a few roses had survived the first frosts of fall, most of the area was covered with a tangle of dry brown mulch that would be the soil's winter coat. Now it seemed like only a moment ago——or a moment altogether—— when my parents were in the full bloom of late middle age and I was in my young adulthood, those few decades that stand as a timeless reference point, free of beginnings and endings.

No one was there that day. The bench was wet, its cracks covered by veins of moss. Though the sun was peeking through the breaking clouds, a cold lake wind had replaced the rain, scattering wet leaves onto the footpath. For several minutes, we stood in silence at the edge of the garden. But the strength of the wind precluded comfort or contemplation, as if announcing that the bramble-covered garden, like the archival boxes in the library, was not a place to look for what had been lost, at least not today. We soon left.

Bau had already turned toward the parking lot, walking at a strong, brisk pace. *"Fortwuschtelt!"* I said, repeating his directive. I was a connoisseur of Tante Ida–isms, but invariably, her words developed little twists under my jurisdiction, dropping or gaining letters and syllables.

Traffic was slow as we pulled out onto the street. "The driver in front of us drives just like me!" my father said. "Maybe it is me!" He chuckled as I passed the car and he waved out his window to the driver. "Hi Paul!" he said with sly hilarity.

"Vhat direction ve take to ze famous Pancake House?" he asked me, his eyes searching and tired.

"Davis Street to Ridge Road to Green Bay Road," I replied, knowing Bau was a stickler for planning the route. He nodded, pulling his flashlight from his side pocket and setting it in his lap, making himself comfortable for the ride. Then the look returned to his face, the one that said his world had become right once again.

CHAPTER SEVENTEEN

Optilenz

Spring 2001

Bau is scowling into the screen of Optilenz, his swollen hands gripping its platform as if it were the steering wheel of a car in a downpour. Optilenz, a machine designed to help people with macular degeneration to read, looks much like a computer but has a lens capable of magnifying any text or picture up to fifty times its normal size. A salesman named Bob Schwartz arrived with it this morning. If my father buys it, Bob, who used to teach blind children in a public school classroom in Chicago, will not only teach him how to use it, he will also be available whenever my father has questions or difficulties.

Optilenz was recommended by Bau's ophthalmologist as a last resort for his failing eyes. "Dr. Heller," Dr. Rosen said yesterday when we were in his office, "it's either the machine or never reading again. I wish I had better news." He led my father out of his office, his arm around his shoulder; the comradeship of doctors and of old men. "Call Bob Schwartz. You'll like him." Dr. Rosen must be nearing eighty himself, yet is still in command of his professional life, practicing medicine, walking tall. Little by little over the last couple of years, my father lost all that—shrinking into himself more each day, walking with difficulty, losing more of his hearing, then more of his sight, and lately, though his vital organs remain strong, his wish to live. He's told me this several times in the last few weeks. Even if he hadn't told me outright, it's a truth I'd guess. Sometimes my father slips in his wish not to live as a little joke, an endearing play with language. If there's anything that keeps his blood moving now, it's his language play. Yesterday, as the two of us cleared old papers and outdated medical books from his study, and I hauled them away in boxes and huge black garbage bags, Bau, having been peevish and ill-tempered all day, broke into a sly grin as I hoisted the last bag over my shoulder and walked out his study door. "Vait!" he called after me. "I forgot to put myself in!" That little grin! Like his beautiful letters, making me forgive yet again the dark self-absorption that's been his signature mood all my life and seems to be getting worse.

I like Bob Schwartz immediately, his buoyant hopeful manner: "You're going to be amazed by this miracle machine, Paul." Bau hates it when a stranger calls him Paul. One has to earn that right. To strangers he is Dr. Heller. Cringing, he puts up his hands as if to tell Bob he's already stepped over a line. "I'm going to have you reading in no time," Bob continues, either not noticing my father's reaction or choosing to ignore it. "Though it won't be like holding a book, it will be better than you ever imagined."

My father frowns, unconvinced. *"Mám na to kursy,"* he says to Bob, who continues to set up the equipment, not stopping to ask for a translation. I knew that it's a phrase the Czech comic Werych was famous for saying on the streets of Prague when my father was a young man. Werych positioned himself on a street corner, where he freely dispensed counsel to all who didn't ask, then used the encounters in his comedy act. *"Mám na to kursy,"* he would say, when people asked him how he could be so sure of the advice he offered. "I took a course!" My father says it when he thinks someone is a charlatan. He says it often.

Once Bob sets Optilenz on its own table in a corner of my father's study, I marvel at its design and ease of operation. Bob asks me to bring a book with which to practice. I choose one from the pile on my father's night table. Under the lens, the small, grainy letters of Milan Kundera's *The Art of the Novel* become magnificent and bold on the machine's screen. The two men fiddle with the knobs as Bob shows my father how to change the magnification and the texture of the background until the letters are as well defined as he can make them. My father looks increasingly sour.

The previous night, trying to fall asleep in the little basement bedroom of my father's house, I combed through an ancient *New Yorker* lying on the nightstand, a leftover from a visit by my brother, or by Tony or Rick, Anna's sons. I came upon a cartoon of a man with a pompadour haircut, wearing a formal suit. He is sitting in an armchair holding a newspaper—or rather, fisting it, and glaring at a woman sitting in the neighboring chair, toward whom he casts the most dreadful look, his tongue hanging out of the corner of his mouth, one eye squeezed shut as if what he might see if he opened it would be unbearable, the other eye bulging from its socket as if to attack. The woman asks with the calmest imaginable look on her face, "And just exactly what is that expression intended to convey?"

I am nothing like this woman. Bau—who, for most of this week that I've stayed with him while Anna is on a trip with one of her grandchildren, has resembled the man in the cartoon—is driving me crazy. Everything, every day, has been "catastrophic" in his eyes: the weather; our failed plans to go to the symphony (because of that weather); my clothing (*"fürs schlechtere,"* or messy clothing, in his eyes); my preparation of the garbage and recycling for pickup; the dreadful motives of Elizabeth, the woman who has cleaned the house weekly for ten years and who he believes has broken the toaster when he can't find the right lever to toast his bread, has broken the slide-out trash can when he pulls it off its hinges, has thrown out his right slipper when he can find only his left. "Vat has she done again?" he asks under his breath as he emerges from his bedroom, holding the lone slipper and giving me a look that implies that in Elizabeth's absence, I should consider shouldering the blame.

Now he glares at the screen, looking nearly as distressed as the *New Yorker* man, the rims of his eyes red with fatigue. *"Es ist alles für die Katz!"* Not for humans!—literally, for the cat. Throughout my life, he's used that phrase to describe many things—a bad restaurant meal, a bad book, a bad day. *"Für die Katz."* As a child, I would jump to my feet, wanting to remedy instantly whatever was wrong, as if my sheer will and good intentions could make the book improve or a meal please him more. Even now an anxiety so great that it causes my shoulders to lift sometimes comes upon me when I feel his unhappiness. It's a sensation that has never fully left me, waxing and waning over time, its intensity dependent on my father's proximity and mood.

Now Optilenz is *für die Katz*. But Bau continues practicing, moving the platform, reading the words from the page of Kundera, slowly, like a schoolboy. "Ah, Kundera," he says, momentarily brightening. "I own zis book, too!" He breaks my heart.

"It *is* your book," I tell him. "I took it from your night table." I look at his hands, vigilantly, indiscriminately adjusting knobs and pushing buttons even after he's told Bob that the level of magnification is to his liking. As a child, I always saw Bau's swollen bluish hands through the prism of my own needs and feelings, registering mainly that they weren't like the long, slender-fingered hands of my classmates' fathers— those that gripped hammers, pliers, baseball bats, or their children's hands with such confidence. Almost more than his sad gray-green eyes, Bau's hands always seemed to me a mirror of his soul—in spite of his vast accomplishments in medical research, his hold on life uncertain, in need of daily renewal.

"How do I make it bigger?" he asks Bob, softening a little, becoming more interested, almost against his will, in how he can make this machine do his bidding. Bob directs him to the button that enlarges the size of the letters on the screen. "How do I make it smaller?" Bob leads him to the correct button again. "Vat else will it make smaller?" Bau asks, that slight look of mischief appearing—the look that always redeems him in my eyes, the endearing Bau who all my life has regularly peeked out from behind the other Bau. "When I write you the check to buy it, will it make the amount smaller?"

"Eyes bad, humor good," Bob says.

My father reads the opening paragraph of Kundera, haltingly, with great deliberation:

In 1935, three years before his death, Edmund Husserl
gave his celebrated lectures in Vienna and Prague on the
crisis of European humanity. For Husserl, the adjective
"European" meant the spiritual identity that extends beyond geographical Europe (to America, for instance)
and that was born with ancient Greek philosophy. In his
view, this philosophy, for the first time in History, ap-
prehended the world (the world as a whole) as a question to be answered. It interrogated the world not in
order to satisfy this or that practical need but because
"the passion to know had seized mankind."

"*Ja*, vell, that is certainly an opinion that needs to be hon-
ored and discussed, but Kundera is wrong about the date,"
Bau says, looking to his left and fixing his stare on the wall. "It
vouldn't have been 1935. It must have been 1933. Husserl
vould have been an emigrant, and it vas harder to come into
Prague after 1933." He speaks now in his lecturer's voice, in
which he is always at his best, turning from the wall to his real
audience, taking Bob on as a student (along with me, always
me), explaining to us that Husserl was a famous phenomenol-
ogist. "I barely remember now if I went to his lectures," he
says, "but I probably didn't, because I had many other things
to do then. I probably studied for my exams. This was always
the case. I don't remember whatever became of Husserl. *Na*,
this is terrible that I can't remember! This happens to me always!"

From here he tells us about Rudolf Carnap, one of his favorite philosophers when he was a student in Prague. Then
everyone had a favorite philosopher. They were the currency.

Philosophy, literature, politics—almost interchangeable, catalysts for all things worthwhile. Rudolf Carnap was a neopositivist, my father explains. Carnap always debated Husserl's ideas in his Saturday-morning lectures, which Bau regularly attended and, he turns to remind me, where he sometimes spotted my mother sitting closer to the front, next to Erich. "Carnap believed that everything could be solved by an equation, and somehow this was absolutely fascinating to me," Bau tells us, Bob leaning on the bookshelf, his face filled with interest, I sitting cross-legged on the floor. "The board was covered top to bottom with equations. Absolutely incredible! Always an idea underneath!"

My father no longer looks anything like the *New Yorker* man. Next to the zipper of his tightly belted, floppy pants is a patch of dried jam from his breakfast, and the lapel of his white sport jacket—which he wears for guests and hastily put on for Bob's arrival—is dotted with caked egg. But to me, he looks forceful and professorial. I suspect Kundera got his dates right (though for most of my life, I would have put my money on my father), but never mind. Bau's world is up there on the screen of Optilenz—his prewar Central Europe, its celebrated ideas, its great debates, its eminent men: a time and place that still delivers his sense of meaning; a world in which, before the war that ended it, he was a young player.

Minutes after Bob leaves, Bau makes a trip down the hallway to his bedroom, challenges to Bob Schwartz's integrity echoing in his wake. "He's a pushy businessman. Vy does he sell these machines? I suspect he's not to be trusted. The world has become a bad place." Before I can respond, Bau is asleep.

Later, in the middle of the night, I'm awakened by footsteps above my basement bedroom, and I go upstairs to check on Bau. From the door to the kitchen, I see him sitting perfectly still at his place at the breakfast table, eating a slice of toasted Sara Lee pound cake and sipping a gin and tonic from a tiny Winnie-the-Pooh tumbler left behind by one of Anna's grandchildren. He looks like a furry little ghost, hair in disarray, his thin, wrinkled torso covered with a mossy white mane, his baggy undershorts accenting the boniness of his scarred, hairless legs. "If you see couple of eyes lying around," he says as if I'd been standing there all along and there'd been no interruption in my attention to his eyesight, "I take them!" He laughs at his joke and, with a look of pride, points to the hallway, now cluttered with odds and ends from his study—a small metal shelf filled with medical reference books; a cardboard file box crammed with letter paper, stamps, and old keys; a set of mahogany drawers that once belonged to Uncle Erich, overflowing with photographs and old clippings. Bau lifts his glass and raises it to the hallway, then leads me to his study. While I was asleep, from midnight until now, four in the morning, Bau was busy rearranging his study to make a home for Optilenz, which Bob had offered to let him try out on his own before deciding whether to purchase it. "I did some cleaning," he says. "*Kviet* like a *Kirchenmaus*." There is an old German word, *verbissen*, that my brother and I heard from the time we were very young. Bau said it to us when we were weary of a task we had to complete for school or a chore he wanted us to do at home. *Verbissen:* Once you commit to something, you sink your teeth into it and hang on. My father is the epitome of *verbissen*, all my life, in spite of his self-doubt, in spite of his daily need to recommit himself to life, showing the strength and energy of two men if he wanted to accomplish something, never allowing himself to relinquish the hidden but persistent optimism that kept him going.

And now, in spite of his doubts that anything can help him read again, Bau's *Verbissenheit* has brought Optilenz to a moonlit corner by the window of his study, where on its platform lies a tiny cloth volume of Stefan Zweig's *Sternstunden der Menschheit,* its old German script filling the screen. Arranged in a row on the floor next to Optilenz, as if in line to be read, is an old yellow cloth book of German nonsense poems by Christian Morgenstern, an equally old collection of poems by Joachim Ringelnatz, and two volumes of *Joseph and His Brothers* by Thomas Mann. Sixty-one years ago, my father had wrapped these books, along with his medical books and several other favorites, and sent them to Liese Florsheim in New York for safekeeping.

In the upper-right corner of the title page of the little Zweig book is my father's name, written in youthful, bold fountain-pen script, and the date of the purchase: 1929. "I vas bright then and now *ausgewiegelter Schwachsinn,*" he says when I note the date. "*Schwach!* Feeble! I need to get a new head." He presses down on top of his thick white hair as though trying to release something, answer something. "I'm interested to know what Zweig wrote about Goethe. Goethe came to Marienbad when he was seventy-four years old, and he fell in love. He wanted to begin life again. I want to know what Goethe found there. Seventy-four years old! He wrote the famous poem 'Marienbader Elegie' there, near Komotau. I visited there often as a boy. '*Sternstunden.*' Kind of *Schmockerei*! You can't really translate zis! Zweig tries to be original—starry hours, decisive moments. One about Napoleon, one about Dostoyevsky, and zis one about Goethe coming to Marienbad and falling in love and writing this famous elegy. *E-LE-GIE . . .*" he repeats after a long pause, drawing out, singing, its syllables, while he holds his little cup of gin high in the air, as if toasting the word, the poem, or saying good-bye.

SOURCE NOTES

CHAPTER ONE

The content of this chapter comes mainly from the tape-recorded conversations with my mother to which I refer in Chapter Fifteen. Among my mother's recollections was Erich's preoccupation with Goethe and the idea of tragedy. He later published an essay, "Goethe and the Avoidance of Tragedy," in his book *The Disinherited Mind: Essays in Modern German Literature and Thought* (Bowes and Bowes, Cambridge and London, 1952, 1971, 1975; Farrar, Straus and Cudahy, New York, 1957; Harmondsworth, Penguin Books, UK, 1961).

Various content also comes from conversations with my father late in his life, during which he talked about the day he met my mother and other details about their group of friends.

Further content was provided in tape-recorded interviews with Paul (Schülle) Seton in London, May 2003, who was present on the day my parents met; and Alice Gollan, the daughter of Franz Gollan and Edith Abeles Gollan (also present on that day), in Boston, spring 2006.

In 1982, with my parents, and again in 2003, a year and a

half after my father's death, I traveled to Komotau and visited
the Alaunsee. The dressing cabins my mother described were
still there.

During the 1982 trip I took to Prague, Komotau, and
Frankfurt with my parents, my mother showed me the former
location of Café Continental. By the time I visited Prague
again in May 2003, the building had been further modernized
and subdivided into offices. Conversations with Paul (Schülle)
Seton and Eve Adler Road during that trip, and again when
Eve joined me on a research trip to Cambridge, UK, in October 2004, provided further descriptions of the café's interior.

During their late-in-life reminiscences, my parents described Erich Heller's admiration for Karl Kraus, the Viennese
journalist, creator of aphorisms and feuilletons, and publisher
of the magazine *Die Fackel* (*The Torch*). In the years just before his death in 1936, my parents told me, Kraus frequently
performed scenes from Offenbach's operettas and Shakespeare's sonnets at the Palace Hotel (which was still there at 12
Panská, just off Wenceslas Square, when I visited in 2003), and
he and Erich became friends.

Erich Heller's book *Die Flucht aus dem zwanzigsten Jahrhundert* (*Escape from the Twentieth Century*), which stemmed
from his earliest essay on Kraus, was published by Saturn Verlag, Vienna, in 1938. Erich's later essay "Karl Kraus: The Last
Days of Mankind" appeared in *Cambridge Journal: A Monthly
Review* (Michael Oakeshott, ed.), March 1948, vol. 1, no. 6,
Bowes and Bowes, Cambridge. Another version of that piece
was published in the 1957 edition of his book *The Disinherited
Mind*. Still another Erich Heller essay on Kraus, "Satirist in
the Modern World," appeared in *The Times Literary Supple-*

ment, May 8, 1953, and was included in later editions of *The Disinherited Mind*.

Northwestern University's June 13, 1978, issue of *Arts and Sciences Review* included an interview with Erich in which, among other topics, he discussed his hope to bring Kraus's work to the attention of the English-speaking world.

My interview with my mother's childhood friend Lilo Oshinsky Leland in Miami, Florida, April 2004, added to my knowledge of my mother's friendship group, *Kränzchen*.

Late in his life my father described the pain of seeing Liese and Erich together at the Mayers' parties and told me that for this reason, after the party described, he didn't attend a Mayer event until Liese's Prague farewell party (described in Chapter Six).

CHAPTER TWO

In my mother's late-in-life reminiscences, she described Erich's Železná Street apartment, as well as the evening she began to recognize Erich's edge of condescension toward her and his capacity to overwhelm her voice and confidence.

She also described Erich's early notes of apology, often accompanied by flowers. Many years later, when Erich lived in Evanston, my brother and I witnessed the arrival of his flowers, accompanied by notes of apology, which usually came after political quarrels (Erich became politically conservative in his later years, while my parents remained left-leaning liberals) and were usually addressed to both my mother and father.

Literary quotes alluded to in this chapter are taken from Erich's early quote notebooks, some of which are part of his files at the Northwestern University Archives, and some of which my father kept in his own files after Erich's death.

Erich describes his early affection for Thomas Mann's first novella, *Tonio Kröger,* most poignantly in his introduction to his literary biography of Thomas Mann, *The Ironic German: A Study of Thomas Mann,* London: Secker and Warburg, 1958. *Tonio Kröger* was a touchstone not only for Erich, Liese, and Paul, but later, in the story's evocation of feeling like an outsider to mainstream culture, for my brother and me as well.

CHAPTER THREE

A 1929 photo of "Kavarna Union" can be seen in *World of Prague* by Pavel Scheufler, Prazsky Svet Publishing House, Prague, 2000. That café, like Café Continental, no longer exists, and the building on Na Perstyn that once housed it has been modernized.

My father provided information about Freie Vereinigung meetings (including his early attempt to tell Liese of his feelings), as did Paul (Schülle) Seton. Both recalled that Erich frequently devoted meetings he chaired to discussions of his literary and political heroes, particularly Kraus. In this chapter I borrow extensively from Erich's essay "Satirist in the Modern World" (*The Times Literary Supplement,* May 8, 1953). The reference to Confucius also appears in "Literature and Political Responsibility: Apropos the Letters of Thomas Mann," Chapter 6 (p. 124), in Erich Heller's *In the Age of Prose* (1984). I drew from my father's and Paul (Schülle) Seton's descriptions in order to imagine what such a discussion might have been like.

CHAPTER FOUR

The content of this chapter comes from my mother and father's reminiscences, and also from letters my grandparents wrote to my mother, which were among those she gave me shortly before her death. John Wherity, a scholar of Old German script, translated them.

My father's short autobiography, "Autobiographic Sketches: The First Forty Years," which he wrote in longhand in 1989 and which his medical secretary, Arlene Sullivan Adams, typed out in 1994, provided additional information.

In summer 2001, I interviewed my uncle Ernst Florsheim at his home in Milwaukee, about his early life, including his journey to Prague. After Uncle Ernie's death in spring 2002, his son, Rick, scanned one of my grandfather's wine bottle labels, which Ernie had kept, and sent it to me.

CHAPTER FIVE

Neither my brother nor I remember exactly when we learned that our mother was involved with Erich before she married our father, but we both recall that conversation with her sometime in our early adulthood. At the time, she asked that we not let our father know she'd told us. My mother often visited me in California; on one of those visits, she told me about Capri and her abortion. In the months before her death, she shared more details about her first breakup with Erich.

Erich's references to Nietzsche and Weininger are taken from his quote journals from 1936, described in Chapter Two source notes, translated by Paul (Schülle) Seton.

My grandparents' letters to my mother, described in Chapter Four source notes, are excerpted in this chapter.

CHAPTER SIX

The Goethe quote *naught to seek . . . that is my goal* is taken from Erich's "Literature and Political Responsibility: Apropos the Letters of Thomas Mann," Chapter 6 (pp. 105–127), from *In the Age of Prose: Literary and Philosophical Essays*, Cambridge: Cambridge University Press, 1984.

In addition to my mother's reminiscences, I learned details of Masaryk's funeral from *Prague in Black and Gold: Scenes from the Life of a European City* by Peter Demetz, New York: Hill and Wang, Division of Farrar, Straus and Giroux, 1997.

Kafka, Love, and Courage: The Life of Milena Jesenská by Mary Hockaday (U.S. edition), Woodstock, NY: The Overlook Press, 1997, describes Milena's friendship with the Schlamms. Hockaday's account, rendered from interviews with Steffi Schlamm before her death in Salzburg in 1995, indicates that Milena found it so difficult to say good-bye to Willi that she left on a holiday just before the Schlamms left Prague. My mother's account of the farewell, on the other hand, indicated that Milena was with them at the train station.

CHAPTER SEVEN

Description of the events in Prague in fall 1938 comes from my father's reminiscences, as well as from his unpublished autobiography, described in Chapter Four source notes.

Erich's life and thoughts shortly after Liese left Prague are taken, in part, from his letter to my mother dated October 1938, entitled *"Du, Mein Leben"* and among those she gave me shortly before her death. From the content of that letter, which my stepmother, Anna Novak-Heller, helped to translate, as well as from reminiscences of my father and Paul (Schülle) Seton, I try to imagine Erich's state during those months.

CHAPTER EIGHT

To my knowledge, the Northwestern interview of Erich (see Chapter One source notes) is the only public occasion when he discussed the circumstances of his escape into Poland. In it he names the prison where he was held and discusses giving the Gestapo his employer's second address. Erich describes the Gestapo at the second prison releasing him with the words "Out with you!"

My mother's late-in-life reminiscences describe the "miracle" of Erich getting out, the three men's suffering, and the fact that neither Erich nor Hans Posner ever discussed with her their weeks in prison or what happened at the border.

My father's unpublished autobiography (see Chapter Four source notes) describes Erich's plans with Hans and Karl, what my father calls "the unbelievable action of the Gestapo" with regard to Erich's escape into Poland, and the likelihood that his cousin Karl perished in the second prison.

Late in his life, my father several times contemplated the connection between Erich's escape and his own arrest, and gave more details of Erich's descriptions of the prisons. Because of the extreme Nazification of the border between Moravia and Poland, Erich's political work, and the efficiency of

Nazi intelligence, Bau thought it nearly impossible that Erich was released without some sort of bribe being involved.

George Cohen—who, along with his wife, Connie, was Erich's closest friend during the years he taught at Northwestern and at whose home he had dinner every week for thirty years—suggested even more strongly that some sort of bribe was involved in Erich's release, and indicated, hinting but not actually saying, that Erich had told him it was sexual in nature.

While the first part of the escape efforts of Erich, Hans, and Karl has been largely confirmed, for the incomplete and sometimes contradictory reports about the circumstances of Erich's escape into Poland, I put particular weight on my father's and George Cohen's theories to surmise what may have happened.

In my October 2004 tape-recorded interviews with Eve Adler Road and Helen Fowler, both of whom were close to Erich during his early years in Cambridge, they recounted that only once did Erich discuss his weeks in prison, and his words began and ended with a description of a guessing game the three men played in prison to pass the time.

Graham Storey, whom I interviewed at his home in Meldreth, near Cambridge, UK, in October 2004, told me that Erich never talked to him about the circumstances of his escape other than to say that it was "miraculous." Graham, Eve, and Helen told me that during his early years in Cambridge, Erich rarely talked about his family and that they were reluctant, because of what Helen called "the English good manners, you know," to ask him questions.

An obituary of Erich that appeared in *The Cambridge Times* on November 14, 1990, written by Peter Stern, recounts that Erich left Poland from the Port of Gdynia, and that he arrived at Tower Bridge in London on August 26, 1939, five days before the Nazi invasion of Poland and the beginning of World War II.

In my interview with Hans Posner's son, Richard, in May 2012, in Cambridge, MA, and in my correspondence with Richard afterward, he told me that his father never talked about his escape, nor Erich's. "It was as though my father dropped from the sky into England," he recounted. Richard said his father once told him that he believed Paul Heller's arrest was based on mistaken identity; that the Gestapo in Prague thought he was Erich Heller.

Paul (Schülle) Seton told me that after Erich was released in Morava Ostrava, Hans was sent back to the first prison, then taken again to Morava Ostrava, then back to the first prison, where, in desperation, he slashed his wrists.

CHAPTER NINE

Trying to understand Erich's capacity to study in the relative idyll of Cambridge while his brother and mother were still in Prague, I turned to his essay "Literature and Political Responsibility: Apropos the Letters of Thomas Mann," Chapter 6 (pp. 105–127), from Erich's *In the Age of Prose: Literary and Philosophical Essays,* Cambridge: Cambridge University Press, 1984, a book he dedicated to my parents.

Documents and letters from Erich's Cambridge days, including his letter of acceptance to the Ph.D. program in literature, dated October 1939 and signed by W. J. Sartain, secretary of the Board of Research Studies, University Registry, University of Cambridge, as well as a typed description, signed by Erich, of the intended scope of his proposed research work, were part of the files my father kept after Erich's death; they are now part of the Northwestern University Archives.

Other information in this chapter comes from interviews with Eve Adler Road, Graham Storey, and Helen Fowler, who led me to *Cambridge Commemorated: An Anthology of University Life* by Helen and her husband, Lawrence Fowler, Cambridge: Cambridge University Press, 1984; from my father's reminiscences; and from interviews with Frank Schwelb (son of Egon and Karla Schwelb, who frequently saw Erich in England) in October 2010 (by phone) and with Richard Posner, described in Chapter Eight source notes.

Information about my mother's early life in New York City comes from my mother's late-in-life reminiscences, interviews (in Miami Beach and New York City on several occasions between 2002 and 2005) with Lilo Oshinsky Leland and Adele (Fath) Larschan, daughter of Uncle Hermann, and scores of letters from Erich Posner to my mother, which were among those she gave me shortly before her death.

CHAPTER TEN

While my father recovered from his broken hip in the hospital in Bayreuth, Germany, he wrote his account of what happened the morning of his arrest in 1939 and as much about the following years as he could put to paper. He would call his account "Fragments from a Concentration Camp Diary." Much of what he wrote from his Bayreuth hospital room was an elaboration of the notes he'd scribbled on a calendar (from which hung a pencil) that he took from a wall of a barn where he slept in Neustadt, Germany, during one night of the death march in January

1945. "Though written post hoc," he wrote in the Bayreuth hospital in July 1945, "[these fragments] reflect my thoughts as I would have put them to paper had I been fully able to do so." "A Concentration Camp Diary" was published in *Midstream Magazine*, April 1980, pp. 29–36 (see Chapter Four source notes), and much of the content of this chapter comes from that diary.

Content for this chapter also comes from letters from Erich Heller to Graham Storey, now at the Northwestern University Archives, and Erich Posner's letters to my mother, which were among those she gave me shortly before her death.

CHAPTER ELEVEN

Descriptions of my father's life after the liberation of Buchenwald are based on his autobiographical writings (see Chapter Four source notes), as well as his late-in-life reminiscences.

Descriptions of the Murrow broadcast, as heard by Erich and Sinclair and Eve Adler Road, in addition to Erich's interactions with Rose Campbell, are taken from interviews with Eve Adler Road as well as from Erich's published interview (see Chapter One source notes).

The full text of Edward R. Murrow's "Broadcast from Buchenwald" (April 15, 1945) can be found in *In Search of Light: The Broadcasts of Edward R. Murrow, 1938–1961*, New York, Alfred A. Knopf, 1967 (New York: Da Capo Press edition, 1997), and on the RCA recordings, *A Reporter Remembers: The Broadcasts of Edward R. Murrow*. Further description of the scene of Murrow entering Buchenwald can be found in A. M. Sperber's 1986 biography of Murrow (*Murrow: His Life and Times*, New York: Freundlind Books), pp. 248–253.

Letters from Paul to Liese from October 1945 to June 1946, and from Erich to Liese, which were among those my mother gave me shortly before she died, and the letter from Paul to Erich (June 1946), which were among the letters in Erich's files that my father kept after Erich's death, were translated by Stephanie Pollender, a graduate student at Lesley University.

Nowhere in my father's files, or among the letters my mother gave me, could I find her responses to the letters Paul wrote between October 1945 and June 1946.

CHAPTER TWELVE

Chapter content comes from late-in-her-life conversations with my mother, from my father's unpublished autobiography (see Chapter Four source notes), and from letters (from Erich Heller) that I found in my father's files after his death, along with others (from Eve Adler Road and Erich Posner) that were among those my mother gave me just before she died.

Vielfache Heimat, which roughly translates as "manifold homeland," refers to the way of life many Europeans of the late nineteenth and early twentieth centuries consciously chose, a kind of "cosmopolitanism" that Goethe lived and advocated. The pogroms and genocides of the twentieth century began to give the phrase a very different meaning.

CHAPTER THIRTEEN

The E. O. Wilson quote is taken from the opening chapter of his autobiography, *Naturalist*, called "Paradise Beach" (New York: Warner, 1995).

CHAPTER FOURTEEN

The idea of the "unthought known" (unconscious knowledge that has not yet been sewn to word or concept) was part of a theory put forth by the British psychoanalyst Christopher Bollas in *The Shadow of the Object* (New York: Columbia University Press, 1989).

CHAPTERS FIFTEEN, SIXTEEN, SEVENTEEN

Chapter content comes from notebooks I kept during the time of my mother's illness and, later, my father's decline.

W. H. Auden gives his unpublished poem the title "A Gobble Poem" in his correspondence with Erich Heller. Edward Mendelson, literary executor of the estate of W. H. Auden, offers the correct title of the poem as "The Platonic Blow." Mr. Mendelson's book *Later Auden* describes the poem in more detail.

"Optilenz" was originally published in a slightly different version in *American Scholar*, spring 2002, pp. 53–58. Just before his death, my father encouraged me to publish that story. "Carrroooline," he said (after my brother encouraged me to read it to him), "you zhould zubmit zis zomevhere." Its appearance in *American Scholar* led to this book.

Books by Erich Heller

Die Flucht aus dem zwanzigsten Jahrhundert (An Essay on Modern German Literature), Vienna: Saturn Verlag, 1938. (One of the few available copies is archived in the Library of the University of Vienna.)

The Disinherited Mind: Essays in Modern German Literature and Thought, Cambridge and London: Bowes and Bowes, 1952, 1971, 1975; New York: Farrar, Straus and Cudahy, 1957; Harmondsworth, UK: Penguin Books, 1961.

The Hazard of Modern Poetry, Cambridge: Bowes and Bowes Publishers Limited, 1953.

The Ironic German: A Study of Thomas Mann, London: Secker and Warburg, 1958.

The Artist's Journey into the Interior and Other Essays, New York: Random House, 1959, 1962, 1964, 1965.

Franz Kafka (edited by Frank Kermode), New York: Viking Press Series on Modern Masters, 1971.

Franz Kafka Letters to Felice (edited by E. H. and Jurgen Born, translated by James Stern and Elisabeth Duckworth), New York: Schocken Books, 1973.

Franz Kafka, Princeton, NJ: Princeton University Press (Viking Press, Frank Kermode series), 1974.

The Poet's Self and the Poem: Essays on Goethe, Nietzsche, Rilke, and Thomas Mann, London: University of London, Athlone Press, 1976.

Nietzsche the Philosopher of Art, Mount Pleasant, MI: Enigma Press, 1981.

In the Age of Prose: Literary and Philosophical Essays, Cambridge: Cambridge University Press, 1984.

The Importance of Nietzsche: Ten Essays, Chicago: University of Chicago Press, 1988.

(Copies of early *Neue Weltbühne* journals, containing essays by Erich Heller and William Schlamm, can be found in the University of Berlin Archives.)

References About Erich Heller

Northwestern University Archives, Deering Library, Rm. 110, 1970 Campus Drive, Evanston, Illinois 60208-2300: Series 11/3/15/3, Boxes 1–13, including correspondence with Conrad Aiken, Hannah Arendt, W. H. Auden, Saul Bellow, Kenneth Clark, T. S. Eliot, Joseph Epstein, E. M. Forster, Michael Hamburger, Werner Heisenberg, Teddy Kolech, C. S. Lewis, Archibald MacLeish, Thomas Mann, Iris Murdoch, Michael Polanyi, Stephen Spender, Graham Storey, Lionel Trilling, among others.

"Erich Heller, 1911–1990" by Joseph Epstein, *The New Criterion,* February 1991, pp. 83–86.

"An Interview with Erich Heller," *Northwestern Arts and Sciences* (interviewed by Steven L. Bates), fall 1979, pp. 8–13 (also available as an unedited audiorecording through the NU Archives).

Versuche zu Goethe (*Festschrift für Erich Heller*), Heidelberg: Lothar Stiehm Verlag, 1976.

Writings by Paul Heller

"A Concentration Camp Diary" by Paul Heller, *Midstream Magazine*, April 1980, pp. 29–36.

"Autobiographic Sketches: The First Forty Years," unpublished typescript, 1994.

Paul Heller's early publications on the treatment of tuberculosis, and his career-long publications in the field of hematology, can be found in the library of the College of Medicine, 840 S. Wood Street (M/C 787), University of Illinois, Chicago, IL, 60612.

Donations for an endowed chair in medical education in Paul Heller's name can be made to the Chair of Medicine, College of Medicine (Attention: Paul Heller Endowed Fund to Support Hematology-Oncology Research), 840 S. Wood Street (M/C 787), University of Illinois, Chicago, Illinois, 60612.

ACKNOWLEDGMENTS

I thank my family, friends, and teachers (many of the following people are all three to me) who read or listened to portions of the book in progress and offered comment—Hal Adams, David Ansell, William Ayers, Susan and Molly Bernstein, John Bethell, Sven Birkerts, Judith Beth Cohen, Martha Cooley, Gianna DeCarl, Janet deSaulniers, Joseph Epstein, Wendy Friefeld, Elaine Fuchs, Camilla Gibb, Paula Grabler, David Hansen, Joseph Hawkins, George Hein, Thomas, Lynn, Gabriel, Noah, and Hannah Heller, Martha Howard, Susan and Bobbi Hulme, Mona Khalidi, Mark Leitson, Phillip Lopate, Kathy and Marc Lubin, Carolyn Miller, Elliot Mishler, Yvonne Mosca, Corey Ohama, George Packer, Therese Quinn, Branca Ribeiro, Eve Adler Road, Judy Salzman, Virginia Samter, Carol Spindel, Jocelyn Stevenson, Deanne Stone, Pam Strauss, and Joy Lynn Wing. Most especially I thank Debbie Danielpour Chapel, Leah Hager Cohen, Lynn Focht, Martha Nichols, and Cristina Rathbone—my beloved Boston writing group members—and Nancy Adess and Lee Whitman-Raymond, for their gifts of writerly insight.

Thank you to my father's and uncle's cousins Ivan Baecher (now Backer), son of Benno Baecher, and Anna Backer Pearlberg and Paul Backer, niece and nephew of Benno; my parents' and uncle's friends George Cohen, Eve Adler Road, and Paul (Schülle) Seton; my uncle's friends Joachim Beug, Joseph Epstein, Helen Fowler, Graham Storey, and Barton Wolgamot; Graham Storey's caretaker, Stiofan Barker; my uncle Ernst Florsheim and cousin Rick Florsheim; Anna Judi Challiner, daughter of Erich Posner; Richard Posner, son of Hans Posner; Alice Gollan, daughter of Franz and Edith Abeles Gollan; Claudia Perez, daughter of *Kränzchen* member Ille Juergenson; Frank Schwelb, son of Egon and Caroline (Karla) Schwelb; Tom Spitzer, son of Richard Spitzer; Kathy Plowitz-Worden, daughter of Kurt and Lisa (Ertl) Plowitz; Peter Waelsch, son of Heinrich Waelsch; Eleanor Skolnik and Janet Weinrib, daughters of my father's Prague friend Litcy Treuer; John P. Reiner, who was close to the Mayers in New York; my mother's cousin Adele Larschan, daughter of Uncle Hermann; and my mother's childhood friend Lilo Oshinsky Leland, for the time they gave me.

Thank you to the anthropologist Michael Jackson, for sharing with me his scholarship on the politics of storytelling; to Susan Bernstein, Wulf Koepke, Anna Novak-Heller, Stephanie Pollender, Herb Rowland, Paul Seton, and particularly John Wherity, who translated scores of letters and documents; Mary Hockaday, who shared reminiscences of her interviews with Steffi Schlamm; the curators of the Edward R. Murrow Archives (Edward R. Murrow Collection) at Tufts University, who gave me access to my father's early letters to Murrow; the Northwestern University Archives and the University of

Berlin Archives, who gave me access to Erich Heller's letters and papers, including early writings never published in the United States; and Stanislav Ded, curator of the Komotau (now Chomutov) Museum, who took me to places I needed to go.

Thank you to the Spencer Foundation, who offered me a fellowship that allowed me to begin this project, and the Mac-Dowell Colony, who offered one that helped me continue; Mike Durrie, David Kirp, Catherine Lucas, and especially Eve Anne and Richard Pearson, who gave me very real shelter over the final writing summers; the administration of Lesley University, my colleagues, and particularly my students, who model for me over and over the courage it takes to face the empty page; Anne Fadiman and John Bethell of *American Scholar* for publishing "Optilenz"; Anna Ghosh, of the Ghosh Literary Agency, for reading it and sending me a fateful email that led to a book contract; Susan Kamil of Dial Press/Random House for trusting that *Reading Claudius* could be written long before I gave her requisite evidence that it could be; Beth Rashbaum for understanding so much, so quickly, and being the kindest, smartest, most insightful editor imaginable; Sam Nicholson for taking me through the final editing stages with such an acute mind and steady hand, and Jennifer Rodriguez and her team at Random House for their eagle eyes on the final copy.

Thank you, Tobias Steed, and the team at Leapfrog Press and TSB Can of Worms, Mary Bisbee-Beek, Akua Rugg, Rebecca Cuthbert, Shannon Clinton-Copeland, Andy Ward, Clio Seraphim, Edward Buckbee, Anne Mahon, and Anna Ornstein.

Thank you, my Heller family and my Ball/DiBella/Oswald family, for harboring me through this project, including all too often putting up with my absence so that I could keep my nose to the grindstone; my brother, Tom, to whom I dedicate *Reading Claudius;* my mother-in-law, Marie; my stepmother, Anna; my sisters-in-law Lynn, Margie, Judy, and Mindy; my brothers-in-law Tony, Jim, and Neil; my nephews Gabriel, Noah, Greg, and Sam; my nieces Hannah, Sara, Naomi, Natalie, Camille, and Ana; and our newest generation: Anya, Max, and Boaz.

And at the top of all my thanks if at the bottom of this list: For every draft she read, for every comment she offered, for every note she pinned to the door of my study reminding me that however deeply I entered the past, the present—including her love—was still with me, I thank (forever) the incomparable Eileen Wynne Ball.

About the Author

CAROLINE HELLER is director of the interdisciplinary Ph.D. program in educational studies at Lesley University, where she is also a professor in the Graduate School of Education. Her previous book is *Until We Are Strong Together.* She lives in Boston with her family.

About the Type

This book was set in Fournier, a typeface named for Pierre-Simon Fournier (1712–68), the youngest son of a French printing family. He started out engraving woodblocks and large capitals, then moved on to fonts of type. In 1736 he began his own foundry and made several important contributions in the field of type design; he is said to have cut 147 alphabets of his own creation. Fournier is probably best remembered as the designer of St. Augustine Ordinaire, a face that served as the model for the Monotype Corporation's Fournier, which was released in 1925.

CPSIA information can be obtained
at www.ICGtesting.com
Printed in the USA
LVHW110543041021
699412LV00001B/1

9 781948 585217